# Why Arnold Matters

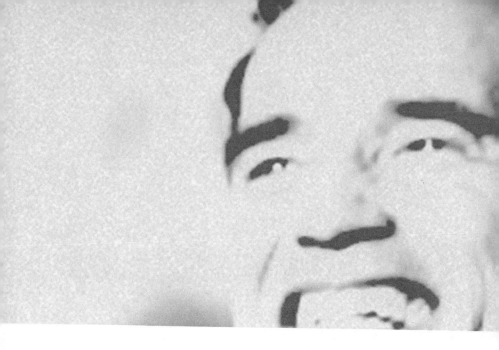

# Why Arnold Matters
## The Rise of a Cultural Icon

Michael Blitz *and*
Louise Krasniewicz

BASIC
BOOKS

A MEMBER OF THE PERSEUS BOOKS GROUP

NEW YORK

Books published by Basic Books are available at special
discounts for bulk purchases in the United States by
corporations, institutions, and other organizations. For
more information, please contact the Special Markets
Department at the Perseus Books Group, 11 Cambridge
Center, Cambridge MA 02142, or call (617) 252-5298, (800)
255-1514 or e-mail special.markets@perseusbooks.com.

DESIGNED BY LOVEDOG STUDIO

A cataloging-in-publication record for this book is available
from the Library of Congress.
ISBN 0-465-03752-6

04 05 06 / 10 9 8 7 6 5 4 3 2 1

# Contents

# Introduction

**TO BORROW, AND SLIGHTLY BEND,** a line from the movie *Kindergarten Cop*, Arnold Schwarzenegger is like the ocean. You don't want to turn your back on him. In 1965, the Austrian army didn't keep a close eye on him, and, to compete in a bodybuilding competition in Stuttgart, Arnold went AWOL. He won the competition and the title—Jr. Mr. Europe. By the age of 20 he was named Mr. Germany and Mr. Universe. Arnold headed to America in 1968 to continue training and winning worldwide recognition as the most significant bodybuilder of all time.

Two years after his arrival in America, Arnold was offered a part in a movie as the demigod Hercules. For the next fourteen years Hollywood made good use of Arnold's incredible body in films from *Pumping Iron,* to the made-for-TV movie *The Jayne Mansfield Story,* to the classic *Conan* tales in which Arnold's nearly-naked physique was on constant display.

There was a comment—still in circulation[1]—that the Guinness World Record people had declared Arnold the "most perfectly developed man in the history of the world." Arnold himself had resolved to "create the greatest, most perfect body anybody had ever seen."[2] Confident that the supermuscled Arnold Schwarzenegger had found his niche in macho movies and would remain there, fixed in celluloid history, the world could now turn its attention to other matters. But the ocean that was Arnold was busy lapping at the shores, buying and selling valuable pieces of American real estate and amassing wealth at an early age. He was also making plans to star in the movie that would dramatically change the course of his career: *The Terminator*.

In the Orwellian year of 1984, *The Terminator* devoured the box office and transformed Schwarzenegger into a Hollywood superstar. While no one forgot his sculpted body, America and the rest of the world could now settle in with popcorn and a soda to watch the blockbuster spectacles Arnold had to offer. And that's precisely what happened throughout the 1980s. One of those hits, not a movie at all, was Arnold's engagement and marriage to Kennedy family star Maria Shriver in 1986. Retired bodybuilder, married movie megastar, entrepreneur... surely it was safe for America to assume that Arnold Schwarzenegger would now become a far more predictable 40-year-old.

But in 1990, President George H. W. Bush named Arnold as chairman of the President's Council on Physical Fitness and Sports. Arnold promptly transformed this largely ceremonial appointment into a personal mission, traveling to every state in the country to promote fitness in schools and communities. Suddenly, and in yet another context, Arnold was, quite literally, everywhere.

By this time, people were already speculating about Arnold's future in politics. Many felt he would make an interesting mayor or perhaps even a senator. But when his box office clout began to fade a bit in the late 1990s, it seemed like it might be time to turn away from Arnold and look—sometimes a bit anxiously—toward the new millennium for what it might offer—or threaten.

While America worked to shore up its defenses against the widely predicted Y2K meltdown, behind the scenes Arnold was shoring up his political base and preparing a run for high office. By the summer of 2003, it was clear that California was likely to recall its sitting governor, Gray Davis, and replace him with someone who could carry the disillusioned voters on his still-mighty shoulders. Arnold's landslide victory in the California recall election came as a surprise only to those whose backs had, once again, been turned.

If you were an anthropologist trying to understand contemporary America, you would do well to pick Arnold as your starting point, paying particular attention to a gubernatorial election that, along with Arnold, featured comedians, used car salesmen, and porn stars. Well, we are those anthropologists, and this is the story of America today as filtered through the lenses imposed by Arnold Schwarzenegger.

Twenty-five years ago, when his name evoked images of an award-winning bodybuilder and little else, there was little reason to anticipate the attachment of Arnold Schwarzenegger to every important issue in American culture at the dawn of the twenty-first century.

But after more than two decades of examining Arnold's domination of American popular culture, we are prepared to argue that more than any other figure in America today, Arnold Schwarzenegger lives and thrives and multiplies at the threshold of diverse worlds: the celluloid of Hollywood, the me-consciousness of self-help and health, entrepreneurship, movie special effects, politics, and all the other arenas in which he has become a major player. It is not simply that he has transformed himself from bodybuilder to businessman to box office monster to politician; rather, he is simultaneously and impossibly everywhere in our culture at all times. Arnold Schwarzenegger defines the essence of the American Dream in a time when Americans have had to recognize the vulnerability and near impossibility of that dream.

If you were to take a tour of our archives, you would find hundreds of magazines featuring cover stories on Arnold; crates full of folders filled with newspaper clippings; mounds of sensationalist tabloids, towers made from Arnold videos and DVDs, shelves full of books with references to, or whole chapters on, Schwarzenegger; also posters, T-shirts, bumper stickers, photographs, games, lapel pins, action figures, bobble-heads, trading cards, transcripts of interviews, mugs, audio tapes, Halloween costumes, scribbled notes about billboards and advertisements, letters and e-mails, electronic databases of our own dreams about Arnold, and Schwarzenegger souvenirs of all kinds.

We have collected these materials not because we are fans of Arnold, but because each item has a place in the constellation called Arnold Schwarzenegger. As we stand in the midst of all these things, casting our attention in every direction like astronomers looking out into the stars, we realize that each of these objects contributes to our understanding of how American culture has invited Arnold to reach into virtually every sector of our society.

As you read this book, you will notice many small endnote numbers in the text. We encourage you to see these superscripts as a kind of subplot to the Arnold story. As the authors, we offer extensive analysis and commentary on Arnold Schwarzenegger and his fascinating roles in American culture. But there is a story within this story, and in fact this embedded story is one of our primary motivations for writing *Why Arnold Matters* in the first place.

The fact is, wherever you turn, you can find Arnold. To illustrate just how widespread his influence is, to drive home how attentively America is watching Arnold, writing, wondering, and worrying about him, and has been doing so since the early 1970s, we have included hundreds of references to him in contexts as diverse as they are numerous, from all over the world. We believe that an important part of why Arnold matters can best be recognized by acknowledging the thorough saturation of American—and to a great extent global—culture with "Ah-nuld." You can prove this to yourself by following the traces in the endnotes. Live links to the references are available on our project Web site www.whyarnold-matters.com. In many cases we have indicated Web sites instead of original texts (for newspapers, for example) so that the reader can more easily access these documents.[3]

We have examined in detail the avenues big and small that Arnold has taken on his way to California's capitol. There are the movies, the magazine covers, the public statements, television appearances, slang expressions, fitness programs and body obsessions, the marriage to Maria, the constant rumors and gossip, the omnipresent merchandising, and the political gamesmanship.

We took it as our task to pay attention to all these things in order to explain how Schwarzenegger has become so thoroughly a part of America's common knowledge. Why, by the end of the twentieth century, was this particular male icon so intricately stitched into the fabric of American culture? Why is he, of all American figures, the one who represents us to the world? Maybe because, as sociology professor Robert Elias put it, to the world, "America is now the Schwarzenegger of international politics."[4] In what ways did Arnold, in effect, lead us into the twenty-first century: cinematically, artistically, physically, psychically, politically, and morally? Why Arnold and not someone else? Why did Sylvester Stallone, for example, never achieve the same cultural status? He had the body, and a similar funny way of talking, and the cinematic presence. What was missing that Arnold readily supplied? Why does Arnold matter so much? About Stallone, Arnold has said, "He takes himself far too seriously."[5] That may be so, but anyone who fails to take Arnold seriously does so at the risk of overlooking a social and political force that will influence the American scene for many years to come.

Much has already been written about Arnold's celebrity roles, and more will be written in the future. The case has been made that Arnold is simply a gigantic celebrity who has translated this status into all his other successful endeavors.

But celebrity isn't everything, and it is doubtful that much of the civilized world cared when singer and songwriter Sonny Bono became a U.S. congressman in 1994, when actor/attorney Fred Thompson of *Law & Order* fame became a U.S. senator, when Jesse "The Body" Ventura turned in his wrestling trunks for the Minnesota statehouse in 1998, when Ronald Reagan first became California governor in 1967, when astronaut John Glenn became a U.S. senator in 1975, when basketball star Bill Bradley became a senator in 1979, or when Clint Eastwood was elected mayor of Carmel, California, in 1986.

But in 2003, people everywhere *did* care about this episode in U.S. politics. The larger context of the California election represented a monstrous warp in the American political process that made the world sit up and take notice. Politics as usual had morphed into politics-as-unusual when a total of 135 candidates mobbed the ballot in what was universally characterized as a circus or freak show, further evidence that the entire state of California needed therapy. The national pastime of watching California make a fool of itself had entered the championship playoffs.

Arnold Schwarzenegger—in all of his various versions—has fed an appetite in the culture that he has cleverly recognized and nourished. We are not simply the passive consumers of Arnold's contributions but rather coconspirators in creating a nation hungry for the figure of Arnold Schwarzenegger. Whether it is our impatience with real democracy or our seemingly endless search for the Superman who will right all wrongs (especially since our filmic "Superman" is now in a wheelchair), we have opened our imaginations, pocketbooks, and poll booths to the simple possibilities he represents. Whether we are looking for a catalyst that fuses our mundane lives to cinematic reality or are seeking an orderly life in a frightening, chaotic world, America has commissioned Arnold Schwarzenegger to be our cultural tour guide.

Arnold, we find, is very much at home in our heads. He has made a cozy place where his ideas seem to wrap themselves comfortably around everyday thoughts and actions: There must be order, there will be self-discipline, you will all make yourselves fit for the world to come. This fit world, so vividly projected in an imaginative way in all of Schwarzenegger's films, was neatly packaged for the California recall election.

Then, the spectacle of the California election became, for the world, a reflection of America. For that moment in history, America was Arnold, and Arnold was America.

Curiously—and perhaps predictably—we have, at the end of the twentieth century and beginning of the twenty-first, created Arnold as a Leviathan in all the senses of the word that have circulated in the Western world for centuries. In simple terms, a Leviathan is the largest thing of its kind. In Jewish mystical thought (the Kabbalah, so popular with Hollywood stars at the moment) and in the Bible, the Leviathan is a giant creature from the sea, a mythical monster that crushes its enemies who will one day be consumed by the righteous at the "end of days." In political terms it refers to an overblown government that exerts coercive control over its citizens. A Leviathan, in the works of seventeenth-century philosopher Thomas Hobbes, is the State, which is represented by a gigantic man who has more stature and strength than is natural. He is a mortal god in whose hands we agree to place our fate. Californians have elected their Leviathan.[6]

Having outgrown his birthplace ("I didn't like being in a little country like Austria"[7]), outgrown bodybuilding (by getting smaller), and outgrown the movies (by expanding his spheres of influence into politics), Arnold has now taken his place as statesman, wielding new and greater power. As he told us all, in an interview over ten years ago, "My relationship to power and authority is that I'm all for it. People need somebody to watch over them. Ninety-five percent of the people in the world need to be told what to do and how to behave."[8] By placing himself among the 5 percent who will watch over the rest of us, Arnold has, some have suggested, become like the "Golem"—a figure from Jewish mythology of the Middle Ages. The Golem was shaped from clay and programmed to obey the rabbi who had created him for the benefit of his people. But the Golem, who could disguise himself at will and who could appear to be either human or superhuman, frequently became uncontrollable, lashing out not only at the rabbi who made him, but also at the people he was designed to protect.[9]

Thomas Hobbes? Sylvester Stallone? The Golem? Porn stars? The American Dream? Sonny Bono? Bodybuilding? Superman? The Kabbalah? Who else could possibly be directly connected to all of these cultural items? Who else could have so completely redefined the idea of "political muscle"? What other public figure has so thoroughly entered the daily attention and expressions of so many people throughout the United States and the world? It is plain to see that in American culture and beyond, Arnold matters. Why should this be so? To quote Arnold from *The Predator*, "Stick around" to find out.

CHAPTER 1

# Crusade for
# Kahl-eee-fohr-nya

**IF YOU ARE NOT IN THE MOVIE BUSINESS,** or don't have a rabid fascination with movie production, then you probably don't know that rumors about which film productions are under way and which roles a star is considering or "attached to" circulate through the film community like currency through a banking system. These rumors are as real, in many ways, as movies that actually get made because they show who the players are, what connections they are willing to make, and what deals key players are happy to be associated with. While a rumored film may never be made, it may in fact pave the path for, and be used as leverage in, numerous other collaborations and deals.

Since the early 1990s, the project that has kept the rumors flowing in the world of Schwarzenegger films is one called *Crusade*. *Crusade* (not *The Crusades* or *The Crusader*) has been called "the Oak's dream project"[1] (one of Arnold's nicknames is the Austrian Oak) by one well-known fan Web site (www.TheARNOLDFANS.com) that has been watching the convoluted history of this would-be epic. Rumored to be in development with some combination of Hollywood heavyweights Arnold Schwarzenegger, James Cameron, Paul Verhoeven, and Walon Green in acting, producing, directing, or writing roles, *Crusade* is the story of a condemned man who uses his wiles to get sent on one of the eleventh-century Holy Wars. The Holy Wars, or Crusades, had many economic, cultural, religious, and political purposes, but one explicit one was to free the Holy Lands from the Arabs "occupying" these sacred places.

As another film Web site described it, "*Crusade* has gone down in legend as the ultimate potential Schwarzenegger movie, in which the floppy-titted Austrian would play a feudal serf carrying Christ's crucifixion cross back to Rome—hacking his way through hordes of anti-social heathens, as he goes."[2] The property was sold to Warner Brothers in 1995 after the original production company, Carolco, went bankrupt. Even as late as February 2003, it was still rumored that the film was ready to be made.[3] Fans expressed an interest in seeing Arnold make this film more than any other. When polled at one fan site, "Which possible future film would you prefer to see?" the answer was 64 percent for *Crusade*.[4]

In 1995 leaked copies of a purported script described the story fans could expect to see in the theatres. Arnold was to play Hagan, a thief in the Middle Ages who is condemned to die. Hearing that the Pope has declared a call to Holy War and had instructed the people to look for a sign that this is the Lord's bidding, Hagan decides to offer the people what they needed and save himself in the process. In his prison cell he burns the image of a cross into his back. When it is discovered by his would-be executioners, it is recognized as the sought-after sign and he is chosen to lead the Crusade.[5]

The same rumored script caused protest in the conservative Christian community. As one newspaper described it, "HOLY WAR is set to break out in Hollywood over an Arnold Schwarzenegger blockbuster which Christian groups have called 'one of the most vicious anti-Christian films ever.'" The objections were to parts of the script that depicted "graphic scenes of rape, violence and cannibalism, with the heads of Muslims being fired from cannons." The objection was that it made the Christian Crusaders look excessively violent. The head of the Christian Film and Television Commission, a watchdog group that monitors media representations of Christians, complained, "It is extraordinarily one-sided in its portrayal of a horrendous, malevolent and evil Church. The evil and malevolence was on both sides in the Crusades."[6]

Arnold's films, and rumors of films he might make, have a way of entering our everyday culture and blossoming into more than just commercial products. Even just the titles for these films have a way not only of foreshadowing events in the culture, but also, somehow, of influencing them in surprising—and sometimes deeply disturbing—ways. While *Crusade* may never see the movie-light of day, the title and its association with Schwarzenegger seem to have leached their way into the vernacular—a development that adds further evidence of Arnold's remarkable omnipresence in the culture. Ignoring this cultural osmosis is akin to failing to learn the lessons of history.

A crusade, as opposed to just a cause or a stance, is a passionate set of beliefs combined with direct action. A crusade expects results. Crusade as a concept and term has been taken up by those fighting breast cancer (the Avon Breast Cancer Crusade[7]), promoting Scientology (The World Literacy Crusade[8]), working for children's education (the Rhode Island Children's Crusade[9]), or trying to release prisoners (the Patrick Crusade[10]).

Schwarzenegger started using the concept of the crusade when he was chair of the President's Council on Physical Fitness and Sports under the first President Bush. His "self-proclaimed 'fitness crusade'"[11] during which he visited all fifty states to preach fitness and exercise was also a valuable political proving ground. He continued to use the concept and term "crusade" when he was advocating government-sponsored after-school programs in California to keep kids out of trouble. In Washington to lobby for funds, he told reporters, "This is my crusade. I want all the political leaders to know how great results of after-school programs are. We want our kids to grow up smart. We are showing measurable results in California.... For every dollar spent on these programs, the taxpayers saved three dollars in less crime and less drugs."[12]

For reasons that are usually presented as economic but may very well have also been political, Schwarzenegger never made *Crusade*. But like many of his film projects, this one had the uncanny ability to anticipate the mood of a time and the issues that would motivate audiences. The Holy Wars story of *Crusade* was projected for all to see during Arnold's run for governor of California. His campaign was framed as a crusade to save California from the heathens in Sacramento, to rescue the economy from the forces of corruption, and to restore to the righteous the sacred place called Kahl-eee-fohr-nya. This was not a hidden message but the very public face of the campaign.

The press began to pick up the word "crusade" and run with it. The *San Francisco Chronicle,* reporting on the September 24th gubernatorial candidates' debate, observed, "It took Schwarzenegger... several minutes to realize that all order was lost and that [Arianna] Huffington was on a personal crusade to discredit him."[13] Commenting about the recall campaign as the gubernatorial race accelerated toward election day, a dean at the Annenberg School for Communication at the University of Southern California said, "Maybe if you're passionate about the recall or about Arnold, this is really a crusade."[14] *Variety* claimed that "Arnold Schwarzenegger's two-month long crusade to terminate Gov. Gray Davis' reign may be the biggest earthquake to hit California in recent memory."[15]

The *Daily News* of Los Angeles featured a story entitled "Major Crusade for Charter Schools Is On," the main point being that leaders of the statewide charter schools movement were now counting on Schwarzenegger's receptiveness to a crusade for educational reforms.[16] The *Inland Valley Daily Bulletin* in Ontario, California, ran a story about radio station KFI-AM's "VLF crusade," explaining that the station was offering to pick up the tab for one listener's vehicle licensing fee each day.[17] A city councilwoman's efforts to halt what she and newly elected Governor Schwarzenegger saw as excessive raises and benefits for government employees were described in the press as her "crusade against rising salaries" for city employees.[18]

The *New York Times* provided an intriguing analysis of the effect of Arnold's election on the Republican Party image:

"In a mere two months, he did far more than George W. Bush's touchy-feely 'compassionate conservatism' to demolish his party's image as the nation's moral scold. (For starters, it's hard to imagine the White House talking up its crusade for abstinence-only sex education with Arnold on the team.)"[19] Arnold's views on matters of sex and reproductive rights for women became the fuel for American Life League's "Crusade for the Defense of Our Catholic Church,"[20] which questioned his commitment to the principles of Catholicism.

Arnold showed his awareness of the importance of environmental crusades to California voters when he vowed to convert one of his famous Hummers to run on natural gas and hydrogen. According to one *Newsweek* article, "Arnold... isn't the only one getting caught up in this crusade." Venture capital firms and wealthy investors throughout California and the rest of the United States "are starting to contemplate" joining the same alternative energy crusade.[21]

In the afterglow of the California recall election, several U.S. congressmen proposed or re-proposed legislation for amending the Constitution to allow foreign-born citizens to be elected president. For one representative, Vic Snyder (D-Arkansas), "the crusade is personal" because he is "troubled that his niece, adopted from South Korea and raised here since infancy, is denied the promise that any American kid—including her—could someday grow up to be president."[22] As if being associated with the idea of the presidency were not a lofty enough crusade, an article in the *Sunday Tribune* (Dublin) with the headline "Nobel Crusades" speculated, with some irony, "Would it be too far-fetched to expect a future [Nobel] prize to go to Arnold Schwarzenegger?" The same article reminded us that "the Pope was forwarded this year's prize for his opposition to Bush's crusade against the Arabs."[23]

Bush's uninformed use of the word "crusade" after the September 11, 2001, attacks was viewed much more ominously than any of Arnold's uses. A few days after the attacks on New York and Washington, President Bush stated his plans to retaliate against the attackers. "This crusade, this war on terrorism," he said, "is going to take a while."[24] Apparently ignorant of the history of the Crusades and how using the term in this situation was one of the most inflammatory things an avowed Christian president could do, Bush ignited a firestorm. President Bush appeared to some to be "calling for an indiscriminate killing of Arabs."[25] One critic stated that "He was obviously quite pleased with himself for having thought of such a catchy phrase. But he was quickly silenced by his advisers.... After that, the word was quietly dropped from his vocabulary."[26]

Crusades have a way of turning around and attacking the very people who initiated them. This is because of the fear that a victory in a crusade will be diluted if the faithful at home get lax in their commitment while the crusading warriors are away. The historical Crusades of the Middle Ages were often redirected toward fellow Christians at home and not just foreign others.[27] They became a form of "internal police actions,"[28] according to historian Jonathan Riley-Smith, and bear a striking resemblance to current Homeland Security measures.

American-style freedom, with its built-in self-analysis and capacity for tolerating a wide range of stances, doesn't seem to be the place for long-term crusades. Yet crusades against Americans by other Americans have become all too familiar recently as fear or indifference replaces the chaos and creativity of real democracy. This is most visible in the "culture wars" that have been raging for years about the proper behavior for citizens, especially those who engage in the arts. In the culture wars, whoever gets to define the country's goals and priorities, whoever gets to launch its self-styled crusade, can claim leadership.

In a finely worded statement on a military issues and foreign affairs Web site, Austin Bay explains: "By design, America is a radical experiment in letting human beings use their own judgment. Sometimes it looks like a huge mistake. Bad judgments tend to fill the headlines. Drunk drivers, lying CEOs, bungling government bureaucrats, runaway teens, and baseball commissioners halting all-star games... [are] welcome to the daily spotlight of foolishness. It's another paradox, one the authoritarians don't quite get: America's capacity for self-critique—indeed, the liberty to criticize—makes it even stronger."[29] Not everyone agrees with this assessment, and the conservative culture war crusade is against this style of chaotic freedom.

A hallmark of any crusade is making those judgments pre-emptively, not letting people think for themselves. Crusades, then, especially ones spawned by governmental figures, must be approached cautiously, like a bad movie script that maybe ought not to get made. Despite giving up on the movie version years ago, Arnold has indeed begun his crusade by becoming California's crusading governor, encouraging his believers to let him decide how things should be run. This *Crusade,* more than any movie version, will either mightily entertain or thoroughly dismay the fans who have been waiting all these years for its appearance.

# CHAPTER 2

# Total Recall: Conan vs. the Terminator, California 2003

ON OCTOBER 8, 2003, the day after the California recall election, and for many days afterward, newspapers, Internet sites, and magazines across the country—and throughout the world—announced the results in bold headlines:

ARNOLD! (*Los Angeles Daily News*)[1]

ARNIE WINS (*New York Post*)[2]

ARNIE DOES IT! (*People*)[3]

VOTERS OUST DAVIS, ELECT SCHWARZENEGGER (*New York Sun*)[4]

SCHWARZENEGGER WINS AS CALIF. REVOLT OUSTS DAVIS (*USA Today*)[5]

THE PREDATOR; MOVIE TOUGH-GUY ARNOLD SCHWARZENEGGER HAS TURNED POLITICAL PREDATOR (*Western Mail*, Cardiff, Wales)[6]

**VOTER SURVEY BACKS OUSTER OF DAVIS AND A VICTORY FOR SCHWARZENEGGER** (*New York Times*)[7]

**SCHWARZENEGGER WINS, DAVIS CONCEDES** (CNN.com)[8]

**ARNIE THE TERMWINATOR** (*The Sun*, London)[9]

**CALIFORNIA HAS A NEW STRONGMAN: SCHWARZENEGGER** (Reuters)[10]

**ARNOLD, IT'S ME, GEORGE** (*New York Newsday*)[11]

**VOTERS RECALL DAVIS; SCHWARZENEGGER'S IN** (*Los Angeles Times*)[12]

**TOTAL RECALL** (*Orange County Register*)[13]

**TOTAL RECALL: DAVIS OUT, SCHWARZENEGGER IN** (*Long Beach [Calif.] Press Telegram*)[14]

**INLAND EMPIRE BASKS IN SCHWARZENEGGER VICTORY** (*Pasadena [Calif.] Star News*)[15]

**FROM NOVICE TO GOVERNOR IN TWO MONTHS** (*New York Newsday*)[16]

**VICTORY FOR ARNOLD** (*U.S. News and World Report*)[17]

**PRODUCTION STARTS ON ARNOLD'S NEXT BIG ROLE** (HollywoodReporter.com)[18]

**ARNOLD'S EARTHQUAKE** (*Newsweek*)[19]

**ARNOLD UBER ALLES** (*The Weekly Standard*)[20]

However they chose to phrase it, it was clearly a major event with echoes and repercussions across the United States and around the world. Correspondents from Mexico, Canada, Japan, Israel, Uganda, Albania, Russia, China, France, and even Scotland all weighed in with reports and commentary. The *New York Times* noted that "Mr. Schwarzenegger is among the most famous people ever elected to political office."[21]

Why were so many people throughout America, and around the globe, so thoroughly absorbed in Arnold

Schwarzenegger's campaign and victory in California? If we consider that most United States gubernatorial elections are generally of little interest to people in the other forty-nine states, never mind to the Chinese or the Dutch or the Brazilians, then we have an idea of the intensity of the national and international interest in this anomalous ballot vote. This fascination is not just with Arnold the celebrity, but with what the election says about American culture at this odd moment in history.

And yet, the only thing that should have surprised anyone about Arnold's political victory is that it did not happen sooner. Movie critic Mick LaSalle notes that "if 'Gov. Schwarzenegger' sounds strange, well, strangeness is the actor's best friend."[22] Arnold's entire career has been founded upon achieving one surprising milestone after another. Becoming governor was, in a sense, a proper sequel in a series of cinematic cultural gestures Arnold has made for over thirty years. "As an acclaimed weightlifter in real life and a barbarian, a terminator, a commando, a kindergarten cop and the last action hero in the movies, Schwarzenegger enjoyed a pop-cultural incumbency [former governor] Davis never had."[23]

However, it may be a mistake to try to distinguish "real" life from Arnold's life "in the movies" since the two domains have always been intimately connected. It's not that he goes through life shooting his enemies, impersonating school teachers, or wearing loincloths year round as he amasses wealth and women (well, actually, he *has* done some of those things!), it's that, in all of his movies, Arnold plays himself. He may be dressed in military camouflage, he may be built around an "aluminum alloy" chassis, he may play a Russian policeman or a pregnant man, but in all his portrayals, there is never a moment when we forget we are watching Arnold Schwarzenegger—former bodybuilder, Hollywood megastar, husband to a Kennedy, power broker, and, most recently, governor.

But the California recall added a new wrinkle to the idea that Arnold is always playing the role of "himself." Each time the campaign was called the "Total Recall," Americans were reminded that Arnold the candidate was always also an elusive cinematic construction. It might not have seemed important to voters to make any more direct connection between Arnold and the continuous stream of allusions to the film *Total Recall,* but if they had, they might have been struck by the ways in which the recall campaign and election and the film's story about a forgetful man destined to liberate the dry, airless Martian planet intersected.

At the start of the 1990 movie, Arnold plays Douglas Quaid, a man with a memory glitch. It's not that he cannot remember the past; the real problem is that the past he remembers is one that never happened. His true memories have been replaced with "true lies" (not to be confused with his 1994 movie by that name). He "recalls" having been married for twelve years to a woman who has in fact only recently been assigned to act as his wife. Only in his dreams do traces of his real memories tantalize him with visions of another life—one he longs to understand again and to which he is, when awake, strangely drawn to rediscover. When the movie begins, Quaid has just awakened from the recurring dream that he is on Mars with a mysterious dark-haired woman. His "wife," guessing that he has, once again, had the dream, teases him about the other woman and the fact that he keeps having the same dream. Quaid laughs that his wife is jealous of a dream and tells her, "I'm always home by morning."

It soon becomes clear, however, that Quaid is haunted by the sense that his life is not quite his own. He is not "always home by morning" because it's not really his home. The house, like his wife, job, and memories, is part of an elaborately staged sham. Attracted by newscasts about a people's revolt against a tyrannical ruler on Mars, Quaid feels compelled to travel to the red planet. Of course his wife, assigned to keep him from doing just that, objects. But Quaid is adamant. He utters the line that could have resonated right out of the movie and into the collective imaginations of California voters: "I feel I was meant for something more than this. I want to do something with my life. I want to be somebody." He wants, it turns out, to be himself… again.

Against preposterous odds, and by way of a botched experience at the neuro-fantasy vendor, Rekall, Quaid starts to regain enough of his old, real memories to confirm that he must return to Mars, to the work he was doing there, and to someone he left there. But upon his reentry to Martian society, he discovers that he is not Quaid at all. He is someone named Hauser who had once fought with the resistance but who had been co-opted by the cruel dictator, Cohagen. Once again, the trouble is that he cannot remember any of this, as he struggles to persuade the dark-haired woman—his former lover—and the other resistance fighters that he is who he says he is at that moment, not who anyone else says he is or has been. In his role as California's 38th governor, he now finds himself in precisely the same position.

How does Quaid succeed in liberating Mars from a ruthless and greedy autocrat who thinks nothing of cutting off oxygen to the Martian citizens as a way to control them? He must first establish himself as a man to be trusted, and then emerge as the front-runner for leadership among a population of rebels and "mutants" with leadership ideas of their own; he must regain the trust of the slender, dark-haired woman after betraying her both politically and sexually; and he must, ultimately, defeat a colorless, white-haired bureaucrat who has deliberately failed to properly manage the planet's energy resources, environment, and economy. If this all sounds familiar, that's because *Total Recall,* made in 1990, provides a strangely accurate glimpse into Arnold's future—the future that Governor Schwarzenegger occupies now.

It is doubtful anyone believes that Arnold's election has "liberated" California and that now the country's largest state will be free of energy troubles, economic strain, political infighting, or social unrest. But most would agree that a Governor Schwarzenegger represents a significant shift in the political climate not only in California, but in the nation as well.

One could argue that America has ignored his rise to political power at its own peril. In a way, he has been heading for political office, like a juggernaut, since he first realized his commitment to the Republican Party in 1968. It was Richard Nixon who first inspired Arnold. "I listened to President Nixon talk about free enterprise, opening up the borders and… trade with the whole world, getting government off your back, lowering taxes and strengthening the military.… So I turned to my friend… and said,… 'This is the philosophy I believe in.'"[24] Arnold added, "If this guy is a Republican, then I am a Republican."[25] Just a few years later, Schwarzenegger told this story to Nixon himself; Nixon replied, "If you ever run for governor, you have my help."[26]

For Arnold, those early years in the United States were spent winning title after title in the bodybuilding competitions that would secure his place as "the greatest bodybuilder of the 20th Century."[27] By 1976, Schwarzenegger had won the Mr. Olympia competition six times; he'd been awarded the title of Mr. Universe five times; and he'd been named "best built man in Europe," Mr. International, and Mr. World. Arnold had the most prominent body on the planet, and the name "Arnold Schwarzenegger" evoked images of gargantuan muscles wrapped around an exotic foreigner's frame. But in 1977, Arnold told the German magazine *Stern,* "When one has money, one day it becomes less interesting. And when one is also the best in film, what can be more interesting? Perhaps power. Then one moves into politics and becomes governor or president or something."[28] As it turned out, Arnold fulfilled his own forecast and did not need Nixon's help. Life for Arnold had come full circle: Nixon was, in effect, "recalled" by the American people and was replaced, and now Arnold is positioned to be the one called upon to help future Republican candidates.

But contrary to what many commentators have debated, Arnold was not elected on the basis of his politics or his position on issues. Despite his being one of the most familiar personalities in the world, no one knew, with any consistency, what those positions were. As *Los Angeles Times* reporter Joe Matthews pointed out, "Californians have never known more about a new governor.... Californians have never known less about a new governor."[29] He was elected for strange and, to some, ominous reasons. But there is nothing about his politics that has made a dent in American consciousness.

America—and much of the rest of the world—is charmed by Arnold because we don't have to concern ourselves with his political positions on anything. Reporter Annie Brown noted that "most Californians do not care that he is no political veteran. In fact, that's why they like him."[30] Arnold is always himself, always a character from a movie not-quite-made. This is why so much talk about Arnold's politics misses the point. There are no politics in the sense that political scientists would define it. The best journalists from around the world spent months trying to figure out what Arnold's politics were and all failed. That is because Arnold's politics are not about a political machine or a stance on issues. His politics are a cultural politics, an attempt to make the world over in his image.

Arnold never takes clear stands on issues because there are no stands. There is only Arnold, the filter through which we must, in his cultural politics, live our lives. There is no hidden political agenda à la Dick Cheney and George W. Bush because Arnold is a different kind of political animal, driven by the sheer lust to market himself in more and more powerful circles. Journalist Mark Lawson makes a useful distinction between two kinds of politics: retail and narrative.[31] In the case of the former, candidates sell themselves by saturating the media and the "street" with a few simple policy messages that eventually imprint themselves onto America's relatively short-term memory. Simply put, the retail politician shakes thousands of hands and repeats his or her political sound bite thousands of times until it becomes like an advertising jingle—something you recall just enough of to make you think its source must be worthwhile.

In the case of a candidate employing narrative politics, "The victor was likely to be not the man who put in the most hours but the one who told the most extraordinary story about himself." As Lawson explains it, "A rough rule of narrative politics is that the candidate whose life story makes the best Hollywood movie wins the race."[32]

In Arnold Schwarzenegger's case, both kinds of politics come dramatically into play. For over twenty years, Arnold has engaged in "retail politics" without necessarily intending to. Every time his name has appeared on a marquee, each time his larger-than-life cinematic character saved the day or society itself, every time his movie titles have somehow predicted, or attached themselves to, events and ideas circulating in American culture, from *Pumping Iron* to *The Last Action Hero,* he was, in a sense, deploying retail political strategy.

What is most remarkable about Arnold's political ascendancy is that his retail politics not only ran parallel to these narratives, but became intertwined in such a way as to produce the most muscular candidacy America has ever seen. Here was a celebrity powerhouse who had already made a movie called *Total Recall* thirteen years before the political event. Here was an icon whose original claim to the public eye—bodybuilding and becoming Mr. Universe—had already been made into a Hollywood narrative in *Pumping Iron,* way back in 1977. Here was an immigrant whose knowledge of English was as minimal as his body fat, who later married the niece of one of America's most popular presidents. America has always loved a good story, a suspenseful tale full of surprises, heroes, and strange characters. The 2003 California recall provided all of the above and made it possible for Arnold's election to seem both inevitable and a perfect fit for the culture.

In the California recall election, the world-famous Arnold Schwarzenegger—champion bodybuilder, Kennedy in-law, fitness czar, box office superstar, successful entrepreneur, model of masculinity, and, as he has said about himself, "the living, breathing incarnation of the American Dream"[33]—provided an air of magic and excitement to what has traditionally been a dull political event dominated by boring talking heads and professional policymakers. After all, there certainly was entertainment value and humor in an action movie election, a "total recall" in which "Conan the Republican" threatened to "terminate" his wimpy opponents and become "Governator" of the Golden State.

The election not only featured the iconic Schwarzenegger but also tickled audiences with a list of players that included a retired meat packer, adult movie actress, porn peddler, former child star, filmmaker, Indian tribal leader, denture maker, screenwriter, marijuana lawyer, railroad switchman, energy consultant, retired police officer, teacher, college student, gay rights attorney, visual effects artist, unemployed engineer, prizefighter, (not *the*) Michael Jackson, (not *the*) Edward Kennedy, (not *the*) Bob Dole, (not *the*) Richard Simmons, Vietnamese radio producer, middleweight sumo wrestler, Persian-American Ph.D., bounty hunter, golf professional, firefighter, doctor, comedian, set designer, ButtMonkey beer producer, punk-rock vocalist, used car dealer, mortgage broker, private investigator, a guy who calls himself the "Bumhunter," and a man dressed all in blue.

If the world was anxious to know about American politics in an era of intensified American influence, it was getting a bizarre eyeful and earful. While Schwarzenegger cautiously provided carefully staged speeches and rallies, the 35-year-old miniature, ex-*Diff'rent Strokes* actor Gary Coleman read a poem on the Game Show Network special called *Who Wants to be Governor of California? The Debating Game.* Serious candidates like Arianna Huffington and Tom McClintock were heavily overshadowed by the likes of smut king Larry Flynt in his wheelchair, or comedian Leo Gallagher smashing watermelons.

Porn star candidate "Mary Carey" jiggled her breasts in excitement when she announced her platform, which included a plan to tax breast implants, make lap dances a tax-deductible business expense, and legalize ferrets.[34] In her concession speech, she also offered to let Arnold grope her. In his postelection Web site, Gallagher lamented that with only 5,306 votes to Carey's 10,919 he did not even beat *one* of Mary's breasts. He is now running for president of the United States. Gary Coleman came in eighth with 13,978 votes but got edged out by Larry Flynt with 17,019.[35] One could argue that, despite their weak showing in the election, many of the 135 candidates presented extraordinary stories to the voting public, and at least one or two have made it to Hollywood. But narrative politics requires a compelling story that would make the *best* movie, one that will stay in the minds of voters long after the projector lights have dimmed. Candidate Arnold's thirty-plus years in the spotlight left his competition in the shadows.

Throughout his brief and intense campaign, Arnold was able to keep the attention focused on his goal to be Gray Davis's "term-eliminator," receiving 3,743,393 votes (49 percent), over a million more votes than the runner-up, Lieutenant Governor Cruz Bustamante. From the moment Arnold craftily announced his candidacy on Jay Leno's *Tonight Show*, he had everyone, ranging from the mainstream TV to radio and print media to the most edgy Web site producers, comedians, and political commentators, seriously addressing his "Running Man" status. No other credible candidate could afford to ignore him and even the sitting governor fruitlessly challenged him to a man-to-man, or manly, debate. When the first candidates' debate was held on September 3, Schwarzenegger refused to take part. "We're holding a chair and will accommodate Arnold if he chooses to come," said Michael Kelly, executive producer of KTVU. But in the end, the organizers opted not to actually have an empty chair on the stage to represent Schwarzenegger's refusal to appear.[36] Arnold's absence, and the absence of his symbolically empty chair, did little to diminish anyone's awareness of him. Even the joke that the empty chair might actually win the debate was a reminder of this.

During the eight weeks of the recall campaign, both gleeful comedians and sober reporters filled the airwaves with imitations of Ah-nuld's Austrian accent. It was sometimes hard to distinguish standard network news, which regularly sprinkled catch phrases from Schwarzenegger films into their reports, from news spoofs like Jon Stewart's *The Daily Show* on Comedy Central or the political debates on *Real Time with Bill Maher.* Late-night comedians bubbled with commentary that was often more critical and insightful than many of the standard news programs. Conan O'Brien joked that "Earlier today, Arnold Schwarzenegger criticized the California school system, calling it disastrous. Arnold says California's schools are so bad that its graduates are willing to vote for me."[37] The California recall was also an inspiration to thousands of artistic types who flooded the Internet with satires, animations, joke lists, songs, faux film posters, and pseudo editorials. The election became the most significant shared cultural event of the year and served as further confirmation of the endless cultural productions directly related to Arnold Schwarzenegger.

While America was mightily distracted by the spectacle of 135 candidates for governor certified by the California Secretary of State's office to run in the recall election, we would argue that the election was really only about Arnold Schwarzenegger. More specifically, it was a contest between two candidates who did not appear on the ballot at all: the mythological Conan and the technological Terminator. Conan the Barbarian dazzled the media and America with his noble savagery, his relentless pursuit of power and justice, and, of course, his big, exposed muscles. Conan the candidate looked like the sure bet for election to California's highest office. (Though not to everyone; an article in the *New York Times* referred to Arnold as "Conan the Deceiver.")[38]

We should pause for a moment to appreciate the cognitive dissonance in the idea of Conan as a Twenty-first-Century political candidate. Arnold's character, Conan, "lived" around 12,000 B.C.E. Among the barbarian tribes, one becomes victim to Thulsa Doom (played by James Earl Jones), leader of a band of raiders who kill everyone in Conan's tribe except the children. The latter are taken as slaves to Doom. Hard labor throughout his childhood makes Conan a powerful adult, and before long he is "promoted" to performing gladiator. His successes lead to his release from captivity, and he vows revenge upon Doom for destroying his family and his people.

The image of Conan the candidate also brings to mind one of the most famous lines in the movie: When Conan and some of his fellow warriors are discussing the things that make life good, Conan declares that living the good life is "To crush your enemies, see them driven before you, and to hear the lamentation of the women." Arnold's victory in California was decisive enough to be seen as crushing his opponents; the media made sure to parade the other, losing candidates before Arnold and America, and from a week or so before the recall election until many weeks after, a number of women raised their own "lamentations" about Arnold's allegedly abusive treatment of them.

Except in the most superficial ways, there are few parallels between Conan the Barbarian and Arnold the Candidate. Still, something must have clicked for dozens of journalists and media pundits to keep referring to Arnold in this way. Even the *Sunday Times* from as far away as The Republic of South Africa made this connection in the article "Pass the Popcorn Please—It's Conan the Governor."[39] In that article, at least one important, if also amusing, link is made between Conan and Arnold: Conan becomes the man capable of seeking justice, vengeance, and power by getting big "pushing a huge wheel around for 20 years."[40] Arnold made himself big by pushing huge (round!) weights around for many years, and it has been the history of his muscular massiveness that has fueled so much of both his celebrity and his image as a man capable of accomplishing anything. Still, it's a long way from speaking a barbarian's lines in a movie to speaking the victory lines of a governor-elect in a thunderous recall election. All those headlines reflecting such a startling event must mean that Arnold's election caught America at least a little by surprise.

For those who are still wondering how Arnold Schwarzenegger could have persuaded nearly four million people to vote him into one of the most powerful elected positions in the country in the most populous and wealthy state in the Union, let's go back in time. Back to the future of Arnold's successful political campaign. Back to the year that Arnold came "bahck" as the second Terminator in *T2,* the year after he transformed a bunch of unruly 5-year-olds into a troop of obedient and efficient soldiers in *Kindergarten Cop,* the year after his brain-wiped character in *Total Recall* managed to wrest power away from the despot ruling the entire Martian planet. In 1991, critics were suggesting that Arnold had "already outgrown the movies."[41] Ironically, earlier that same year, at the annual Arnold Classic in Columbus, Ohio, Arnold had told the crowd that to properly fit into the film-frames *of Terminator 2: Judgment Day,* he'd had to shrink his body down from its overlarge proportions. But what he may have outgrown so many years ago was the idea of a frame itself. Just when Arnold had reached the pinnacle of earning power and movie stardom, he found himself ready to break that frame and begin rebuilding himself for a new kind of competitive achievement: politics. John Milius, Arnold's director in *Conan the Barbarian,* pointed out that Arnold had "always said he's going to be governor of California some-day.... This is part of his plan, you know."[42]

Part of that plan had to include putting to rest any idea that he was anything like the barbarian he portrayed in the movies, that he was somehow the toxic product of a Nazi father, that his admitted use of steroids during his body-building career weakened his potential candidacy in any way, or that his brawn camouflaged an inadequate intellect. Early on, he had important people vouching for him. In 1991, Rabbi Marvin Heir, dean of the Simon Wiesenthal Center, listed three reasons why Arnold would be a good governor: He hates to fail, he's a workaholic, and he started out poor and can still remember those days. "Too many politicians," Rabbi Heir noted, "don't come from that sort of background and forget the important things to strive for."[43]

That the dean of the Simon Wiesenthal Center would speak so glowingly of Arnold told Arnold's detractors that having a Nazi father did not make Schwarzenegger complicit in his father's—and his birth-nation's—anti-Semitism. When President George Bush (senior) named Arnold as chair of the President's Council on Physical Fitness, the message was clear that Schwarzenegger's steroid use decades earlier was simply part of a vague history that no one need recall. Of course his marriage to Maria Shriver served to dispel any ideas that he was "uncivilized" like Conan. And Arnold's tremendously successful real estate investments have helped to show him to be a man with considerable brain power and business acumen. *Los Angeles Times* editorial-page editor Tom Plate explained that Arnold is "smarter than Reagan, and he sounds like Kissinger."[44] For Arnold, running California provides the next powerful transition in a life punctuated by achievement and that now punctuates the American story.

But what about the charges of sexual misconduct? Why didn't the allegations undo Arnold's campaign? Why wasn't Arnold more concerned that these charges could sink his candidacy? One reason may be that while one of Arnold's most popular phrases is "I'll be back," his true motto, according to Peter McGough, senior editor of the well-known bodybuilding magazine *Flex,* is "Don't look back."[45] Always looking ahead, Arnold was able to ignore the facts of his own past, and despite the allegations of "groping" and harassment, Schwarzenegger's vision of his future never wavered.

Ironically, the allegations may actually have helped his campaign. They provided Arnold with an unusual and surprisingly useful new role—that of the victim. In a fascinating piece of commentary, *Los Angeles Times* reporter Jill Stewart addressed the possibility of anti-Schwarzenegger/pro-Davis bias in the *Times*' handling of the harassment allegations. In particular, Stewart responded to what she described as *Times* executive editor John Carroll's "decisions to run eleventh-hour bombshells" intended to undermine Schwarzenegger's campaign and to discredit Stewart (and other reporters) in their attempts to expose this bias. One of Stewart's sources told her, "It became a Capt. Ahab and Moby Dick thing where they felt an increasing need to nail those points that could most hurt Schwarzenegger."[46]

Stewart's contention that Arnold was under unfair attack by the *Times* suggests that Californians may have found the eleventh-hour allegations to be, themselves, unfairly delivered so late in the game. According to Stewart and the reporters with whom she spoke, the *Times* reporters on the groping story had ample time to publish something long before they did. Stewart's source, a reporter who had been part of the Schwarzenegger coverage, told her, "Toward the end, a kind of hysteria gripped the newsroom. I witnessed a deep-seated, irrational need to get something on this guy [Schwarzenegger]. By Wednesday before it was published, I counted not fewer than 24 reporters dispatched on Arnold."[47]

One man, two dozen reporters (from a single newspaper), and a story about behavior that people described, variously, as primitive, Neanderthal, misogynist, and barbaric. Arnold was the "running man" dressed up in the ordinary guise of his more ordinary movie characters—John Kimble, Howard Langston, Adam Gibson, Gordy Brewer, even Julius Benedict.[48] But in the eyes of many, if you stripped away his casual clothes, his savvy businessman's aura, and his

Hollywood smile, we were left with Conan, a barbarian who, despite past sexual misconduct, Californians—and Americans in general—found more and more intriguing as the campaign picked up momentum.

Although Arnold's acting was roundly criticized after the making of this first Conan movie in 1982, many critics acknowledged that Arnold made a most convincing Conan—powerful, independent, clever, and ultimately and inevitably victorious in all of his ambitions. It became possible for Californians, and a nation, to overlook the allegations of misconduct partly because Conan the Candidate conjured images of a man driven by primitive urges who nevertheless has the strength to rise above them.

Despite Arnold's sometime image as the barbarian, few really believed that he was so simple in his thinking. Even from as far away as Pakistan, analysts have followed Arnold's clever economic strategies. As one writer put it in the *Daily Mail*, Pakistan's English daily newspaper, Arnold Schwarzenegger is "no barbarian at finances."[49] Conan was expected to have a sordid past; it was the noble quest of the present that drew the support of the west coasters. With reporter Bradley Gitz writing about the hypocrisy of voters who thought that past indiscretions should disqualify otherwise able candidates, voters may have asked themselves, "How many of us never did anything when we were 20 or 25 that we now wish we hadn't?"[50]

Perhaps more importantly, and foreshadowing the position that has made it possible for Arnold to fight through suspicions, accusations, and allegations, Arnold's Conan speaks the words that characterize his fierce independence from the kinds of influences that typically direct and redirect political campaigns. Toward the end of the movie, Conan and his companion, Subotai, are overwhelmingly outnumbered in a climactic battle. Invoking a deity, Conan says, "Crom, I have never prayed to you before. I have no tongue for it. No one, not even you, will remember if we were good men or bad. Why we fought, or why we died. All that matters is that two stood against many. If it pleases you, grant me this one request—grant me revenge! And if you do not listen, to HELL with you!" In other words, if the gods want to help, fine. But if not, Conan will fight off the hordes and emerge victorious (he returns, of course, two years later in *Conan the Destroyer*).

In the image of Conan, the powerful, passionate, and savage man, Arnold's appeal as a candidate seemed to actually grow. Something happened to Conan in the minds of voters in the early twenty-first century. As Kenneth Turan of the *Los Angeles Times* writes, now "he's Conan the Candidate, not Arnold the Barbarian."[51] Turan recalls Arnold telling him that Conan "has learned to defend himself in every kind of situation.... No one else gives him a break; he has to do everything himself."[52] Some Californians may have embraced the idea of the lone warrior Conan; for others he became "Conan the Auditor" who promised to "find out where the waste is" and restore the state to financial solvency.[53] Conan, the character, amassed vast wealth through stealing his way across the countryside. Arnold, the governor, has amassed comparable wealth through timely business transactions, relentless self-promotion, and by "stealing" the attention of Americans as we find ourselves unable to ignore Schwarzenegger's ubiquitous, cinematic presence.

The only problem with the theory that Conan was elected governor is that he wasn't. For reasons we explore later, it was the image of the Terminator that finally compelled voters to choose the postmodern, posthuman cyborg over the ancient muscleman. Of course, the election of Arnold the Terminator as governor of California also tells a compelling story about America, the choices we make, and the reasons for those choices. Arnold's election to governor signals just the infancy of his political power. It is that story that drew the attention of people around the world.

# CHAPTER 3

# Around the World in (Almost) 80 Days

**NOT MUCH IS KNOWN,** as of this writing, about Arnold's cameo role in the Warner Brothers 2004 remake of the Jules Verne tale *Around the World in 80 Days.* What we do know is that he plays the part of the Turkish prince, Hapi, who falls in love with a beautiful French artist, Monique, who is accompanying Passepartout and Phileas Fogg on their high-stakes, less-than-three-month journey around the world.

It's a multicultural story with the always-ironic twist of having Arnold, with his stronger-than-ever Austrian accent, playing the part of a foreigner from a vastly different land. As has been the case with so many of Arnold's movies, this one, for which production plans and filming began over a year before the California recall election, seems to anticipate an important cultural event or phenomenon: Arnold's own improbably brief and intense campaign to become governor of California. In fact, Arnold's campaign aroused the appetites of media far beyond American borders; by the time he was elected, he had, indeed, made it around the world in 80 days!

Actually, it took only 63 days. Arnold Schwarzenegger announced he was running for governor on August 6, 2003. Sixty-three days later, he was elected, and around the world, the news was all about Arnold and the California vote:

**MOVIE HERO BECOMES CALIFORNIA GOVERNOR** (Pravda.ru)[1]

**LA-LA LAND LOONY OVER SCHWARZENEGGER** (*Winnipeg Sun*)[2]

**SCHWARZENEGGER WIN: "IT'S OK FOR AMERICA"** (*Moscow Times*)[3]

**SCHWARZENEGGER OVERPOWERS DAVIS** (*Taipei Times*)[4]

**WORLD IS WIDE-EYED AS STATE ELECTS FOREIGNER WITH VERY LONG NAME; GLOBAL GRINS, SOME RAISED BROWS GREET SCHWARZENEGGER'S CALIFORNIA VICTORY** (*Austin American-Statesman–International*)[5]

**AUSTRIA HAILS ARNIE VICTORY** (BBC News)[6]

**DAVIS OUT, SCHWARZENEGGER WINS IN CALIF.** (Muzi.com–Chinese/English)[7]

**ARNIE—IT COULD ONLY HAPPEN IN AMERICA** (*Australian Financial Review*)[8]

**THOSE CRAZY CALIFORNIANS; A CANUCK TRIES TO MAKE SENSE OF 'MERICAN POLITICS—LIKE ARNIE AS GOVERNOR** (*Edmonton Sun*)[9]

**ARNIE STEALS UGANDAN THUNDER** (BBC News)[10]

**ARNOLD, DE POWERMAN** (*De Morgen*, Brussels)[11]

**FROM MOSCOW TO HIS HOMETOWN, WORLD MARVELS AT SCHWARZENEGGER'S VICTORY** (Associated Press)[12]

**ARNOLD SCHWARZENEGGER EST ÉLU GOUVERNEUR DE LA**

**CALIFORNIE** (*Le Monde,* Paris)[13]

**HASTA LA VISTA** (*Business Day,* Johannesburg, South Africa)[14]

**HASTA LA VICTOR!** (*Daily Mirror*)[15]

**UGANDAN POLITICIANS SHOULD TAKE NOTE OF THE CALIFOR-
NIA RESULT** (Global News Wire)[16]

**DROMEN VAN ARNOLD** (*de Volkskrant,* Amsterdam)[17]

**CALIFORNIA'S JEWISH REPUBLICANS HAIL SCHWARZENEGGER
WIN** (*The Jerusalem Post*)[18]

**THE TIDAL WAVE THAT SWEPT SCHWARZENEGGER TO VICTORY
WAS POWERED BY A POLICY OF LETTING ARNOLD BE
ARNOLD** (*Scotland on Sunday*)[19]

**SCHWARZENEGGER's VICTORY BODES WELL FOR REPUBLICANS
IN 2004** (Agence France-Presse)[20]

**TERMINATOR 4: ARNIE's VICTORY IS A TRIUMPH OF POPULISM
OVER AN INCUMBENT** (*Financial Times,* London)[21]

Photos of Schwarzenegger appeared on October 9 front pages in Austria, Belgium, Brazil, France, Germany, Holland, Hungary, Italy, Lebanon, Malaysia, Philippines, South Korea, and Spain. On November 17, 2003, when Arnold Schwarzenegger was sworn in as California's newest governor, in addition to the nearly eight thousand people in attendance at the state capitol, millions more around the world watched the event on television. The Associated Press reported that around 740 journalists covered the swearing-in, "numbers similar to a presidential inauguration." Foreign dignitaries from thirteen different countries, including Austria, Mexico, and Egypt, attended the ceremony.[22]

Mary Kay Magistad, of the on-line publication *The World,* reported that, while the Chinese press regarded the California election as a matter internal to the United States and therefore not to be officially broadcast, news spread quickly throughout Beijing and beyond. Chinese citizens, writing in Internet chat rooms, said things like, "No wonder there are so many gun shots and explosions in America. Look, they elected an action star as governor," and "We are so envious of the people of California. They have real democracy." Magistad spoke to a woman in Beijing who said, "I think he will be a good governor because he can use his skills from action films in the political field."[23] President Eduard Shevardnadze of the former Soviet republic of Georgia offered to name a mountain in the Caucasus range after the new governor of California.[24] France's interior minister, Nicolas Sarkozy, is reported to have said, "Someone who's a foreigner in his country, who has an unpronounceable name and can become governor of the biggest American state—that's not nothing."[25]

Reports came in from Vietnam about Arnold's winning "control of the nation's richest state, capping an improbable rise from Austrian farm boy to unexpected bright new hope for California."[26] New Zealand's *National Business Review* reported not only on Arnold's victory, but also on the various media reactions to it. While Radio New Zealand featured a cynical morning-after program in which the hosts mocked Californians for electing someone so intellectually deficient, the *National Business Review* counterargued that "Schwarzenegger's real sin was to be a hugely popular actor in blockbuster Hollywood movies. Given that Hollywood is a major economic powerhouse of California, why shouldn't California elect a film actor to be governor? They've done it before with Ronald Reagan."[27]

Even before the election, the foreign press was hot on the trail of the Schwarzenegger-for-governor story. Israeli media ran stories about Arnold's commitment to the Simon

Wiesenthal Center and his significant investments in, for example, Israel's CellGuide, a company founded in 2000 that has since patented a technology for locating cell phones in an emergency.[28] A week before election day, Michael Blitz received a call from a reporter from the Brazilian newspaper *Folha de S. Paulo*, requesting an interview about the impact of Arnold's candidacy on American politics and society.[29] The same week, we both received calls from one of the leading newspapers in the Netherlands called *de Volkskrant*, published in Amsterdam. Again, the request was for an interview about what it meant about American politics and culture that Arnold was the front-runner for governor.[30] A day or two later, we received an e-mail from a journalist for the Belgian newspaper *De Morgen*. The reporter explained that he was researching the cultural impact of "Mr. Schwarzenegger."[31] A Dutch television station sent a producer and crew to Michael's house prior to the election to interview him about why Arnold matters so much to the American people.[32]

The media requests continued from around the world, and the questions all had to do with Arnold's unique role in American culture. It was clear that Arnold Schwarzenegger was big news in countries throughout the world, but Arnold's candidacy and subsequent election were perceived, by the foreign press, as an opportunity to learn significant truths about American political life. For one thing, as one pair of interview questions indicated, Arnold's election had considerable economic implications worldwide. As *De Morgen*'s Maarten Rabaey asked, "Is Arnold's election good/bad for Californian/American politics? Is someone with such a popular cultural history and impact able to swap his role as body-pop-icon and rule over the sixth [largest] economy in the world?"[33] Our responses to these questions seemed to confirm, to several reporters, a view of American politics as a strange blend of public relations and hysteria.

To the first question, we responded that Arnold's election represents a unique and powerful moment in the history of American politics. In fact, even if he had lost the election, his campaign alone would have been sufficient to cause a significant shift in the American political landscape. Californians will probably benefit in some ways from the ouster of Gray Davis. They will likely also find themselves wondering, at times, why they thought Arnold could lead the state government. But American politics now has a new wrinkle: The recall election itself opened the door to further attempts, by both parties, to undo and/or warp the election process to suit their political agendas. Perhaps more importantly, as many argue was the case with the election of George W. Bush to the presidency, Arnold's victory demonstrates the willingness of Americans to put control of government into the hands of those with "no experience of politics and no discernible policies."[34]

To the second question ("Is someone with such a popular cultural history and impact able to swap his role as body-pop-icon and rule over the sixth [largest] economy in the world?"), we suggested that Arnold has done just that. The choice of the word "rule" is appropriate. Arnold's persona, the image we carry of him in our cultural imaginations, is one of ultimate power and strength—attractive traits for a storybook hero, perhaps, but disturbing traits for a political leader in a democratic society.

Again and again, the foreign press made sure to mention that California is the fifth or sixth largest economy in the world. There was recognition, far and wide, that Arnold was now the leader of a state whose budget dwarfed that of nearly every country in the world. Described as a "political ingenu [*sic*],"[35] Arnold Schwarzenegger has captured global attention precisely because he represents what the *Financial Times* of London has characterized as "a trend in Western democracies from the U.S. to France and the Netherlands" to harness their disillusionment with ineffective incumbents and install "populists" into high office.[36]

Populist, centrist Republican, or political ingenue, Governor Arnold Schwarzenegger's significance to the world beyond America is considerable. In Mexico, for example, Eugenio Elorduy, the governor of the Mexican state of Baja, made immediate diplomatic overtures to Arnold following the California election, hoping to lay the foundation for friendly relations between the two.[37] Governing a state where Hispanics account for a third of the population of 34 million, Schwarzenegger is uniquely positioned to be a champion, or an adversary, to Latinos throughout California and Mexico. Following Arnold's election, Mexican federal legislators expressed deep concerns that Schwarzenegger's history of antimigrant comments presented a potential problem for Mexican migrants.[38] Arnold had said, several times during the campaign, that he supported Proposition 187, an initiative introduced in 1994 and then rejected by a federal judge. Proposition 187 denied a variety of services to illegal immigrants living in California. Arnold had also opposed one of Gray Davis's last pieces of legislation allowing illegal immigrants to apply for driver's licenses.

From across the Atlantic, the Arabic electronic newsletter *Al-Bawaba* ("The Middle East Gateway")[39] took special note of Schwarzenegger's election and his ties to Israel and Jewish causes, including the Simon Wiesenthal Center: "If Schwarzenegger wishes to follow in the footsteps of Ronald

Reagan, on his way from movie actor to California governor (and who knows, maybe U.S. president?...), perhaps it would be wise for him to be a bit more balanced in his political approach and endeavors by taking into account California's significant Arab constituency in a more profound manner." Offering advice from the Arab world, *Al-Bawaba* reporters suggested that "It would be a fair and clever step to research the Arab voters' interests and needs and to perhaps, 'pump' some 'iron' into various Arab causes as well."[40]

In India, Arnold is regarded as the "most popular action hero" whose *Terminator 3* was India's highest-grossing film of 2003.[41] His election to governor created a second boom for the movie, as marketers promoted it as Arnold's last film appearance. "So is it curtains for our favourite hero who always says 'I'll be back' as he starts a new career as a Republican politician?"[42] Understanding the tenuous relationship between cinema and politics well, India film star Amin Hajee observed, "The pitfall for actors-turned-politicians was that voters believed the screen image is real.... An action actor could be a mouse in real life.... What he portrays is not what he is."[43]

It's clear to everyone that Arnold is no mouse. What is perhaps also becoming clear is that in many ways, Arnold is precisely what he portrays: a man of relatively few words, broad strokes when it comes to explaining fiscal and political issues, and an almost mystical charisma whose effects are felt even in India's parallel to Hollywood, Bollywood. Ironically, Jay Leno reinforced the Arnold–India connection one evening prior to the election, when, commenting on Schwarzenegger's pronunciation of "Kahl-eee-fohr-nya," he remarked, "California. California with a—where is he from, *India* now?"[44]

Continuing our "voyage" around the world, Southeast Asia has not been immune to Arnold's global aura—indeed, he is perhaps more popular and revered in Japan than anywhere else. The Japanese have their own name for Arnold: Shuwa-chan. It is common in Japan to refer to celebrities by nicknames easier to pronounce and/or more fun to say than the real names. "Shuwa" is simply the easiest-to-pronounce syllable of Arnold's last name, and "-chan" is a common Japanese suffix. A survey of Japanese Web-logs and chat-room transcripts about Arnold yielded the native explanation that "-chan" can be affixed to anyone's name and usually expresses "affection or awe of cuteness. Most of the time, 'chan' is used for girls, children, heartthrobs, and other cute machines."[45] This particular writer quickly pointed out that "You needn't be female or even cute."

It became clear from reading through these various journals and Web-logs that the Japanese had followed the recall election closely. One contributor to KEC Journal, Lagniappe from Hokkaido, Japan, wrote to an American friend, "So, *Shuwa-chan* is much easier to spell than Schwarzenegger.... The recall election in *Kariforunia* [*sic*] has been big news here in Japan, too, because *Shuwa-chan* was running for it. And, now that he has been elected, it has given a very interesting phenomenon. That is, most of the Japanese now know who the California governor is, while nobody seems to know the name of, say, the Hokkaido governor. Wow."[46]

Like many Hollywood stars, Arnold has done a number of wacky commercials for Japanese television. But because Arnold is such a gargantuan star there, his ads tend to be so over-the-top as to render the product secondary. The commercials are really always about Arnold himself. In one ad for DirecTV Arnold played at least four different roles, including a political candidate. " 'What are you planning to export?' asks a reporter, also played by Arnold. 'American entertainment!' replies Arnold the candidate, as the crowd roars and we see a family man, also played by Arnold, watching on TV. Finally we see Arnold in quasi-Terminator mode, at an airport and in a big crate."[47]

Japanese broadcasters have scrambled to make sure Arnold gets plenty of airtime, feeding a widespread cultural appetite for the mighty Shuwa-chan. The *Los Angeles Times* noted, "Anything that is not popular on Japanese television is immediately pulled off the air, but Arnold Schwarzenegger's run for governor of California has been a huge winner in a nation that has intense ratings wars."[48] According to *Japan Media Review* writer Helen Baek, "The Tokyo Broadcasting System in Japan sent a news crew to follow Schwarzenegger around from the premiere of 'Terminator 3' to his inauguration."[49] The *Los Angeles Times* reported that "the Tokyo Broadcasting System team has been all Shuwa-chan, all the time."[50]

In Tokyo, at Japan's 2003 annual exhibition of decorative "hagoita battledores"—traditional paddles used in a Japanese New Year's game somewhat resembling badminton—images and caricatures of Arnold Schwarzenegger were among the top choices for adorning the paddles.[51] Typically, the ornamental battledores feature caricatures of the top newsmakers during the year. One tradition is to give these highly decorated battledores as a gift upon the birth of a baby girl as a symbolic charm for the baby to grow up healthy and strong—a fitting purpose for a paddle with Arnold's image.

Singapore, too, felt the impact of Arnold's big political win. As reported in the *New Straits Times Press* of Malaysia,

"It seemed that Arnold Schwarzenegger's triumph as Governor-elect in California was more prominence [*sic*] than the International Tribunal for the Law of the Sea's (ITLOS) decision to allow Singapore to continue its reclamation works."[52] The reclamation work, permitted by a Tribunal decision in early October 2003, involves building up additional land for Singapore—a vital project from the point of view of Singaporeans who "need every inch of soil we can get," but one that is hotly opposed by Malaysia[53] (thus necessitating the International Tribunal). But Singapore's broadcast company, Mediacorp, opted not to run the Tribunal story; instead, "the only big news was Arnold Schwarzenegger."[54]

Once of the first people to call Arnold to congratulate him on his election victory was former South African president Nelson Mandela. Mandela and Schwarzenegger had worked together in South Africa, promoting Special Olympics. Of President Mandela, Arnold said at the time, "he is one of my heroes."[55] In other parts of Africa, the political implications of the California recall election became an object lesson in surprising places. Nigerian political scientist Tonye David-West, Jr., noted, "The election of Schwarzenegger is very instructive for a number of reasons, but most importantly for the reason that an immigrant, an Austrian-born immigrant with an accent worse than those of most Nigerians, can become governor of arguably the most powerful state in the U.S. with the most electoral votes of 54."[56] In contrast, Professor David-West observes, "in Nigeria, even today, in the year of our Lord, 2003, a Yoruba man, for example, who is also Nigerian, not a foreigner with an accent, but a bona fide Nigerian, born and bred in Nigeria, cannot be governor of Imo State or an Ijaw woman the governor of Kano State even if she was born and bred in Kano." David-West argues that the election of Arnold Schwarzenegger, without regard to his "'foreign' background and deep accent," should serve as a sobering reminder to Nigerians that they "should be working towards unity not division if we are really serious about one Nigeria."[57]

In Kenya, one reporter saw the California recall election as the result of a well-informed and energized public. Mr. Kagwe took up the issue that the Kenyan press devotes too little coverage to "the single biggest challenge" of poverty, instead allowing "sterile political duels, rumor and innuendo… to dominate our daily discourse and media coverage."[58] Mr. Kagwe pointed out that the press in other parts of the world plays an important role in shaping public opinion about economic factors and politicians' responses to these factors. For Mr. Kagwe, an excellent example of media-fueled political health "is the recent state of California gubernatorial contest, in which voters recalled a non-performing governor and elected renowned movie personality Arnold Schwarzenegger, on a platform of economic reform. What role can we in Kenya's Fourth Estate play in making this paradigm shift?"[59] The Kenyan on-line newspaper *East African Standard* published an editorial following Arnold's election entitled "U.S. Recall Ballot a Lesson for Our [Legislators]."[60] The editorial argued, "If recall clause is good for democracy, then it's good for Kenya. It would be the voter's weapon against deceit."[61]

Media writers from Uganda clearly understood many of the implications of Arnold's victory, and saw his election as a warning of a "fundamental shift in the way that politics is conducted the world over."[62] As reported by the BBC, Uganda's liberalization of electronic media is an indication that the country "is following that same road that leads to California. It was noteworthy that Arnie had no clearly stated political or economic policies. He merely said that he was going to terminate the woes of California." As noted in the Ugandan press, "all Ugandan politicians should take note of the California result. It is not good enough to just have a good policy package, you have to have good public relations as well."[63]

The election of Arnold Schwarzenegger is a much more complicated matter than simply one of good public relations. He is more than the sum of his various professional and/or public or even "private" incarnations. As analysts around the world have been quick to note, "Arnie" is, despite his immigrant beginnings, a uniquely American phenomenon. And yet the worldwide attention to Schwarzenegger's rise to power and influence underscores how universal the interest in him really is. He is more universally recognizable than even the densest collection of worldwide headlines could suggest. He is a constellation of activity, philosophy, iconography, and influence that causes both fascination and fear in American culture. As parts of that constellation may change or disappear, the overall powerful effect remains fairly constant. It is only when we begin to examine what George Bush (elder) might have called Arnold's "points of light" that we can begin to connect the dots and grasp how deeply embedded in American culture the man now known as the Governator has become.

# CHAPTER 4

# Collateral Damage: Connecting the Dots

CONNECT-THE-DOTS is a familiar children's pastime. A picture composed of unconnected dots is presented in a partially completed scene. The idea is to connect the dots in the correct order so that a coherent picture is completed. Connect-the-dots is also the basic way that humans come to understand things. Any new experience, any new piece of information has to be put into a picture that compares it with other known elements. If that new element can be connected somehow to what is already known, it too becomes knowable.

This is a familiar strategy in the reporting of the daily news. Quite often news stories are illustrated or punctuated with examples drawn from fiction, fantasy, or motion pictures. For example, any flocking of birds in a community conjures references to Alfred Hitchcock's 1963 classic *The*

*Birds.* Any failure to adequately care for children by forgetful or selfish parents results in a reference to *Home Alone* (1990). One thing that a comparison to popular and well-known films provides is a sense of a known, shared experience. The need to explain the scenario, the characters, or the outcome is eliminated and instantaneously the news story is put into context and adequately illustrated.

Often when an event is particularly violent or aggressive, an Arnold Schwarzenegger movie is used as the comparison or illustration. The reaction to the terrorist attack on the World Trade Center provided an especially unnerving example of this process. During the earliest moments of 9/11, people seemed compelled to describe the attacks as "just like a Schwarzenegger movie."[1] As the somber reality of the event unfolded, this comparison apparently became too crass to repeat. Yet at the very same moment, Schwarzenegger's new antiterrorism movie *Collateral Damage* was being advertised on billboards all over New York City. It even appeared in one video shot of the Twin Towers attack: As the operator of the camera entered a tunnel that blocked the view of the towers, the camera was turned to show a *Collateral Damage* advertisement. Citing the chilling similarities between *Collateral Damage* and the attacks, the studio decided to postpone the movie's release until 2002. But Schwarzenegger returned to New York when Mayor Giuliani appointed him to the board of one of the 9/11 relief foundations. And to complete the connection, Giuliani later made a campaign ad for Schwarzenegger's California candidacy.

One reason Arnold has become a prototype for many of our cultural categories is not only because his films are useful for illustrating news stories, but because they often offer an eerie foreshadowing of important events and contentious cultural issues. Instead of being mere entertainment, these films can be mined for their anticipation of burgeoning concerns that the broader culture usually has not yet addressed directly. This apparent foresight has led to the impression that Schwarzenegger is always ahead of the curve.

Arnold's ability to blur the line between his film personas and his flesh-and-blood presence provides unusual resonance to these prescient narratives. Since the cinematic Arnold is now used as an indispensable key to understanding and even predicting the future of America, it would be useful to use the connect-the-dots strategy to guide our analysis of the political and social formations that are the collateral damage of his cultural incursions.

The connect-the-dots metaphor seemed to be a favorite way for political commentators during the California gubernatorial campaign to express one simple idea: that Arnold Schwarzenegger was coming onto the political scene with many "dots" in play. Understanding how the election happened and what it meant seemed simply a matter of connecting the dots that were already there (though not always visible). It was assumed that Schwarzenegger was part of a larger political picture and that the dots were scattered among Republican Party politics, the California energy crisis, the disputed 2000 presidential election, and the presumed liberal leanings of the media. But the dots actually were spaced much wider than that, and all the elements of mythology—the bigger than life, self-made man—as well as many elements from popular culture, from Siegfried and Roy (Arnold's longtime friends) to the Hummer and the Mouse, needed to be brought into the picture.

The dots popped up everywhere and were so varied in their expression and constitution that political observers constantly urged each other to make the connections so that a better picture emerged:

- Arianna Huffington, who called Arnold a "Bush Republican," campaigned that she would "connect the dots between the disastrous economic policies of the Bush administration and the plight of California."[2]
- A comment on a political Web site: "You know the routine: '… a power grab that started with Clinton's impeachment, continued in Florida 2000, and now repeated in California.' I'm sure one of the nitwits on the *LA Times* op-ed pages will try to connect those dots."[3]
- A CNN REPORT:
  *Wolf Blitzer, CNN anchor:* "The California recall vote goes to court today over the nightmarish prospect of, get this, hanging chads. CNN's Bob Franken is over at the U.S. District Courthouse in Los Angles. Bob, hanging chads in the California recall, connect the dots."
  *Bob Franken, CNN national correspondent:* "Connect the dots. Well…"[4]
- Jack Fritscher, a writer of gay erotic fiction and chronicler of San Francisco gay history, auctioned $24,000 worth of his "Schwarzenegger Shrine" on eBay—including a photograph of Arnold taken by the late Robert Mapplethorpe. Fritscher said his purpose had been to raise questions about Arnold's views on homosexuals and government funding of the arts. "It was not to embarrass Arnold at all, just to connect the dots so the conversation can occur."[5]

- A satirical Web site, All Hat No Cattle, depicted Kenneth Lay, George W. Bush, and Arnold Schwarzenegger, each with a big red dot for the knot in their neckties. The caption reads, "What a difference a Lay makes… by connecting the dots!"[6]
- Bill Bradley, correspondent for *LA Weekly*, wrote an analysis of "the long tentacles of the get-Arnold campaign" entitled "Connecting the Dots."[7]
- A "BuzzFlash Reader Commentary," examining the probability that George W. Bush would seek Schwarzenegger's support for his 2004 reelection campaign, was entitled "Connecting the California Dots: Rove to Arnold."[8]
- In response to an October 5, 2003, Reuters story, "LA Times Faces Anger for Schwarzenegger Coverage," a member of the conservative Web forum Free Republic wrote, "I'd love to connect the dots."[9]

Connecting any of these events and issues started to create a picture that disturbed many seasoned politicians. The efforts to make the recall election look like business as usual for the Republican Party was echoed by many prominent Democrats who came to California during the short campaign to support Gray Davis. Former president Bill Clinton warned that the recall was a threat to democracy and the election process.[10] Hillary Clinton sent a message to a women's rally that stated, "Let's make it absolutely clear that California is not going to be stampeded by the same right-wingers that gave us the election in Florida and are trying to do things that are really against our interest."[11]

But if the California recall election proved anything, it is that the dots we have to connect to make sense of Arnold Schwarzenegger are painted everywhere outside the political arena even more significantly than inside. The manifestations of Arnold Schwarzenegger, large and small points on the cultural map, are amazingly prolific, widespread, and varied. His extensive influence and remarkable presence in contemporary American culture have gone beyond celebrity, hero worship, politics, and entertainment. He permeates our lives—persistently, invisibly, quietly, in small ways as well as large. His name and the character names from his movies have so thoroughly entered into cultural production that well before the California election not a day went by without the likelihood of encountering Arnold through some form or another ranging from jokes and children's videos to courtroom testimony and food supplements. His election to office represents not a departure from this pattern, but simply the production of additional traces that help create a more complex and unsettling picture.

In order to understand how Arnold became so pervasive, and to measure the range and impact of this omnipresence, we can look at any number of ways in which he has dotted the landscape of the American imagination, of American merchandising, of American social life, and of American language. There are connections between all of these elements besides their references to Arnold. Connecting Arnold to these things both limits the way we can imagine the world and opens up a new view of America. Why it is Arnold who appears in all these different realms and not someone else is the key to understanding this phenomenon. The following examples demonstrate some of these connect-the-dot scenarios.

- On the *Today Show* during the first Gulf War, the father of one of the hostages taken in Iraq comments that if he were Arnold Schwarzenegger, he would go in himself to rescue the hostages. What connection was that father making? He could have been acknowledging Arnold's physical strength, his movie characters' notoriety, his vast wealth and Hollywood power, his reputation for setting out on a mission and achieving it, or all of the above. In fact, although it may be a little of each of the aforementioned associations, Arnold Schwarzenegger, in name and persona, has come to mean a kind of indestructible—and undeniable—force. Even recalled California governor Gray Davis is susceptible to the impression of Arnold as an immutable force. About his loss to Arnold, Davis said, "I've beaten back plenty of wealthy people, but they were just mere mortals."[12]

- During the O. J. Simpson criminal trial in 1995, the prosecutor claimed that Nicole Simpson said to her abusive husband for the last time, "Hasta la vista!" Whether she actually said these words, or the prosecutor was using poetic license to describe Nicole Simpson's attempt to end her marriage, there is still an eerie and macabre connection to *The Terminator* here. Before deciding on Schwarzenegger to play the first Terminator, James Cameron had considered casting O. J. Simpson in the title role. In what would become, in hindsight, a moment of perverse irony, Cameron then decided that people would not take O. J. seriously as a ruthless bad guy; instead Arnold was given the part of the cold, calculating killer.

- In the Disney movie *Aladdin* (1993), as well as the TV cartoon and theme park show derived from it, Aladdin's genie regularly puts on a Schwarzenegger accent and recites his catch phrases. Clearly a Mickey Mouse accent would not do, even though Mickey has the same recognizability and can-do attitude. The generator of so many of our other pervasive cultural icons, The Disney Company, nevertheless relies on Arnold for certain tough guy effects.

- In an article about Democratic politics and the party's search for presidential candidates in 1991, Michael McCurry laments, "Unfortunately, Arnold Schwarzenegger is taken."[13] People know Schwarzenegger is a Republican, even if he takes centrist positions, and even if he is married to a member of the high-profile Democratic Kennedy family. Still, for years the powerful Arnoldian magnetism has attracted the interest of the Democratic Party. McCurry's expressed disappointment that Schwarzenegger was not available to be a Democratic presidential candidate is an indication that Arnold's political potency is desirable in bipartisan ways. The fact that Arnold wasn't, and still isn't, eligible to be president took nothing away from the sense that an Arnoldian candidacy would be a tough one to beat.

- Marjorie Newlin is "the Arnold Schwarzenegger of grandmothers" because, at age 72, she entered her muscular form into a bodybuilding competition.[14] Aged grannies who go into bodybuilding demonstrate not only how plastic the human body is, but also that the model for fitness, even for the elderly, is one we've inherited from Arnold. When Schwarzenegger was chair of the President's Council on Physical Fitness and Sports, he engaged his cigar-smoking buddy Milton Berle to develop fitness programs for senior citizens. In an article in *Cigar Aficionado,* Berle said, "Recently I've been going around to all the senior-citizen places.... I tell people that I smoke cigars, but tell them to lay off cigarettes. And I mention that I keep healthy by exercising. Every day I run on the treadmill and punch the bag."[15] At the time of the interview, Berle was starring in a video called "The Milton Berle Low Impact/High Comedy Workout for Seniors" in which he leads a group of seniors from 70 to 101 years old in a series of exercises.

- A man is arrested in connection with a triple murder in Long Beach, California. Police say he was "ranting about cyborgs and terminators."[16] Did the killer of three people in Long Beach in 1993 have Arnold on his mind when he was arrested? We may never know why he was thinking about cyborgs, but it isn't difficult to imagine reasons why he would be muttering, in confusion, about "terminators." Between the first Terminator movie and the sequel, *T2,* Arnold's character morphs from ultimate bad guy to ultimate defender of the good. The Terminator kills—or protects—without passion. Whatever the Long Beach killer thought he was doing, the idea of a terminator could easily be fit to his plans.

- In 1991 and again in 1997, Schwarzenegger was honored with the Simon Wiesenthal Center's "National Leadership Award" for his support of the organization's Holocaust studies and programs fighting intolerance. The first award came soon after Arnold commissioned the center to confirm that his father had been a member of the National Socialist Party during World War II. On September 11, 2003, during the gubernatorial campaign, Arnold chose to appear at the Wiesenthal Center for memorial services. His Wiesenthal Center contributions came in handy during the recall election when people started to scrutinize several favorable comments he had allegedly made about Adolf Hitler.

- In 2000, radio station KCRW featured a magazine program called "Studio 360" that each week provided a "one-hour look at the myriad intersections between the arts, popular culture, and everyday life."[17] The show's host, Kurt Anderson, explained, "Most of us have cultural passions that extend all over the place, and this show is an attempt to connect those dots." The show's co-producer, WNYC's Vice President of Programming Dean Cappello, elaborated: "Whenever Shakespeare and Schwarzenegger end up in the same show, you know you have something engaging and provocative and entertaining." Three years later, one more "dot" was connected when *The Daily Standard* asked, with regard to people's speculation about Arnold's participation in the California debates, "Is Arnold Schwarzenegger the recall Hamlet?"[18]
- A member of the University of Virginia computer science department put up a program that encourages users to "name any actor or actress and I can construct the shortest list of links that terminates with Arnold Schwarzenegger."[19] If you type in a celebrity name, you discover that, somehow, Arnold is "linked" by no more than two or three degrees of separation to virtually everybody.

Other examples, while perhaps less complex, show the range of these connections, their appearance in odd and unexpected ways, and the zero degrees of separation between Arnold Schwarzenegger and American culture:

- Pectoral implants for men are called a sign of the "Schwarzeneggerization" of society.[20]
- The Swiss franc is called "a Schwarzenegger among currencies."[21]

- During her visit to the Veterans Medical Center in Washington, D.C., first lady Hillary Clinton told one veteran who was lifting some weights, "You're going to have arms like Arnold Schwarzenegger."[22]
- *Sesame Street* in 1999, in a segment on what a jacket is, a black leather motorcycle jacket says, in an Arnold accent, "I'll be back."
- Warren Olney, a TV reporter and anchor for over twenty years in Los Angeles, hosted a monthlong radio series after the LA riots called "Which Way, LA?" An *LA Times* article called Olney's "one of the most recognizable voices this side of Arnold Schwarzenegger's."[23]
- A 1993 piece in the *Village Voice* discusses MIT linguistics professor Noam Chomsky's one-time support of a Holocaust revisionist, his six- or seven-year-long "ban" from the American press, and his return to prominence in the media. "Today the guy is risking Schwarzenegger-style overexposure."[24]

Only an idea as flexible as Arnold Schwarzenegger could have appeared in all these places and forms. These connected dots trace the path of a kind of contagion: Arnold seems to get passed from one arena to another without any referee raising a red flag. Arnold is used to enhance our understanding or appreciation of a voice, a piece of clothing, a currency, a sports career, body enhancement, physical rehabilitation, and media appearances. Sports fans expecting "an Arnold Schwarzenegger-like performance" from a star athlete[25] or the state of Ohio seeming "to have libraries in an Arnold Schwarzenegger-like grip"[26] combine with Arnoldian jackets on *Sesame Street* to show that the contagious idea called "Arnold" has entered every unprotected aspect of our collective lives.

Arnold is a uniquely American idea, and ideal, whether in the movies, in business, in bodybuilding, or in politics. While Arnold seems in America to be immune to everything from political opposition to accusations of sexual misconduct, Americans themselves are not at all immune to the spread of Arnold into everyday life. We only need look at the history of the all-terrain vehicle called the "Hummer" to see how Arnold can be connected to any object or idea. Arnold was the first American civilian to obtain the military vehicle, the HumVee that was popularized during Operation Desert Storm in the 1991 Gulf War. Since then Arnold has been machined into the super SUV itself in a powerful ad campaign. Once the HumVee was changed into the Hummer (which is what Arnold dubbed his unique pet vehicle) and Arnold convinced General Motors to make the Hummer available to the general public,[27] the cyborg connection between the car and the man who gave it its new stylish name was forever fused. The advertisement for the first retail model of the Hummer tells the tale:

Think of it as Arnold on Wheels.

Almost nothing on the face of the earth is tougher than Arnold.

Almost nothing. Meet HUMMER for 1994. Tougher, stronger, more powerful than ever. Like Arnold, it can go places the others wouldn't dare to go. Or maybe even want to. It can do things the others wouldn't think of doing. It will take you there. And, like Arnold, it will be back.

HUMMER: Nothing is tougher. Hasta la vista, baby.[28]

As if this connection between man and machine were not already as strong as it could be, announcements for the 2001 luxury edition of the Hummer effectively dissolved any distinction between the two. One article in the *Los Angeles Times* called the new Hummers "Sport-Brutes: Like Schwarzenegger with Bumpers."[29] A promotion of the new Hummer—the H2—on *Good Morning America* featured Arnold popping out of one of these "brawny four-wheel-drive boulder crawlers with military roots" and proclaiming that the Hummer is a truck with hair on its chest.[30] *Motor Trend*'s review of the 2003 Lingenfelter Hummer H2 describes it as having "Schwarzenegger muscle to go with its Schwarzenegger looks."[31] The Hummer was now human; Arnold (with bumpers) was the Hummer. Once again, Arnold had been paired with a twin of only superficially different proportions. Both combined "ruggedness with luxury."[32]

This fusion of Arnold and GM's largest sports utility truck foregrounds the aggressiveness of Arnold's diffusion into mass culture. More than anything else, Arnold Schwarzenegger is an *idea* that has spread not because it is good or valuable or true. It has spread because of the appetites it creates in the culture for a neatly packaged daily life that makes sense. Arnold guides us to make our world coherent so that that there will be no doubts if we are decisive, no disappointment if we seek specific goals, no hesitation if we want to win. We construct our world with these instructions provided by Arnold Schwarzenegger, and in this fit world there is no democratic messiness, no compromise, no wimping out, and clearly no denying Arnold.

It is not that we admire or idolize him (although many people do), but rather that we recognize that he is the essence, the very definition of a special category bearing his name that carries with it enormous power and influence. This category is one in which he is the easy-to-use reference point for things that are powerful, tough, violent, successful, expensive, and big. We use these evaluations, these models of behavior, these "prototypes," these dots in the cultural landscape when we want to make judgments about the quality of something, or have to decide on a course of action, or have to figure out who we are and where we belong.

Arnold Schwarzenegger is an American icon in the most complex sense because he is our premier cultural prototype. Cultural prototypes are rare but necessary entities. A prototype is the best example of a category, the standard against which all other comers to that category are measured. Not all items in a category match the prototype but rather are compared to it and judged as being good or bad fits for the category. In the Galápagos Islands, of the thirteen species of finches that Darwin found to be indigenous to the area, the large cactus ground finch is referred to as "the Schwarzenegger of these amazing birds."[33] About sheep that are now bred for dramatically increased size and muscle density in their buttocks, we are told that "if they were people they'd look like Arnold Schwarzenegger. They're big, and all muscle."[34] In Fairfield City, California, a candidate for city council is praised for turning her lack of political experience into an effective and earnest effort "to lead Fairfield back into the light." She is called "the Schwarzenegger of Fairfield."[35] And when we want to talk about a powerful new car we can say, as the *Los Angeles Times* did in 1991, that "The Dodge Viper is the Arnold Schwarzenegger of sports cars." Could we substitute "George W. Bush" for Arnold in this line, or Clint Eastwood, Michael Jordan, Martha Stewart, or

Madonna? None of these notable figures compares with Arnold as our reference point for the most fitting example of power and self-possession.

If Arnold is our prototype or model of behavior, he claims it is because *he* has made it so. Arnold has always promoted himself as a self-made man, not someone beholden to his culture like the rest of us. In the recall election, his wife Maria Shriver drove this message home in a series of speeches and in a campaign brochure aimed at reassuring women that Arnold would be their champion. The brochure, addressed to "Remarkable Women," states, "Don't think for one second that there's some genius out there engineering Arnold's various successes. It's all him. Nobody lifted one weight for him—learned one word of English for him—saved any money for him—bought one piece of real estate for him—took one business class for him—navigated the shark-infested waters of Hollywood and now politics, for him."[36]

In his 1977 autobiography, however, Arnold does in fact credit many people with helping him train as a bodybuilder, develop his business sense, and learn to become an American. He also acknowledges the role his girlfriend Barbara played in helping him learn English. Dependent on these others, he was still Hercules, the flawed hero he played in his first movie (*Hercules in New York,* 1970) who was half mortal and prone to needing help. But years—and many successes—later he seemed to have morphed in Maria's eyes into Hercules' half-sister Athena, who popped out of the head of Zeus fully armed and ready for combat. His image was now that of a completely self-sufficient hero who was steadfastly accumulating greater strength, notoriety, and accomplishment. Arnold once said, "Everything I have ever done in my life has… stayed. I've just added to it… muscles will always be in the movies. I will never ignore or avoid them. I will add to them. I will add to my acting ability. I will add to the types of roles I will play. I will add to the kinds of responsibilities I take on with my movies. But I will not change. Because when you are successful and you change, you are an idiot."[37] Perhaps what Arnold really meant was something more like what poet Charles Olson once wrote: "What does not change/ is the will to change."[38]

It may be an "idiot" who changes a successful formula, but Arnold apparently has had the brains, the brawn, and the foresight all along to transform himself in order to keep himself in the foreground of American life. But it is not in the foreground but the *background* where we find some of the most compelling examples of Arnold's inoculation of America. Every time someone says "Hasta la vista, baby" or "I'll be back" or that something or someone is "pumped up," he or she is both echoing and reinforcing Arnold's uniquely influential sculpting of the language. Every time pundits referred to the California recall election as the "total recall" or to Arnold-the-candidate as "the running man" or to Arnold in his role as promoter of Proposition 49 (the after-school program he supports) as "the Kindergarten Cop," they were offering proof of the profound ways in which the very idea of Arnold Schwarzenegger—the constellation of all of his cultural productions, and especially these high-density expressions—has become part of the very texture of American conversation.

Whether it's the way he speaks, the history of his hyper-developed body, the power of his movie character portrayals, or the authority his name alone invokes, Arnold has moved into American consciousness like no other public figure. We have seen similar but not equal effects with Elvis Presley, or Mickey Mouse, or Michael Jackson, or Jackie O., or in earlier times Rudolf Valentino, Marilyn Monroe, Mae West, Sigmund Freud, Adolf Hitler, or Cary Grant. But each of their effects was confined and circumscribed by the circumstances of their bodies, or their times, their talents, or their peculiarities. Arnold, on the other hand, has been adopted and co-opted for purposes as diverse as they are widespread.

You could look at Arnold as a brand name that has branched out, that has created product spin-offs designed to efficiently pass on variations of the original message. Spin-offs are easier to accept than something totally new and can go in multiple directions. It is an approach relished by Edward Bernays, the inventor of public relations (and Freud's nephew): It involves "lateral thinking" that spreads an idea or product into the wider economy or society rather than just in its original market. The strategy is referred to as "Big Think" and it requires defying conventions, assuming that the ordinary rules don't apply, and even "reshaping reality."[39] Arnold has taken "Big Think" to the next level, making connections to things so seemingly remote from his original packaging that there is no question he has reshaped our realities while breaking every rule.

Like a good movie sequel, every dot, every new appearance now not only extends and widens the story, it corrects errors or embarrassments from the earlier appearances. Never was this put to better effect than in the recall election. When asked by longtime friend Tom Brokaw in an interview right before the election if the accusations by women of a "kind of mischief" against him were true, Schwarzenegger answered "This is not me,"[40] redefining not just the issue but even the characters in the earlier event. It was apparently convincing: Reporters repeated for weeks after the election that that was a different Arnold, a younger Arnold; how many of us would want our youthful actions to define us today? No one asked, "If that was not you, who was it?"

The answer may be on the cover of *People* magazine. Of all the twists and turns in the California recall election, and all the talk about the cultural significance of the campaign, perhaps the most surprising development was Arnold's failure to dominate the cover of *People* magazine the week after the election. His identification as the most significant pop cultural event of the moment was usurped by "Tiger Terror!"—the attack on Roy Horn of the illusionist team of Siegfried and Roy by one of his own freaky white 600-pound cats. Arnold was relegated to a small picture in the right-hand side of the page, sandwiched between Halle Berry's separation and Renée Zellweger's Snicker's diet.

After the Las Vegas tragedy on October 3, Arnold's election campaign had to share radio, TV, newspaper, and Larry King space with the mauling of one-half of the flashy, "breathtakingly weird"[41] duo even as Arnold was facing his own "mauling" charges. Oddly enough, the next day another wild animal story appeared, this time about a 425-pound tiger and an alligator found living together in a Harlem apartment. The day after the election, newspapers reported that bears had killed two bear enthusiasts in Alaska. Was it coincidence or had the California political circus somehow precipitated the coast-to-coast revolt of traditional circus performers, provoking real flesh-eating events so humans were no longer certain of their role as top predators?

The *New York Times* asked about this coincidence too, but felt the events were inevitable, not only because we have displaced wild animals from their realm, but because of their "distorted replacement within ours."[42] Siegfried and Roy were the absolute masters of this distorted replacement both on stage and off.[43] Their popular Las Vegas show combined clever and dramatic illusions with wild beasts. As one fan explained, "The appeal of the show is that these two dudes impose control over animals that could tear them to shreds."[44] But the "dudes" were also living and sleeping with these tigers if not each other and their entire approach to animal raising and training, wild cat "conservation," and being the "most openly closeted celebrities"[45] was also a grand illusion.

The real significance of *People*'s cover is that although the recall election was a show of masterful illusions, the Siegfried and Roy story was actually the best choice for representing the battle between reality and illusion that had been occupying the country for two months. At any other time, Arnold's recall election would have won for the best display of manufactured reality; Siegfried and Roy just happened to have been at it longer; they also had better sequins and lots more blood. Their ability to knock Arnold off the front page of the weekly bible of celebrity illusionism is not so surprising, then, and doesn't take away from the magnificent reality-warping machine that was the California recall election. Both events were attempts to reach across time and species and history as if none of those landmarks mattered. Arnold's election has convinced many that they don't. Edward Bernays and his uncle Sigmund Freud would recognize in this the successful connection between previously unrelated fragments that got added to the larger picture. This connection was confirmed on the cover of the February 2004 issue of *Esquire,* which featured the heads of Arnold and the white tiger as well as Michael Jackson, Britney Spears, and Saddam Hussein along with the text "Dubious Achievements! 2003."

This was an election of the wrestling ring, a pseudodrama, and Arnold was the main contender of mythic proportions. As in professional wrestling (which, after all, produced one other governor, Minnesota's Jesse Ventura), the voters only wanted "the perfection of the iconography,"[46] not real action. Nobody really wanted the 135 candidates in the ring to debate or do anything more than stand up and wave on the *Tonight Show;* nobody was really longing for Arnold to say anything concrete about any issue; nobody was really surprised when the referees were looking the other way when the rules were broken. And "It wasn't me" is the age-old defense of wrestlers caught making an illegal move.

What we expect of our mythic models is not perfect behavior or obsessive truth-telling; we expect them to create what the French literary critic Roland Barthes called an "intelligible spectacle,"[47] one where the actions and words and appearances work together to form a pleasing or interesting narrative, a story to ponder or share, to rant about or cry about. In these mythical stories, people are not really concerned with contradictions as long as the story provides a reassurance about the necessity of continuity in the narratives that define our lives.

This is why the accusations of sexual harassment against Arnold did not have a chance. The mythic candidate— Arnold the Magnificent—needed this type of moral challenge and display of passions to prove he could conquer and prevail. As in wrestling, and in theatre and film, the issue is not "truth." Rather, as Barthes told us back in the 1950s, what we expect from our favorite myths is the "intelligible representation of moral situations" that becomes a model for certain issues rather than a telling of real events.[48] We should have expected, if not this particular story, then something like it. It is not an issue of whether the *Los Angeles Times* favored Gray Davis or was trying to undermine Arnold Schwarzenegger; they were merely the messengers in a mythic drama. Arnold's perfect response only perpetuated the mythology machine: The liminal, rowdy nature of movie sets, where all rules are suspended for the creation of more myths, was all the explanation anyone needed.

That this election/wrestling match was between stereotypical physical types only enhanced the drama; it is what we wanted and what we expected and what we got. In what kind of world would a thin, bland gray man or a roly-poly brown man win out over a Herculean figure? "I am Hercules. I am Hercules," Schwarzenegger's demigod character in his 1970 film repeated over and over to the citizens of New York until everyone just shrugged, acquiesced, and said a collective, "okay." Today the body may be smaller, the face more masklike, and the accent unchanged, but those encountering his message—I am Arnold—had the same reaction, shrugging their collective shoulders, accepting him, and electing him governor.

**CHAPTER 5**

# Dave

**JOEL SIEGEL SAID DURING HIS REVIEW** of *Total Recall* on *Good Morning America* in June 1990, "Who would have thought one of the biggest international box office stars of the '90s would be named Arnold? Accountants are named Arnold. And Schwarzenegger?"

Quite simply, and certainly ironically, "Arnold Schwarzenegger" has become an American household name. But Arnold Schwarzenegger has also become the seed for a dense harvest of alternative names that seem to be created compulsively by members of the culture. Each one of these names gives Arnold another voice, a dialect in which to speak again and again, in any context, on any subject, at any time. The "Arnold Show" is being broadcast 24/7 in all forms and every language, formal and informal.

Schwarzenegger has only a cameo role in the movie *Dave* (1993). Along with Jay Leno, Arnold plays himself. "Dave"

(Kevin Kline) is Dave Kovic, a humble man who helps people get jobs and who occasionally entertains people with his uncanny talent for imitating United States President Bill Mitchell. When the president has a stroke, his closest—and corrupt—ministers keep it a secret from the nation as well as from the first lady. In their search for someone who can stand in for the president, they discover Dave, who bears a remarkable resemblance to the president, and who proves to be much more presidential than they had bargained for. Dave is all the things that President Bill Mitchell is not: compassionate, sensible, romantic (he ends up charming the first lady, who is at first mystified that her "husband" is suddenly the slightest bit interested in her), generous, and gifted when it comes to galvanizing the emotions of everyone around him.

It's a movie about governmental deception, about a political outsider becoming a political leader without an election, and ultimately about how a simple name, Dave, comes to embody an idea about America that might well chill us all: It is entirely possible to fool an awful lot of us into feeling supportive of a leader even if there is good reason to be deeply suspicious of him. Although Arnold's appearance is a relatively minor moment in yet another Ivan Reitman film (he directed Arnold in *Twins, Kindergarten Cop,* and *Junior*), there is, once again, something strangely prescient about his connection to a movie about the sudden and emotional replacement of the leader of government ten years prior to an election in California that many say should never have been allowed to happen at all.

As we come to understand in the movie, Dave—the man—is always himself, even when he is abruptly made president. It is not as a Bill Mitchell stand-in that he attempts to fathom the intricacies of the federal bureaucracy, or to push through humane legislation that the often inhumane president would have neglected or vetoed. It is always Dave, himself, who navigates the roles forced on him by his cabinet and his "wife." Perhaps this is one of the more intriguing connections to Arnold's career. In each endeavor—athletic, cinematic, political—he has, essentially, played himself. And because he is always "Arnold," it is doubly curious that so many people, in a variety of contexts, call him something else.

There may be a number of ways to explain the proliferation of "nicknames" for Arnold. David Letterman weighed in with one possibility: "President Bush has been silent on Schwarzenegger. Of course, he can't *pronounce* Schwarzenegger.'" We would argue that nicknaming Arnold has become a form of cultural consumption. Americans can have a piece of Arnold by naming him, identifying one or more uniquely personal points of view about a particular image, action, or statement he has made. Each name brings the namer just a little closer to Arnold, staking a minute claim to Arnold's currency in the culture.

This list represents a rich sampling of Arnold's nicknames as they have occurred in print, on-line, and in a variety of other media.

Ah-nuld[2]
Arnie[3]
Arnie Weismuller[4]
Arnie, the class clown[5]
Arno, The[6]
Arnold "no fat, all meat" Schwarzenegger[7]
Arnold "The Hummer-Driving Ninny" Schwarzenegger[8]

Arnold Inc.[9]

Arnold Schmalzenegger[10]

Arnold Schwarzeneggerkopf[11]

Arnold Schwarzenhammer[12]

Arnold Schwarzenheimer[13]

Arnold Schwarzenheimer-Blut-und-Eisen-Achtung-Baby-Aw-
    Idunno[14]

Arnold Schwarzenoodle[15]

Arnold Schwarzeschnitzel[16]

Arnold Smarmynipper[17]

Audio-Animatronic Candidate, The[18]

Austrian Oak, The[19]

Benedict Arnold[20]

Big Arnold[21]

Big Green Governor[22]

Californiator, The[23]

Collectinator, The[24]

Conan the Candidate[25]

Conan the Gentleman[26]

Conan the Librarian[27]

Conan the Republican[28]

Conan the Vulgarian[29]

Deregulator, The[30]

Determinator[31]

Dirty Hansel with a pocketful of Gummy Bears[32]

First Colossus[33]

Fondlinator, The[34]

Gov. Christmas[35]

Gov. Hollywood[36]

Gov. Schwarzenegger

Governator, The[37]

Governor Gangbang[38]

Governor Meathead[39]

Gropinator, The[40]

Herr Gröpenfuhrer[41]

His Oakness[42]

Innoculator, The[43]

Jerkinator, The[44]

Johnny Schwarzenegger[45]

Kindergarten Cop[46]

Kindergarten Cop-a-feel[47]

Kindergarten GOP, The[48]

Manipulator, The[49]

Maria's hubby-egger[50]

Mr. Discipline[51]

Mr. Freeze[52]

Mr. Gobernator[53]

Mr. Muscle[54]

Mr. Musclehead[55]

Mr. Olympia

Mr. Protein[56]

Mr. Shriver[57]

Mr. Schwarzen-Schnitzel[58]

Mr. Universe

Muscle-bound Republican, The[59]

Olympian Oak, The[60]

Presidator[61]

Pres. Schwarzengroper[62]

Republican Terminator, The[63]

Robo-cop with a heart[64]

Schwarzenkopfmannegger[65]

Schwarzenookie[66]

Schwarzy[67]

Self-Made Man, The[68]

Sexinator, The[69]

Shit Wanker[70]

Shuwa-Chan[71]

Sudden Death elfenized[72]

Sultan of Sinew[73]

Teflon Groper, The[74]

Term-Eliminator[75]

Termwinator, The[76]

Tool-E-nator, The[77]

Tweetie-Pie Terminator[78]

Ubermensch[79]

Ungh-nold[80]

Vacillator, The[81]

This long list of nicknames not only reflects the many ways that people have appropriated their share of Arnold Schwarzenegger, but it also serves as an ever-expanding cast of characters in the "movie" continuously being made by Arnold's life and career. Each time a new name is added to the list, the plot of the "movie" grows and changes and Arnold's story increasingly becomes ours as well.

# CHAPTER 6

# Eraser:
# The Schwarzenegger
# of All Metaphors

IN *ERASER* (1996) Arnold plays John "The Eraser" Kruger, an extremely efficient U.S. marshal who provides entry for endangered citizens into the federal witness protection program. Kruger's job is to eliminate all traces of his charges' previous identities. He goes in and takes all forms of identification—driver's licenses, credit cards, trinkets, and photographs—and destroys them, creating a replacement identity that must now guide their lives. In the efficiency of B-moviemaking, Kruger himself apparently has no other existence except for his role in erasing other people's lives. He strips down the lives of these needy souls to a single ordering principle: Delete the past and all traces of it; there is only a future now. It is not simply that he erases their tracks, but as the ultimate historical revisionist he actually lifts them out of history.

In the movie, he has to protect Dr. Lee Cullen (Vanessa Williams) when she agrees to turn on her defense contractor employer and provide information to the FBI about their illegal business dealings. Kruger creates a new identity for her, but meanwhile his own corrupt boss (who is also the man who trained him) is party to a plan to eliminate her. At this point a new identity for Cullen is no longer the issue; now Kruger must rewrite his own history to figure out the plot.

By erasing the past lives of his charges, Kruger thinks he is able to eliminate the chaos and unpredictability that plague their current existence. But such erasure is impossible because humans are not so easily directed into new identities. When the film begins, Kruger is rescuing a mob informer who just had to go to his favorite Italian restaurant to get a taste of his former life. Because he was spotted by someone from his past, the new identity fails. Trying to erase his origins proved impossible. Identity is constructed from the bits and pieces of our lives; an identity is put together into a somewhat coherent story that needs to be confirmed by others. If there is no one to share the sense of identity with, it does not stick.

On his Web site, Arnold describes his reaction to the story idea for *Eraser* this way: "I'd always been incredibly fascinated about the idea of the witness protection program… how people's identities can just be erased and they can end up in different parts of the world, with different papers, different backgrounds… the real you doesn't exist anymore."[1] But it is not the case that a "real you" apart from the papers and the backgrounds and the world can exist. The erasure of origins merely moves the meanings and identity to another temporary location, like the roles an actor takes on with each new movie. The creation of a "you" is always dependent on contact with others who provide reassurance that you are there in the world with them.

In order to live in this world that we share with others, we have to find ways to communicate complex meanings and to extend them to new situations, new people, and new times. One of the most productive ways we do this is by the use of metaphors. Metaphor—where we take one term and apply its characteristics to a second term—is not just something that resides in poetry. Instead, metaphor, according to George Lakoff and Mark Johnson, is the basis of our "ordinary conceptual system," affecting how we think and act every day, and almost all the time.[2]

In Arnold's description of the movie *Eraser,* he uses a metaphor that treats identity as if it were a thing that can be handled and reshaped, located and moved, and read and rewritten. But if identity were metaphorically referred to as an animal, for example, these same characteristics would not apply. The animal metaphor might also seem odd to us because we do not associate human identity with animal characteristics, even though many other cultures do. So the collection of metaphors that a culture uses says a lot about how they organize and interpret the world around them.

In metaphor we take two elements and make a connection between them, often one that cannot easily be traced. Metaphors, like U.S.marshals, have a way of erasing origins, and once a metaphor enters the common vernacular its uses are not restricted or weighed down by the original connection. So, for example, we don't know why we use the metaphoric structure that says an argument is war and as a result we claim things like "He shot down all my arguments" and "He attacked every weak point in my argument."[3] Metaphors like this also structure our actions so we approach an argument as if it were a battle and not as if it were a dance or a race. This way of thinking has become so ingrained we don't even question it anymore.

Not everyone can generate new metaphors that get accepted and generally spread by members of a culture. The ability to generate these shared metaphors is, quite simply, a sign of the greatest power and influence. Metaphors can create new categories of meaning that affect how we think, act, feel, and believe. The metaphors we use, then, are a basic part of our identities. Metaphors, and not the papers and the documents and the photographs, play a major part in creating our identity.

In American culture today, this construction of identity has an undeniable dependence on the metaphors that we generate using Arnold Schwarzenegger. Arnoldian metaphors show up everywhere: when talking about plants and animals, music, religion, computers, children's television, medicine, telephones, food, history, business, and even emotions. In the teen book *What's in a Name,* one character says, "I'm the Arnold Schwarzenegger of sensitivity" because his emotions seem to loom so large.[4] One Web-log writer vows to be "the Schwarzenegger interaction."[5] On a *Sesame Street* fan page, a mom explained that "Herry Monster is the Arnold Schwarzenegger of the Muppet world. He's very strong and proud of his strength, but not boastful. Kids can learn self-esteem without conceit from this guy."[6]

"I'll have the Schwarzenegger du jour," actor. Peter Ustinov is reported to have said in a Manhattan restaurant that does not have such an entrée on its menu: "Austrian mussels, glazed to perfection."[7] A parent described interviewing a somewhat severe pediatrician with a German or Austrian accent as "the Arnold Schwarzenegger of pediatricians" but chose her anyway for baby care.[8] Rock climber Steve Petro is called the "Schwarzenegger of climbing."[9] A woman who acts in adult movies told a crowd at a comedy club that she was "the Schwarzenegger of porn."[10] Even inanimate things come to life under Arnold's power; when he gave a talk at UCLA, the campus newspaper reported that "Biceps and Ballroom Bulge for Schwarzenegger Speech."[11]

To say an award-winning beer has a "unique chocolate/coffee richness to create the Schwarzenegger of our beers"[12] is to annex Arnold as the measure of brewing excellence. A wine is described as "spicy, rich, and loaded with mocha/vanilla highlights." You might want to call it Michael Jackson, but "The fruit is plump, pure cassis—the Arnold Schwarzenegger of Cabernet."[13] The chardonnays have their own representative in the wine muscling contest. In the "Olympic Challenges" category of gift wine, the *Wine Merchant* lists the Patz and Hall vintage 2000 Napa Valley chardonnay as "The Schwarzenegger of Chardonnays. Muscular yet balanced."[14] The WinePros Web site said the best Australian pinot noir, the "Arnold Schwarzenegger of Pinot Noirs," should be drunk with wild boar. But of course.[15]

If there is one performing arts category Arnold has never been associated with in his career, it is music. A few strums on a guitar during his election campaign do not make him a musician, but a few well-placed words make many a musician or musical instrument an Arnold Schwarzenegger. Russian pianist Arkardi Serper played at a recital in Monterey, California, on October 18, 2003. The reviewer commented, "the good news is that whenever Mr. Serper was not role playing as the Arnold Schwarzenegger of piano playing ('I am going to pound your piano into submission—have a nice day!'), he is a magnificent pianist."[16] "He's the Arnold Schwarzenegger of modern jazz," a fan says of DJ Otzi, a popular European musician.[17] Bass guitars seem to have an identity crisis: "Some people use bass to refer to something that looks like an oversize electric guitar, and some refer to the Arnold Schwarzenegger of the violin family."[18]

The way metaphors work is that there is a source of the metaphor and a target, or the thing to which it is applied. In every case we examine here, Arnold Schwarzenegger is the source of the structure and the elaborations that help redefine something else, something not naturally coupled with Arnold and that does not in any way originate with him. One such "unnatural" connection is to nature itself; one would not intuitively press Arnold into the service of defining something about the natural world. In an unintentionally ironic reference, contemporary bodybuilder John Hansen, who prides himself on a steroid-free approach to the sport, says that his long-term ambition is to "become the Arnold of natural bodybuilding."[19] By his own admission, Arnold's physique was enhanced by drugs; still, he becomes a natural metaphoric anchor for naturally built bodies. At the opposite end of the spectrum, even one of the smaller natural citizens, the insect, is given new meaning through an Arnoldian metaphor: North Carolina Extension Services entomologists warn of a type of wasp that looks like "the Arnold Schwarzenegger of the ant world" invading area homes. And they are hard to get rid of: "In all likelihood, when next year rolls around *they'll be back*."[20]

Animals especially seem to need to measure up to Arnold,

whether in the present or in the past. According to *Science News,* the *Tyrannosauridae* is the "Schwarzenegger of dinosaurs."[21] McGill University's alumni newsletter describes a prehistoric wild ox of Neanderthal times that was "forty percent larger than domestic cattle and had a real attitude." The Neanderthals would routinely attack these "Arnold Schwarzenegger of cows" but at great cost to themselves in terms of injuries.[22] A new type of beef just available on the market has more muscle and less fat than its "beefier, bulkier cousins." According to one breeder of the cattle (called Piedmontese), who is also the sales director for this new "double-muscle brand of beef," "It's the Arnold Schwarzenegger of cattle.... It's nutritionally correct meat with a high food value chock full of riboflavin, B–12, iron and zinc. It's the crème de la crème of beef."[23] A report on Iowa Public Television described another "hunky looking" breed of cattle called the Belgian Blue that has more muscle and less fat as the "'Arnold Schwarzenegger' of the cattle set."[24] A report on the genetic engineering of animals to increase productivity refers to a Belgian Blue bull as the "Arnold Schwarzenegger of the cattle world." Originally appearing in the *London Times* as "The Freaks of the Farmyard," the story further explains how the engineered animals cannot normally reproduce, and are often deformed, lame, and diseased.[25] Yet the desire for more muscle and less fat seem to outweigh these unfortunate side effects.

Animals in the wild and animals in captivity all seem to have Arnold Schwarzenegger reflected back at them from their water bowls. A Web site showing lions from an African safari marveled at their size in comparison to zoo animals and captioned a lion photo from the wild as "The Arnold Schwarzenegger of Cats."[26] A woman describing in an on-line journal a dream she had about two dogs calls one of them the "Arnold Schwarzenegger of dogs."[27] Another dog, Wotan, is described on a personal Web site as the "Arnold Schwarzenegger of dachshunds." He is an inbred dog whose deformed back legs won't let him run but he is "muscular and sleek."[28] Scooby-Doo is not your average dog either but that didn't stop one reviewer from choosing not Scooby but his nephew, Scrappy-Doo, as the "Schwarzenegger of canines" for the live action version of the cartoon.[29]

A Web site for tourism in Florida describes a creature in state waters that it calls the "Arnold Schwarzenegger of the soft-shelled turtle world," species name *Trionyx ferox,* which "won't hesitate to defend its space" and has a sharp beak.[30] A discussion group for divers describes a dive off Palm Beach: "One coral hole was the home of the Arnold Schwarzenegger of crabs. This fellow was HUGE (his claws were as big as my hands), and he was not at all afraid of us. He kept pacing back and forth in his home, daring us to mess with him."[31] For the state of Georgia agricultural agents, a new bass appearing in their waters provides a fight for fishermen: "Anglers familiar with its fighting characteristics consider it the 'Arnold Schwarzenegger' of freshwater predator fish."[32]

A Web site defining the "ideal structural styles of llamas and how to select them" describes a "muscle llama" called the "Schwarzenegger of llamas" as a "powerful looking beast" with "medium-width frame, big bone, big muscling, chest muscling ties into forearms, good ground clearance, medium back length" who has to have good ground clearance or he becomes "a short winded heavyweight."[33] The real Arnold Schwarzenegger of llamas is champion llama Domino. His owners say, "We call Domino the Arnold

Schwarzenegger of llamas because he has a fantastically athletic physique, yet has a very gentle personality."[34]

Plants also appear to behave like or resemble Arnold. For lovers of roses, there is a tough, drought-tolerant plant called *Rugosa rosa;* it is the "Arnold Schwarzenegger of the rose family."[35] The Arnold Schwarzenegger of trees, the American hornbeam, is a tough hardwood found in the deciduous forests of the East. Its trunks and branches "look like sinewy muscles covered with a thin blue-gray bark.... American hornbeams don't grow tall or spread their branches far from their main trunk, but they do stand firm and defiant."[36] If you are having trouble with your rhododendrons, it could be because you have *Rhododendrum ponticum,* which is "a Schwarzenegger among plants, a botanical terminator." It contains thirty neurotoxins and is poisonous to mammals, birds, and insects.[37] And it has pretty flowers. Japanese knotweed is a nuisance plant in Alaska. When a local writer saw it "engulf a salmonberry bush" he realized it was "the Schwarzenegger of the plant world."[38] In Texas, a contest by Texas A&M University to find the "tallest, straightest mesquite trees to put into their genetic improvement program" will probably be won by the "owners of the Arnold Schwarzenegger of Texas mesquite trees."[39]

When we teach our children about the plant world, most of us don't think to use Arnold as a prototype for plant processes, but someone did: In a set of guidelines for agricultural activities in the classroom, children are instructed to divide up into groups that represent the parts of a tree's circulatory system. The "Xylem" form a circle and pretend to raise water into the system by raising up their hands and saying, "Pump it up." The "Phloem" lower their hands and chant, "Pump it down." The Bark has a special job: "Have the bark form a circle around the phloem, facing outward, and pretend they are protecting the tree. (Tell the students to be the Arnold Schwarzenegger of the tree!)"[40]

Arnold Schwarzenegger, as a rose, a cow, a tree, a pianist, a beer, a wine, an ant, or a classroom lesson, has dominated the terms of those trying to talk about things big, expensive, valuable, high quality, powerful, violent, tough, successful, aesthetic, and maybe even erotic. According to David Feldman, "If belly dancers looked like Arnold Schwarzenegger, their movements would make their skins appear to be lined with live snakes!"[41] To be the measure of so many important things—right and wrong, good and bad, real and unreal, "real" and virtual, proper or improper, big and bigger, valuable or worthless—is an amazing feat.

And amazing feats are by association an Arnold Schwarzeneggerian phenomenon. In a review of the movie *Showtime* (2002), a criminal "tries to shoot his way out of trouble with the Arnold Schwarzenegger of guns—this thing can literally blow a house down."[42] An amazing sight works just as well. Views of the Hong Kong skyline inspired this comparison: "It is of course at night that the Schwarzenegger of night views really begins to flex its muscles."[43] A politically savvy trash company in Las Vegas, Nevada, "has exercised its local political muscle like the Arnold Schwarzenegger of sanitation" to get long-term contracts.[44]

The V-Max is a motorcycle called "The Arnold Schwarzenegger of power cruisers" and, to cover all bets, "The Mr. Olympia of power cruisers."[45] Another motorcycle makes a similar claim: The Yamaha XVS1100 Drag Star is the "Schwarzenegger of the motorcycle world."[46] A monster truck brought to a sales meeting for a tech company was called "the Schwarzenegger of four-wheelers" even though the monster truck was not "The Terminator." The company's marketing director commented, "It was the best sales meeting we ever put on. It pumped everybody up."[47] The Mercedes S600 sedan, "once just a mighty behemoth, is now an athlete of monumental proportions. Sort of like the Schwarzenegger of sedans."[48] And perhaps least surprising, the HUMMER H2 extended limousine, one of the largest in the world, is called the "Schwarzenegger of all rides."[49]

Metaphors actually serve humans in the most fundamental of ways—they permit us to exchange meanings, thoughts, and feelings. These exchanges transform into social bonding and are the foundation of the social fabric. If it is true, as Jacques Godbout and Alain Caillé propose, that "we must first use words to establish a relationship,"[50] then these utterances filled with Arnold Schwarzenegger are connecting us in a web of relations that always point to Arnold as the basis for making our decisions and judgments. Arnold is immediately recognized as the model of behavior that values persistence, force, self-determination, physical strength, power, positive action, uniqueness, and destruction. Such models, cognitive scientist Mark Johnson explains, "will be the basis for whatever moral principles we have."[51]

Has Arnold, then, become the basis of our culture's morality? Johnson's remark is interesting to bear in mind when we recall that U.S. Supreme Court justice Antonin Scalia was introduced at the Florida Governor's Leadership Forum with the thought that, "if mind were muscle, and court sessions were televised, Justice Scalia would be the Arnold Schwarzenegger of American jurisprudence."[52] Now that these definitions of morality seem so linked to Arnold references, we ought to consider just how thoroughly these links have begun to restructure ordinary thought.

A culture's morality is often revealed in the stories it tells. The sense of belonging to a group takes place through sharing narratives like this one: In a Sunday sermon delivered in May 1998, on "The Art of Christian Nurture," the preacher explained that the first step is to perceive "the image of God in the life of *every* person." He then proceeded to tell the story of Pharaoh, the King of Egypt, trying to destroy the firstborn of the Hebrews by ordering the midwives to kill the babies as they are delivered: "Well, these heroic women cooked up a grand story. They told the Pharaoh that the Hebrew women were sort of like the Arnold Schwarzenegger's [*sic*] of pregnancy. So robust were they that the babies just came POPPING out of them, so fast in fact that the midwives couldn't get there in time."[53] Just like that, Arnold Schwarzenegger joined Charlton Heston in the history of the Jews.

We have found over the past twenty years of research that people everywhere have Arnold Schwarzenegger stories to tell. Sometimes the stories that contain Arnold are parables with metaphors like the "Art of Christian Nurture." Other times, Arnold is a model for the story's characters. In "The Secret Lives of Pastors," we learn that "in his letter 'To the twelve tribes in the Dispersion,' the apostle James, the Schwarzenegger of the New Testament without groping, adds some muscle to the much-aligned [*sic*] notion of works-righteousness: Faith without works is dead. Terminated. DOA."[54] Explaining why narratives are so influential, Leslie Brothers tells us, "a group's narratives organize the thoughts of its members, specifically the categories of their perceptions, especially perceptions regarding persons."[55] Louise was at a snack counter in Santa Fe right before the California election and an inebriated man put down $40 to pay for a soda. Looking at it and realizing what he had done, the man said to no one in particular, "I guess I could do that if I were Arnold Schwarzenegger."

The point is not just that there are a lot of Arnold stories. The idea of Arnold Schwarzenegger now augments story upon story, reference upon reference throughout American culture and far beyond America's borders. The metaphors let Arnold enter stories that have no basis in direct encounters or observation such as stories about llamas or about birthing Hebrews. They give him entrée to stories where he would seem to have no business. Knowing Arnold's politics dramatizes the range of these forced associations and the peculiar results they produce, as when radical political protest organizer Mike Dolan is called the "Schwarzenegger of leftist insurgency"[56] and Catholic cardinal Joseph Ratzinger is called "the Vatican's Schwarzenegger of doctrine."[57]

In the world of medical science, Arnold supplies the yardstick for measuring strength, durability, intensity, or even malignant persistence. At a science Web site, penicillin is "the Arnold Schwarzenegger of antibiotics."[58] At a French medical school, the first topic of a medical seminar is about "myofibroblast bodybuilding: the Arnold Schwarzenegger of connective tissue."[59] A dentist in New Jersey, investigating possible causes for migraines, including the way headache sufferers use their temporalis muscles (for clenching), discovered that he was "the Arnold Schwarzenegger of clenching!"[60] Facial skin cancer cells that returned again and again, despite repeated radical surgeries, to one unfortunate man in Madera, California, were "the Arnold Schwarzenegger of basal cells."[61]

Even at the subcellular level of living tissue, Arnold lends his name and legacy to explanations of the most fundamental and important of cellular functions, endocytosis, the means by which vital hormones, proteins, nutrients, and other materials the cell needs are gathered and transported across the cell's boundaries. These materials are then packed into a kind of sack—the "budding vesicle." The enzyme-cluster that breaks open this sack to "dump" it into the cell is, in one medical article, called "Conan the Dynamin." Dynamin is extra-powerful in that, unlike other "GTPase enzymes" that require "cofactor proteins," dynamin carries its own such proteins. It is, we are told, "the Arnold Schwarzenegger of GTPases."[62]

Given Schwarzenegger's association with high-tech film-making and special effects generated by computers, it might not be surprising that he is used as a metaphor in the computer world. The ways he is used, however, are not direct reflections of this association with computerized production. Rather, they draw on the same repertoire of characteristics that inspired the metaphors in plants, animals, medicine, music, and product advertisements. French writer Gaston Bachelard found that "metaphors summon one another and are more coordinated than sensations."[63]

A system for sharing files across a network was developed "to be the Arnold Schwarzenegger of distributed file systems."[64] A computer reviewer in Australia was "suddenly walking taller" and had a more "commanding voice" when an 800 MHz machine arrived: "No more digital sand in my face, I was now the Schwarzenegger of the computing beach."[65] Serious Sam is the "Schwarzenegger of PC gaming."[66] Mac computer fans have always praised BBedit, a text editor for writing clean code, "the schwarzenegger of text editors."[67] The same Mac enthusiasts' list praises "Debabelizer" for once being the "schwarzenegger of

Image-Conversion and batch-/scripted jobs."[68] Likewise, "Résumé Maker Deluxe is the Arnold Schwarzenegger of résumé-writing software" because "It's a blockbuster—powerful and huge in size and scope, but gentle and friendly once you get to know it ('Kindergarten Cop' Schwarzenegger, not 'Terminator' Schwarzenegger)."[69] In one of the best reference books for Mac computers, the authors explain how to perform a quick task of formatting text. The first step is to "Type a word or phrase, such as, *I'll be back.*"[70]

The Arnold metaphors used by or about politicians are no different from the ones used on fish or motorcycles. Politicians can be more or less flattered when they are compared to Schwarzenegger. We have had the Arnold Schwarzenegger of British politics, Tony Blair,[71] and the Arnold Schwarzenegger of New Zealand politics, Mark Burton.[72] "Maybe I could be the Arnold Schwarzenegger of Louisiana," businessman John Georges said about the possibility of running for governor;[73] and in Ontario, Canada, "physique and charisma aside, Dalton McGuinty could be called the 'Arnold Schwarzenegger of the north'";[74] General Wesley Clark has been called "the Arnold Schwarzenegger of the national scene"[75] and "the Schwarzenegger of the Democratic Party."[76] In a much-quoted editorial from *Der Spiegel* in 1997, America is called "the Schwarzenegger of international politics: showing off muscles, intrusive, intimidating."[77] Meanwhile the German Bundesbank has been called "the Arnold Schwarzenegger of monetarism."[78] The U.S. dollar has been called "the Arnold Schwarzenegger of currencies" because "it will get elected by the people" around the world.[79]

If language, through narrative and metaphors, constructs our reality, then the place of Arnold Schwarzenegger in our language points to his significance as an indisputable influence on our cultural activities, actions, and understandings. Arnold the idea has vast metaphoric manifestations in everyday language, not in some complicated linguistic way that we can't understand, but in some very straightforward ways whose simplicity hides their importance: For one thing, they sell products, and by extension, they sell and resell Arnold himself.

While it's easy to comprehend how a constantly widening context for Arnold references would keep Schwarzenegger foregrounded in the American imagination, it is at first less apparent how deploying Arnold in product metaphors promises improved sales of items far removed from the metaphoric source. For example, AMSOIL 100% Synthetic ATF is considered "the Arnold Schwarzenegger of synthetic lubricants."[80] iPod Armor is the "Schwarzenegger of iPod cases," an iPod being Apple's tiny MP3 player.[81] "Not a saw for the faint of heart" is the Gryphon Miter saw, "the Schwarzenegger of came saws"[82] (came saws cut metal came or bars). In Orlando, "Homeowners bulk up with the Schwarzenegger of contracts" when they are in the housing market.[83] In each case the Arnold reference seems to come out of nowhere yet makes perfect sense because it draws on some characteristic associated with him.

"Boring product description follows: 3M Dual Lock, 1 [inch] wide, black, self-adhesive backing," says a Web site for a Velcro-like product. But it continues, "Big deal, right? Actually, yes! Dual Lock is the Arnold Schwarzenegger of 'hook and loop' fasteners. It's used in applications where Velcro—even the industrial stuff—isn't strong enough."[84] "Given the sheer size and weight of this system," states a buyer's description of the RBH T–2 Signature Speaker

System, "we believe it is properly named and may be the Arnold Schwarzenegger speaker of choice."[85] The "Schwarzenegger of phone plugs" is here: "this is the new wide-mouth jumbo 1/4 [inch] phone connector. Goes where no jumbo 1/4 [inch] phone plug has gone before, terminating even thickly-jacketed 12 gauge speaker cables."[86] Despite the almost slip into Star Trek country, this is an artful connection to Arnold.

Arnold appears as a connection point for this amazing constellation of products, creating new ways to represent things whose attributes draw significance from their metaphoric association with him. Yet somehow the Arnold reference makes sense to consumers, clarifying something essential about the products and broadening and deepening the universal applicability of the Arnold analogy. It is hard to imagine other cultural figures who could cover so much territory: Marilyn Monroe might suggest sexiness and vulnerability but not power, influence, and determination as well as saws and finches. And what, if anything, do stars like Johnny Depp or Julia Roberts evoke? Certainly not the power to protect an iPod or the ability to lubricate better than anything else. It may be possible to compare a llama to Madonna, but not also Velcro, phone plugs, and ants. Arnold is the Energizer Bunny of star metaphors and he just goes on and on. He, himself, is the Arnold Schwarzenegger of metaphors.

All these metaphors give Arnold a podium from which to speak. On the radio, in television, on Web sites, at congressional hearings, in magazines and newspapers, in children's videos and cartoons, at public lectures, or in courtrooms, he can speak without having to make a direct appearance. It is amazing that when he helps define what can count as experience, what can be seen as valuable, what can be allowed as truthful, and what can be acceptable as real, he doesn't even have to show up to enforce his vision of this world. Whether it is through an obscure reference like that of Galápagos finches or the most familiar one of the Terminator, these are impressive uses of Arnold to define our world.

Arnold Schwarzenegger is America's model of a new evolutionary force, one that favors the ability to spread thoughts, imitative speech, behavioral patterns, consumer choices, or metaphors. But as a result of this contagion, we end up limited in the ways we can imagine the world. Arnold has erased our other possibilities, just like John Kruger erased identities by destroying their previous manifestations. Our expectations now are that Arnold will be meaningful for every category we employ, that our memories should be filled with stories generated through Arnold, and that our sense of wonder[87] will be muted because Arnold provides the safest and easiest bet for explaining almost anything we encounter. Metaphors are supposed to be indications of the creativity of a culture, and certainly Arnold metaphors are entertaining and surprising. But they also narrow the ways we judge and categorize the things around us. America's attentions have been turned toward Arnold Schwarzenegger and we don't know how to turn away.

# CHAPTER 7

# The Terminator:
# 3D Icon

**ARNOLD SCHWARZENEGGER DID NOT WIN** the gubernatorial election in California. By most accounts, the election was won by an impressive action figure clad in black leather and cool shades, riding a motorcycle, packing impressive weaponry, and giving the bad guys hell. This figure coolly destroyed his weaker and less focused opponents, physically and mentally dominated the landscape, demanded the curious attention of lesser mortals, and warned us that his way was the only way. The election was won by one of the most familiar, popular, and telling mythical figures produced by late-twentieth-century American culture: The Terminator.

Arnold Schwarzenegger is obviously identified with the Terminator more than with any of his other characters. If it were not for the Terminator, he would not have had that magical combination that transforms man into myth, and movie actors into successful politicians. Imagine Arnold trying to run for governor without having made the Terminator films: Not only would headline writers be struggling with Conan metaphors or Hercules in New York analogies, but the election would not have had such a coherent storyline: Arnold terminates Gray Davis. As the *Los Angeles Times* noted, "Schwarzenegger is the first politician in American history to use the selling of a movie—a worldwide promotional tour for 'Terminator 3'—as the warm-up for a political campaign."[1]

When he first got into politics helping George Bush (elder) run for president in 1988, Schwarzenegger was dubbed "Conan the Republican." Conan the Republican was just what George Bush needed to overcome his widely discussed image as a "wimp" and to put all the other candidates on notice. As Arnold said in an election speech for Bush, "I saw [Ronald Reagan and George Bush] take over an economy that looked like PeeWee Herman and I saw them turn this economy around to make it look like Superman."[2] Arnold, still not identifying with the Terminator in this campaign, also said that "When it comes to American future, Michael Dukakis will be the real Terminator!"[3] It was a statement that was impressive at the time and repeated throughout the media but missed the point of the Terminator's appeal and misplaced its locus. Bill Clinton called a member of the Bush administration in the 1992 campaign "the Terminator" because he ended jobs and added, "We don't need a terminator 2."[4]

Bush rewarded Schwarzenegger for his support with the chairmanship of the President's Council on Physical Fitness and Sports, an obscure and usually ceremonial role. Schwarzenegger took the position and turned it into a passport that allowed him to cultivate the attention of Washington politicians and of policymakers in every one of the fifty states that he visited during his reign. Yet neither Conan nor Schwarzenegger's first political position was sufficient to build a political future. Conan, with his bulging, rippling muscles, furry loincloths, grunting exchanges, tendency to bloody slaughter, and his pumped-up women, was not a good Republican image. And the chairmanship of whatever-that-thing-was may have helped behind the scenes, and did give him the opportunity to exercise with both Willard Scott and Mickey Mouse, but it was not compelling as proof of his ability to get important things done.

All of Schwarzenegger's other film characters are one-shot deals that blur into each other: the Russian police officer in *Red Heat* (1988), the desperate dad in *Jingle All the Way* (1996), the genetically perfect twin in *Twins* (1988), the military men in *Predator* (1987) or *Commando* (1985). *The Running Man* (1987) was really only known as a film title, as was *Total Recall* (1990), in which Arnold was both a construction worker and a spy whose memory was erased. The rest of the films do not form either a cohesive image or provide a great symbolic character from which the culture could generate meanings. In *Eraser* he was a government operative, in *Batman and Robin* (1997) he was the frozen Mr. Freeze, in *The 6th Day* (2000) he was a clone, in *Collateral Damage* (2002) he was a fireman fighting terrorists, and in *End of Days* (1999) he was a policeman fighting the devil himself.

Before Arnold announced his candidacy for governor, a Democratic political consultant who had worked for Gray Davis suggested, and maybe hoped, "He clearly has to run as Kindergarten Cop, not as the Terminator."[5] *Terminator* and *T2* director James Cameron commented about the character that same summer, "The Terminator's so last millennium."[6] One reviewer of the movie *Terminator 3* advised, "Seriously Arnold: Forget politics. You're much more fun on the screen."[7] But a counterview presented by a Republican consultant was reported as "Schwarzenegger's violent record on celluloid won't hurt him if he runs, says Republican consultant Don Sipple. 'If he played a well-known serial killer character it might be a problem,' Sipple says. For instance, Anthony Hopkins of 'Silence of the Lambs' fame, might struggle to expand his base beyond cannibals."[8] The Terminator as the candidate's alter ego turned out to be the correct choice. His wife, Maria Shriver, while campaigning in the recall election, called the Arnoldian qualities the three D's: He is disciplined, determined, and decisive. California elected a three-dimensional Terminator, and politics-as-usual was now targeted for termination.

The first Terminator movie came out in 1984, right in the middle of the Conan phenomenon. For a while, Schwarzenegger was caught in a time and image warp between crude, violent, and fleshy barbarians from the past and smooth, violent, and efficient killing machines from the future. The Conan path could not have led any further in politics because it was not a prolific referent. What can you say about Conan the Barbarian and Conan the Destroyer that would lead anyone to think, gee, this guy should run for governor of California? Any attempt to change the path or nature of Conan would have led to disappointment, especially for his "bloodthirsty fans," as one critic quipped, who would not find "Conan the Vegetarian" acceptable.[9]

The Terminator path, however, even with a series of unpredictable and surprising changes to the character through the years, led Arnold to Sacramento. Remember there are several types of Terminators, and although Arnold has not played all of them, he has absorbed the qualities of each. He has somehow maintained the aura, and the notoriety, of the Terminator even as the roles he plays in American culture and the movies have evolved.

If you have never seen any of the Terminator movies, it may be hard to connect these particular points, so a rundown of the plot lines of the Terminator series will be useful here. These descriptions also raise the question, "Which Terminator are people referring to when they call Governor Schwarzenegger 'the Terminator'"?

In *The Terminator* (1984), the first movie in the series, Arnold is an unstoppable killer cyborg sent back in time from the year 2029 to terminate Sarah Connor, a woman who will give birth to the leader of the human resistance against the machines that, she learns, have taken over the world of the future. As the movie describes it, "The Terminator is an infiltration unit, it's part man, part machine. Underneath it's a hyper-alloy combat chassis, microprocessor controlled, fully armored, very tough. But outside it's living human tissue, flesh, skin, hair, blood, grown for the cyborgs." The model number of this first and subsequent Terminators that look like Arnold is of great interest to fans who attend Terminator conventions, exchange Terminator trivia and merchandise, and who debate whether there are real Terminators in our future.[10]

In the second movie, *Terminator 2: Judgment Day* (1991), Sarah Connor has had her son but is in a mental institution because she tried to blow up the machines that would attack humans on Judgment Day, which was coming soon. This time two Terminators are sent back from the future: a protector Terminator that still looks like Arnold Schwarzenegger and the T–1000, a liquid metal morphing machine determined to eliminate 10-year-old John Connor. The highly touted "kinder, gentler" Terminator frees Sarah, saves mother and son from the T–1000, and becomes John's surrogate father.

In *Terminator 3: Rise of the Machines* (2003), the now really obsolete Arnold/Terminator model is again sent back to protect John Connor but this time is followed by the T-X, or Terminatrix model, a sexy-looking blond cyborg who can not only transform her liquid metal body but also turn it into various weapons of destruction. Judgment Day finally occurs as the machines blow up the world with nuclear weapons. John Connor survives with the help, again, of the original Terminator, although he is warned that in the future this same Terminator will be reprogrammed and will kill him.

The Terminator is the most prolific symbol spawned by Arnold Schwarzenegger and it has generated numerous metaphors that our culture uses freely and creatively. In his analysis of the dead Elvis Presley as a similar, very prolific icon, Greill Marcus explains that there is a "necessity existing in every culture that leads it to produce a perfect, all-inclusive metaphor for itself."[11] Elvis was one such metaphor from the 1950s and 1960s and past his death in 1977. He provided numerous ways to talk about authority, sex, repression, and guilt in an era that had just begun to develop widespread outlets for these conversations. When Elvis died, people continued to use him and some even to see him. Arnold's Terminator metaphor gets used across his multiple lives, too.

The Terminator is an example of what anthropologists call a dominant symbol: It appears in many contexts and guises, it can perform many cultural tasks, it can condense many meanings into one image, and it provides a window onto the rest of the culture.[12] In recounting some of the uses and variations of the Terminator here, we trace ideas in American culture about violence, dominance, metamorphosis, power and political effectiveness, mothering and paternity. There aren't too many other symbols that can carry this burden.

The Terminator doesn't work as a cultural metaphor merely because it is a cyborg, though that combination of human and machine is inherently fascinating. It works because a cyborg is a liminal figure, one that crosses boundaries—in the Terminator's case, those boundaries are between the future and the past, reality and fantasy, reality and film, beginnings and ends. And at each crossing, the Terminator imports a volatile mixture of creation and destruction. The destructive powers are obvious; its goal is, after all, "species-cide." But the creative power may at first be less apparent. More than anything else, the Terminator is a creature of order; its goal is to eradicate human unpredictability. It is a creature of violence and relentlessness, metamorphosis, lethal skill and craft, and, in the permutations we see in the Terminator trilogy, renewal—but the "new" must reflect the hybrid soul of the Terminator itself. The Terminator seeks to create a world with logical programs, not hearts and souls, at its core.

For the past two decades the label "Terminator" has become synonymous with Arnold Schwarzenegger himself, not just with a film character, and no matter what he is doing or how removed it is from a cyborg in a science fiction film.[13] Of course, Arnold is not the first Hollywood figure to become identified with a particular character or character-type. Clint Eastwood is, for many people, Dirty Harry. Sylvester Stallone has, at various times, been referred to either as Rocky or as Rambo. Christopher Reeves was, on occasion, referred to as Superman. But nothing that Stallone or Eastwood has done in ordinary life has blurred the distinction between the men and the characters they played in the movies. And while some have described Reeves' efforts, after his crippling accident, to regain more and more function as "superhuman," no one mistakes Reeves for the Superman he portrayed.

Nobody but Arnold has been as seamlessly attached to his cinematic persona. Arnold has recognized this phenomenon and exploits the way Americans accept the fusion between the man and his movie portrayal. "In Terminator, they laughed when I reached into a guy's chest and pulled his guts out.... I can get away with things most people can't."[14] As one writer for The Age put it, "He is the Terminator, an outsider who'll keep on coming until he has completed his mission: saving the human race from the Democrats."[15] Calling attention to the potentially enormous irony of the election, a VH1.com article entitled "'The Terminator' Wins California Governorship" predicted, "No doubt Hollywood will eventually make a movie out of this bizarre, dramatic escapade, and it won't be too hard to secure Arnold Schwarzenegger to play the lead role."[16]

The Terminator appeared in many forms in the recall election campaign and continued to be a powerful image right up to the closing of the polls, and then even after the election. A few days before the vote, Arnold staged an elaborate demonstration that so clearly illustrated the power of the connection between the actual person, the one running for governor, and the Terminator character from his best-known movies.

Arnold's campaign was at one of the first stops on a four-day, statewide bus tour called the "California Comeback Express" that took place the week before the election. Looking at a wrecking ball dangling from a crane, he told the crowd at the Orange County Fairgrounds, "In the movies, if I played a character and I didn't like something, you know what I did? I destroyed it." The wrecking ball was then dropped onto a car, symbolizing the way in which Arnold intended to terminate the newly imposed car tax that was one of the major issues in the election. "Hasta la vista, car tax," he said.[17]

Arnold continued to promote his Terminator agenda throughout the campaign. In his speeches he often deployed a variation of these phrases: "Gray Davis has terminated hope. Gray Davis has terminated opportunity. Now it is time to terminate Gray Davis."[18] In the one candidates' debate in which he participated, he sarcastically offered the loud and contentious Arianna Huffington a role in his next movie, "T4," presumably a role that included another female terminator being stuffed in a toilet. On the day he announced his candidacy he is quoted as warning all American politicians, "Do your job and do it well or else... hasta la vista, baby." He later told the same news conference, "I'll be back."[19] By the end of the election, headlines announced "Arnold Poised to Terminate Davis"[20] and "'The Terminator' Wins California Governorship," followed by the comment that "the man who served three terms as a cold, metallic 'Terminator' has been elected the next governor of California."[21]

The Terminator had qualities that made him a formidable candidate. Opponents sometimes reacted as if they were fighting the cinema character instead of a political rival, and indeed they were right. Robert Novak commented in his column entitled "Bush's Terminator" that "Longtime Democratic hitman Bob Mulholland talked about shooting 'real bullets' at Schwarzenegger (though State Chairman Torres said he cautioned him against 'using that word again')."[22] A Republican analyst noted that Arnold was a "kick ass kind of guy," one who could "go to Sacramento and take charge. So in effect the movie persona that he has had seems to go beyond the fantasy into reality here."[23] *Newsweek* mixed it all up in a story about Arnold's bus tour of the state one week before the election: "The big-budget thriller that began with Arnold Schwarzenegger's dropping a bomb on 'The Tonight Show' ends with next Tuesday's recall vote—but not before a climactic chase scene that's one part 'Terminator 3' and one part 'Meet the Press.'"[24]

It is not only the Terminator character itself that helped create the victory in the recall election; it is the combination of the Terminator with all that Schwarzenegger represents through his body and his personal history. The Terminator alone is not enough, as a candidate in the 1993 Texas special election learned. Democrat Bob Krueger was defeated by Kay Bailey Hutchinson in a run for the U.S. Senate even though he appeared in a political ad wearing Terminator sunglasses and leather. In the ad the former English professor quipped, "Was it Shakespeare who said, 'Hasta la vista, baby'?" in an attempt to appear less stuffy, but the ploy backfired. First Lady Barbara Bush commented (echoing Lloyd Bentsen's put-down of Dan Quayle in the 1988 vice presidential debate), "I know Arnold Schwarzenegger, and Bob Krueger's no Arnold Schwarzenegger."[25]

That the Terminator became the framework for Arnold's election seemed inevitable. This was both reflected in and shaped by the news coverage of the campaign, which invariably reinforced the idea that it was the Terminator who was running for governor of California. As one reporter put it, "Schwarzenegger's political experience is exactly zero.... But as an incarnation of his on-screen presence, he is unbeatable."[26] It is Arnold's ability to continually resurrect this on-screen image, and to become the living embodiment of it, that much of America finds so compelling. Arnold-as-Terminator presents a profile that offers something for everyone: He is unstoppable; he answers to no one; he is the strong and nearly silent type. The wide path of cinematic destruction he causes is justified because the fate of the world hinges on his actions. And he is often funny—however accidentally—when the language of his machine-logic tangles with the human emotions of those in whose world he is a time-traveling foreigner.

Across America, it was definitely the Terminator running for and winning the statehouse in Sacramento. And if international headlines are any indication of the way American politics is perceived, then the world also thought that America's most populous state was going to be run by an action figure. The *Toronto Star* published the headline "Terminator Wants to Be Governor." The article began, "The Terminator wants to clean house in California."[27] Across the ocean, in the United Kingdom, *The Observer* speculated that "The Terminator might soon emerge from the Governor's residence in Sacramento, stripped to the waist and, mad as hell."[28] In the Philippines, analyzing the upcoming Filipino presidential election, one news magazine quoted candidate Paul Roco: "Healing wounds [of division] needs experience. You can't get that from a [movie script]." The article then continues, "Gray Davis said as much about

Arnold how-do-you-spell-his-surname 'The Terminator' during the recall elections in California. But Mr. Terminator won anyway."[29]

In the self-proclaimed "The Number One News Resource of Pakistan" (*The News International–Internet Edition*), the regular feature "Media Watch" led the story on Schwarzenegger's election victory with the headline "Enter the Terminator."[30] Australia's national daily newspaper reported, on October 9, 2003: "Terminator Wins Toughest Battle."[31] The Czech Republic's *Mlada fronta Dnes* reported, "Iraqis want a strong leader like Arnold Schwarzenegger.... Terminator Arnold Schwarzenegger wins elections in California amidst public uprising against the Democrats." Slovakia's *Pravda* noted the "Metamorphosis of Terminator into Gubernator." Malaysia's *Utusan Malaysia* commented, "People across the world are in shock: one of America's most prosperous states is to be governed by The Terminator." Even the London-based pan-Arab newspaper *Al-Quds Al-Arabi* noted, "They were voting for the Terminator, the legend they had seen on the cinema screen."[32]

Variations of the term "Terminator" during the campaign provide a sense of how productive it was to think of Schwarzenegger's candidacy in this way. Arnold became the "Governator" even before he was elected. "The Governator?" questioned one newspaper back in June 2003.[33] "Recall numbers show Governator about to be real," claimed another news source; "Arnold—contemporary political shorthand for 'actor in over his head'—is going to win. All the jokes and Leno appearances and Governator snickers and working his movies into headlines are about to become the new reality."[34] "The Terminator became the 'governator'" was the common description.[35] In a spoof on the term and the election, a talking Governator doll was accused of groping Barbie.[36]

The Internet's Urban Dictionary created a forum in which people could post definitions of this new term:

governator "guv-urn-ate-er":

- A machine sent back in time to terminate Gray Davis and become Governor of Caleefornia.
- A ruthless cyborg killing machine (Schwarzenegger) created by SkyNet (Republican Party). SkyNet will send this killer cyborg back in time to kill our founding fathers before they can write our Constitution that gives rights to every American.
- California's answer to Minnesota's former governor Jesse "The Body" Ventura. Now maybe California's governor can kick the Minnesota governor's ass. We'll see if Gray will be back.
- Half governor, half cyborg... a hyper-alloy combat chassis surrounded by living tissue, sent back by SkyNet to become governor of California.
- Large Austrian man who won the election for Kaleefohnya, and all of deese tings.
- A robotic humanoid sent back from the future to rule the human race with his Scandinavian accent and hidden weapons of mass destruction.
- A robotic groping machine sent back from the future to terrorize womankind.
- Supreme ruler of Kal-lee-four-niah.
- Governor who can only be elected during Total Recall.[37]

If a name is, as social scientist Harold Isaacs argues, the "simplest, most literal, and most obvious of all symbols of identity,"[38] then the other Terminator variations are just as revealing. A French magazine called Arnold the "Californiator"[39] and the Scottish took possession of him by dubbing him the "Tartanator."[40] Even Maria Shriver was captured in the spread of this phrasing, being called "The Inoculator" by *Newsweek* for her ability to keep Arnold from being infected by ugly rumors and accusations.[41] *Newsweek* asked if Arnold was going to morph from the Terminator to the "Great Communicator" and perhaps along with Maria the two of them could be called the "Twin Communicators."[42] Arnold himself told *USA Today,* "At home, Maria is The Terminator."[43] The "Gropinator" appeared in media everywhere as well as on protest signs after the sexual misconduct accusations surfaced. It morphed into "Herr Gröpenfuhrer" in Garry Trudeau's *Doonesbury* cartoon. The Governator also became "The Deregulator" after the election for his interest in eliminating public oversight of energy markets.[44]

But the Terminator commanded a place in the culture well before the recall election and it is this relentless productivity of the Terminator that reveals America's complete absorption of the phenomenon. The Terminator has penetrated the American consciousness in ways that are remarkable not only for their frequency but for their diversity as well.

The Terminator has spawned several catch phrases that people around the world find themselves using with regularity. "I'll be back" was one of the few things the original Terminator bothered to say in the first film. Coming to a police station to terminate Sarah Connor, he eyes the wall surrounding the officer on duty and then states without emotion: "I'll be back." He returns by smashing through the glass wall with a car and proceeds to decimate the police in the station. The phrase has come to be repeated endlessly in

American culture, always with the same dual message of a plan to return and a threat to incite mayhem. But the original line for the movie was supposed to be, "I'll come back,"[45] a statement of the intent to return with a passive rather than aggressive bent. It never would have become an iconic phrase like "I'll be back."

"Hasta la vista" has become as common as "I'll be back," with the same double connotation of return and threat. "Arnold Unplugged—It's hasta la vista to $9 billion if the Governator is selected," states one commentator.[46] "Hasta la vista, Davy!" exclaimed one Christian Web site;[47] "Will Schwarzenegger say 'Hasta la vista to showbiz?'" an entertainment Web site asked.[48] "Hasta la vista, baby" made its first appearance in the second Terminator film. Young John Connor is trying to teach his protector Terminator how to be more human. "You gotta listen to the way people talk," he says to the Terminator. He tells the Terminator that if someone has an attitude you say, "Eat me." And if you want to "shine someone on" you say, "Hasta la vista, baby." The Terminator tries it, but gives too much emphasis to the word "baby." Learning his lesson well over time, the Terminator looks into the camera later in the film and tells the bad Terminator as he attempts to eliminate him, "Hasta la vista, baby."

Beyond these familiar catch phrases, the Terminator has entered the language, and thus our way of thinking about the world, by being a metaphor that is useful across an amazing variety of fields. In the world of science and medicine, the Terminator is an allusion to both disease factors and the scientists who fight them. In an article on the ability of HIV to mutate when it replicates, the virus can fight for survival "not unlike the morphing android of the movie 'Terminator

2.'" In the next paragraph, the scientists are similarly compared: "Every time the Arnold Schwarzeneggers of science have the virus in their sights for destruction by a drug, it transforms into something else and shrugs the drug *off*."[49] The power of nature seems to be of Terminator proportions. One house during a large earthquake outside of Los Angeles was described as looking "like it had been trashed in a 'Terminator' movie."[50]

Steven Clarke, of the Department of Chemistry and Biochemistry and the Molecular Biology Institute at the University of California, published a study entitled "The Methylator Meets the Terminator."[51] The metaphor Clarke and his colleagues use refers to the chemical termination of protein synthesis at the cellular level. Robert Forward (et al.) published an article about something called "The Terminator Tether," a device designed to assist in the "end-of-life deorbit" of a spacecraft.[52] There is also a controversial agritechnology called "The Terminator" that is designed to "genetically switch off a plant's ability to germinate a second time."[53] In this instance, the Terminator brings about the end-of-life for plants and, by extension, for those who plant and those who consume plants.

The Terminator is a perfect metaphor in these arenas of science not only because it signifies the ultimate end of a process, but also because it signals the thoroughness with which the image of the relentless, emotionless, Arnoldian Terminator has spread in the culture. Of course, sometimes the metaphor gets used against its source. In late August of 2002, conservative columnist Michelle Malkin wrote, "Terminate This, Arnold"—a piece forecasting the doom of Arnold's dawning political career. In California, virtually anyone can put forth a ballot initiative in hopes of attracting the interest of legislators. According to Malkin, Arnold's ballot initiative, the "After School Education and Safety Act," would be so costly and was such a "warmed over Hillaryism" that he had sabotaged his own electability. She warned, "Hear me now, Arnold, and believe me later: The Hillary costume will scare away Republican voters faster than your last box-office bomb." For emphasis, Malkin added, "Hasta la vista, baby."[54] Malkin's fluent use of Terminator terms and language bears witness to their potency. The problem with Malkin's logic was that she was wrong; Arnold's popularity only increased as a result of the After School ballot initiative.

You would think that with all the mayhem and violence he incites the Terminator would not be a welcome guest in Christian worship services. But he has proven to be a useful character for those trying to convince others of the proper Christian life. One broadcast sermon called "The Terminator of Truth" asked, "If you are not entirely sure what happens to the soul when a person dies, what should the church do about that?... Should the church send The Enforcer after you?"[55] In an on-line lay journal of Catholic thought, an article entitled "The Splendor of Truth: Terminator of Proportionalism?" asks the question, "John Paul II says 'Hasta la Vista' to Popular Moral Theory. But Richard McCormick says, 'We'll be Back!' Who's Right?"[56]

A worship series at the Covenant Community Church in Florida called the "Terminator of Pain" was introduced by two homemade videos featuring metallic Terminators chasing the worship planners in order to stop their activities. In each video the group is saved by the "Timonator," a member of the congregation. The topic for the series was "Living with Pain and Turning It into Praise"; in the first week the focus was on "Your Pain Is Your Gain," and the second week "Moving from Pain to Praise." In his own unique interpretation of the Terminator movies, the leader of the worship service explained after the first video that the movies show a future where robots do everything for humans and they won't have to work, think, or have pain (an idea that is not in the films but does show up in the Terminator 3D ride at Universal Studios). The Bible does teach, he explains, that at the end there will be no pain, that pain will be terminated, but several television ministries are trying to teach that the belief in Jesus Christ now would eliminate all pain. "That is a lie from the pit of hell," he warns them, and the "Terminator of Pain" series shows how to deal with the pain that is here in their lives now.[57]

On a less positive note, the "Crusade for the Defense of Our Catholic Church" printed a series of ads in the Sacramento Bee during the election that was headlined "Wanted: One Catholic Governor, Not Three 'Catholic' Terminators." Referring to the pro-choice stance of Schwarzenegger, Bustamante, and Davis on abortion, the ad continued, "Hasta la vista—BABIES."[58]

Many products also claim Terminator affinities. "The Terminator of security appliances"[59] is a computer network security device to fight off software attacks on the system. An older computer interface called SCSI (pronounced "scuzzy") was described as having "a lot in common with Arnold Schwarzenegger. It's powerful. It's hard to understand. And its terminator keeps coming back, even after you're sure it's a dead issue."[60] A Portland, Oregon, brewery makes "Terminator Stout," which is described as "Black as the blackest night. Rich as the most decadent dessert."[61] "Terminator II" dumbbells are to be expected, but paper and CD shredders, the "Media Destroyers," are also headlined as

"Terminators."[62] The Therminator is a "wooden man bearing $30,000 worth of electronic sensors," very much like his Terminator namesake, who is used by the Ford Motor Company to research climate control in the factories.[63]

The "Terminator of telecommunications" is a name for the automated dialing system that, "Coldly working its way through the phone directory," just like the original Terminator, can autodial 1,500 numbers a day. "Telling a machine to stop calling is useless," the description concludes.[64] "Hummers: Terminator of All-Terrain Vehicles"[65] is the description of the HumVee that Arnold is so closely identified with. Vehicles that are not Arnold's Hummer also try to identify with the Terminator. "The Terminator of SUVs" was the claim made for Mercedes' G-wagon, another all-terrain vehicle originally designed for the military.[66] "The Terminator" is a real Monster Truck, but a miniature remote-control version of it called "The Raminator" was in stores for the 2003 Christmas holiday season.

Back in the human realm, Terminator names can also indicate being the best in a career. Tough politicians can take on the name: Attorney Warren Christopher, head of the Christopher Commission set up to investigate the Los Angeles Police Department after the Rodney King incident and subsequent riots in 1991, was called the Terminator.[67] So was the Los Angeles police chief, Daryl Gates, who was in charge at the time: "It's not Chief Gates behind the desk; it's Terminator Gates: he can't be reasoned with, he can't be argued with, he's programmed only to go forward."[68] Chairman of the Federal Reserve Alan Greenspan was called the "Inflation Terminator" and people who did not believe in his policies were described as the same people who "saw Elvis a couple of weeks ago."[69] The best noodle maker in

Rowland Heights, California, has been visited by Arnold Schwarzenegger himself, so Mr. Chu can now be called "The Chu-minator II."[70]

Proving to be as malleable as the T–1000 of *Terminator 2,* the Terminator metaphor has found its way into careers less "naturally" related. Cher's husband calls her the "Cher-inator," "the feminine version of the Terminator," when she gets very businesslike.[71] In an ad for the movie *Toys* (1992), Robin Williams calls himself the "Toyminator." The tooth fairy in the movie *Santa Claus 2* (2002) is sensitive about his name and wants to change it. Rejecting the name "Roy," Santa suggests "The Molinator," and sure enough the Molinator saves Santa and Christmas. Poor Dennis the Menace, always getting blamed for something, got named the prepubescent Terminator by one reviewer because "everything this Dennis touches is marked for extinction."[72]

Sports stars are also often Terminators. Nancy Reno's friends call her "the Terminator" in women's professional volleyball.[73] Jeff Reardon of the Atlanta Braves is the Terminator of batters for his ability to choke off late-inning rallies.[74] In the 1998 Winter Olympics, Tara Lipinski's unexpected win in figure skating got her christened "The Taranator" for her aggressive freestyle program.[75] The Austrian skier Hermann Maier was called "The Hermannator" for a similar approach in his sport. The "Tiny Terminator" is a UCLA gymnast who, like Arnold, will be back after her injuries.[76]

In Arnold's own films, his characters were sometimes treated as spawn of the Terminator and renamed appropriately. "The Terminator becomes the Germinator in Junior," one reviewer states.[77] A character from *Collateral Damage,* talking about Arnold's character, John Armstrong, tells a fellow guerilla, "You know how Germans are. They're like cyborgs." To a reporter in the movie *The 6th Day,* Arnold's character, Adam Gibson, tells a salesman at RePet (where dead pets are cloned), "I might be back." The salesman responds, more to himself than Arnold, "You'll be back." "I'll be back" is also threatened by Arnold's character in *The Running Man.*

Entertainment, politics, science... where else can the Terminator show up? It might be more appropriate to ask, where hasn't he shown up? The Terminator—the great antagonist (the original Terminator) and hero (T2, T3)—has been adopted, co-opted, and adapted in so wide a variety of venues, it could give us—as nearly happens to the overwhelmed Doug Quaid in *Total Recall*—a "schizoid embolism." Speaking of productive, fertility specialist Cecil Jacobson was dubbed "The Sperminator" when he illegally impregnated up to seventy-five women with his own sperm instead of donor sperm or that from the women's spouses.[78] The idea of the "Sperminator" has taken off like a new strand of recombinant DNA. In addition to the infamous "Sperminator" physician the world has seen (or heard):

- Peter Van Tol and Maurice Hickendorff's rock band/album "Sperminator" (featuring their hit song "No Women Allowed")[79]
- An episode of the television show *L.A. Law* entitled "Sperminator"[80]
- One of actor John Leguizamo's characters, from his award-winning one-man show *Mambo Mouth,* a 13-year-old homeboy named "Sperminator"[81]

- A made-to-order bicycle company offering a super-tricked-out bike called "The Sperminator"[82]
- A pornographic film entitled *The Sperminator*[83] (another X-rated video entitled *Inside Porn* features a performer named "Candy Cockinator")
- An injectable contraceptive for men—called by its bio-medical engineer inventor, Sujoy Guha, Reversible Inhibition of Sperm Under Guidance (RISUG)—colloquially referred to as both "the Sperminator" and "the De-Sperm-inator"[84]

Is this an idea borrowed from Arnold himself? At a *Terminator 2* fan convention in Los Angeles in 1991, Arnold announced to the deliriously energized crowd, "Jim Cameron and I have just decided that we're going to do another *Terminator*. The title will be *The Sperminator*. 'I'LL COME AGAIN!'"[85]

Not to be left off of the Terminator train, many others have warped the "Term" slightly to come up with their own unique handles. To name a few:

- Verminator! A music video by the band The Hamsters. One of their feature songs is "I'm Bad, I'm Nationwide."[86]
- Verminator: a custom-built robot to enter the new Drag Rat Race of the Micromouse Y2K Grand Prix[87]
- Verminator Predator Calls ("At the Verminator shop, we can custom make your calls to sound like you want them to. For example… The Big Dawg Howlers…")[88]
- "Fleshbiter the Epiderminator": a skin-care product to be used with men's shower gel[89]
- Worminator Lures: the "finest designed soft plastic lures on the market today"[90]

- "Der Sexinator": a reference to Arnold in the German newsletter Bild.T-Online[91]
- Bob Sturm, a.k.a. "The Sturminator" of KTCK-AM ("The Ticket" 1310). It is ironic to note here that talk-show host Max Miller had been in Sturm's time slot, but after going on vacation, he was "never heard from again."[92] Miller had actually been fired, but the impression was that The Sturminator had terminated his predecessor.
- Der Sturminator: a would-be German army "super trooper" of World War II—these were the soldiers who broke ranks to try to be heroes but whose actions placed their "kumpelen" (buddies) at risk. Sturminators are "those who think they can flammen everyone themselves."[93]

Arnold himself has always understood the appeal of the Terminator: "Everyone would like to be a Terminator.... Everyone would like to be a person who can take care of the job. Whoever makes you mad, you can get even," he has said in numerous magazine articles and television interviews.[94] He has also said, "I like the Terminator... I'd like to be as resolved as he was and have that kind of power."[95]

What kind of creature is the Terminator that it would be the appropriate reference point for everything from athletes and nasty politicians to computer parts, fishing lures, and porn videos? From its conception, the Terminator is first and foremost, through all its iterations, a cyborg, a cybernetic organism, part(s) human, part(s) machine. But Arnold's Terminator is not simply a cocktail of living tissue and machine guts; it's not just a man with steely character. The Terminator is the realization of pumping iron: flesh on a metallic chassis with enough visible and hidden power to change the way the culture understands human limitations.

Arnold's plan has always been to grow beyond limits, to move ahead, to make a lot of money, to maintain an efficiently organized life, and to be the last word in each of his professional endeavors—to terminate the possibility of being surpassed. Some find this inspiring; others, like journalist Knute Berger, see it through darker glasses, arguing that California's choice of the Terminator for governor means that "We are being told that the 'chaos' of a multicultural world—and society—is unacceptable, that order and safety can only be restored with the discipline that a strong hand can bring."[96] Arnold's project has always been to be single-handedly fighting the border wars between the cybernetic and the organic. Starting with bodybuilding, where the melding of machines and bodies is the essence of the "sport," to his most familiar melding with machines in the Terminator movies, and even with the political machines of the recall election, we have seen him challenge what is considered a believable joining of humans with their mechanisms.

The easiest way to think about a cyborg is that it is a fusion of some kind of intelligent machine with organic life. It's not a robot, and it's not a robotlike human being. As Arnold's three Terminators have shown us, cyborgs are hybrids that defy separation into the two constituent parts. But our culture's resolute blurring of the boundary between Arnold Schwarzenegger and the Terminator prompts us to consider somewhat more complex ideas about cyborgs.

"Cyborg," as author Dani Cavallaro explains, refers to the "myth of the perfect body and the dread of human incompleteness" as well.[97] The queen of cyborg theory for both geeks and scholars alike is Donna Haraway, a professor of the history of science. Haraway attempted to create a feminist approach to cyborgs in an article that was widely circulated and discussed in 1985, right after the first Terminator (1984) movie. She called the attempt ironic because the two things—cyborgs and feminists—seem so, so different.[98] From this article emerged the basics of cyborg theory: that a cyborg is a synthesis of machine and organism, that cyborgs are about confusing the boundaries between technology and humans, and that we are all cyborgs whether we like it or not.[99]

Haraway says we *should* like it, that we should take pleasure in this odd coupling because it can help us subvert traditional, stale categories by which we rule our lives. If you think of yourself as a cyborg, then old oppositional categories like male/female, nature/culture, and public/private can be rendered meaningless. *Terminator 3* (2003) features a female cyborg, but this superficial surface decoration does not really change anything. As a morphing terminator, "she" is no more female than Arnold's Terminator; in *Terminator 2* (1991) the liquid-metal cyborg can change into any type of figure, male or female, living or inanimate. Cyborgs of the Terminator class open up every possibility of boundary crossing and category destruction.

What does Arnold gain and what does he lose by being seen as a cyborg, perhaps as the most important cyborg ever? Arnold's highest compliment is when he says of another, "He's in control."[100] Few cinematic characters have taken more control over people, the environment, and circumstances than Arnold's Terminator. Arnold the candidate demonstrated similar power—"with a wave of the hand he could dismiss charges that he had once admired Adolf

Hitler, or used drugs."[101] As T3 producer Mario F. Kassar has said, "The Terminator has become an icon.... The character has this quality about him that makes you want to see him more. You want him to win. You want him to survive."[102]

But can it be true, as Arnold proposes, that "everyone would like to be a Terminator"? If California elected the Terminator, and we'd all like to be terminators, does it follow that everyone would want to be like Arnold? Despite what his detractors say, this may be truer than anyone would want to believe. As John Milius, director of *Conan the Barbarian* (1982), observed, "Arnold is the embodiment of the Superior Man.... There's something wonderfully primeval about him, harking back to the real basic foundational stuff: steel and strength and will."[103] To be a Terminator is to be, in this sense, a Superior Being—someone who can dispose of anyone or anything that bothers them. "It's a release," as Arnold tells us, "especially when you throw in a few cool lines of dialogue that always signal that you're not even concerned about the danger."[104] Terminator creator James Cameron put it even more dramatically: "There is a little bit of the terminator in everybody. In our private fantasy world we'd all like to be able to walk in and shoot somebody we don't like, or kick a door in instead of unlocking it: to be immune, and just to have our way every minute.... People don't cringe in terror from the terminator but go with him. They want to be him for that moment."[105]

Now that Arnold Schwarzenegger is California's governor, it is unlikely that he will appear in a *Terminator 4*—unless he serves only one term, in which case he would have to come back as a 60-year-old Terminator. But even if he hangs up his leather jacket and dark sunglasses, Governor

Schwarzenegger will remain the Terminator in the eyes and minds of Americans. Weeks after the election, the world was still reading headlines like "Dean Takes Tip from Terminator with Power Lunge"—the idea was that at least one presidential hopeful was talking very tough, distancing himself from "politics as usual," and referring to both Republican and Democratic opponents as a "bunch of cockroaches" that his victory would scatter.[106] What would he do as T4? Some have argued that in his capacity as governor he is already in his fourth role as Terminator.[107] Each of the previous two Terminator episodes had a subtitle ("Judgment Day" and "Rise of the Machines"); what will be the subtitle to this newest Terminator action saga? In one political cartoon, the title was "Terminator 4: Deficit Demolition."[108] In another, the movie marquee read "Arnold Schwarzenegger in Terminator 4: Eliminating Wasteful Spending While Maintaining Fiscal Priorities in a Stagnant Economy."[109] In both cartoons, people observing the movie titles muttered that Arnold had been more interesting in earlier versions. Oddly enough, in the way Arnold's films have always anticipated, or linked to, political, social, and scientific ideas, the very prospect of a T4 movie resonates in some deeply unsettling ways.

During World War II, before the creation of Nazi concentration camps, a secret organization known as the Reich Work Group of Sanatoriums and Nursing Homes (Reichsarbeitgemeinschaft Heil-und Pflegeanstalten, or RAG) based their operations at the Berlin Chancellery located at Tiergartenstrasse 4. The code name for this organization was "T4," and the purpose of the group was to develop methods of euthanizing unfit adults and children including those mentally and physically handicapped. The T4 program was abandoned when its secret was leaked. (Heinrich Himmler had argued that the program might have survived had it been entrusted to the SS.)[110] In 1941, the director of the T4 program agreed to allow Himmler to use T4 experts and facilities to dispose of adults from the concentration camps who were deemed too physically or mentally ill to maintain in the camps.[111] To make a T4 movie may conjure up some of these historic connections.

At the end of *Terminator 3,* a nuclear war has been launched by a worldwide artificial intelligence (AI) super-computer, SkyNet, which had been made so sophisticated it had become "aware of itself." The AI program has effectively terminated humanity—an inevitable consequence of the war between humans and the satellite web of intelligent machines they created. The network has determined that humans are unfit. John Connor and his female companion, Kate, are safe, for the moment, deep inside the mountain-bunker designed to protect the American leaders in the event of just such nuclear destruction. But, in typically human fashion, the leaders were caught unawares, and they never make it to safety. If there had been a *T4* movie, it would have been up to John and Kate to restart Genesis. The catch is that John Connor has been forewarned that he, too, is destined to be killed by a Terminator. The T4 program, in other words, would continue into the twenty-first century and beyond.

What, finally, can account for America's utter fascination by the idea of the Terminator working his way up to higher and higher office and greater and greater political influence? It may come down to something as simple as America's worst consumer habits: Everything, and everyone, is disposable. The Terminator's most refined skill is the control and disposal of people—unruly, unpredictable, and needy human beings. In the case of Arnold the Terminator, America has installed an effective cure for ordinary human chaos; a *governor* on human disorder.

**CHAPTER 8**

# Stay Hungry:
# Appetites for Arnold

**WINNING HIM A GOLDEN GLOBE** award for "Best Male Acting Debut," Arnold's 1977 movie *Stay Hungry* was a story about a young bodybuilder's struggle to become Mr. Universe. It was an otherwise forgettable movie, despite starring roles for both Sally Field and Jeff Bridges, but the theme of the film has been one of the philosophies driving Arnold's career: stay hungry—for success, fame, wealth, and power. Even more significant, the movie echoes an effect that Arnold's career has had on the culture at large: America (and much of the rest of the world as well) long ago developed a powerful appetite for each of Arnold's incarnations, and the culture has *stayed* hungry for more than three decades.

During the summer of 1991, the year we'd gone to the Arnold Schwarzenegger Classic in Columbus, Ohio, we began either to record or to take extensive notes on our phone conversations about Arnold. One of those "transcripts," from July 1991, included the following:

LOUISE: [Arnold] doesn't have *political* ambitions, just [an ambition for] cosmic ubiquity.... What it is about is Arnold being everywhere and how that has affected our everyday lives. Most people don't take note of it but he is still everywhere affecting them in some way or another.

MICHAEL: It's true he's everywhere, everyplace. [Everyone] has a story about him. Everyone has an opinion about him. And everybody, in theory [according to] him goes to see his movies. Twice, because he tells them to. This is the whole basis of [our project research], the connection he makes you have with him... the kind of intimacy we're talking about, this fantastic intimacy or phantom intimacy. In our case, more than people obsessed as fans, we're occupied in a terrorist fashion and we have to learn how to negotiate this occupation.

LOUISE: We have to make the distinction between us and fans. We are clearly not fans in a conventional way. I really feel like I've been occupied. There's been a coup of my daily attention over the last couple of years. Even though we deliberately go out and look for things... I'm drawn... what will happen is I'll be in the stationery store buying a card and I will feel something in the newsstand, and I'll go over and there will be something. Now part of it is that I know there will be something there but I'm really accurate most of the time, I can usually go right over to the magazines and there he is. So how do we talk about this without being mystical?

MICHAEL: There is a kind of magic going on here. It is partly the result of literally tuning in to every media event we can though we've actually become pretty good about weeding out ones we don't need to pay that much attention to. Part of it is that like a parent we have one ear that we somehow have fine-tuned, one corner of our peripheral vision tuned in so thoroughly that we don't have to actively [search]. Every newscast I watch I expect there to be something remotely connected. And I'm surprised when he is *not* on the cover of a dozen magazines. Of course, he often is.

In a bookstore with a very large magazine section, Michael looked through the racks for Arnold, expecting of course to find him in at least one or two different kinds of periodicals. How do celebrities get into the public eye? And how do they stay there? One obvious way is through magazine covers. Staring out at you from the newsstand or the supermarket checkout, arriving with your mail or keeping you company in the doctor's office, the cover of a periodical reaches a wide audience, far wider than those who actually read it. Since the early 1970s, Arnold Schwarzenegger's face has been on the cover of hundreds of magazines. Sometimes he has been the cover image on many editions of a single magazine (he has, for example, appeared on the cover of *Muscle and Fitness* many times). Taken as a single phenomenon, we might think of all these magazine cover images as a long-term installation in the Arnold museum. Whatever the particular story or intent of the specific magazine may be, the cumulative effect of seeing Arnold's face on cover after cover, month after month, year after year, on newsstands everywhere in the world, is to reinforce the idea that the culture cannot seem to get its fill of Arnold.

For more than thirty years, on any given day, people across America and around the world would have encountered Arnold Schwarzenegger's face on one or more of these magazines:

*Action Heroes*
*Action Movie Heroes*
*After Dark*
*American Cinematographer*
*American Enterprise*
*American Film*
*Black Belt*
*Boston Phoenix*
*Box Office*
*Bravo* (Germany)
*BuyMagazine*
*Cable Guide, The*
*Cigar Aficionado*
*Cinefantastique*
*Cinefex*
*Cinescape*
*Cracked*
*Cybersurfer*
*Disney Adventures Magazine*
*Drama-Logue*
*Electronic Game Monthly*
*Empire* (UK)
*Entertainment Weekly*
*Esquire*
*ET Magazine (Entertainment Today)*
*Fangoria*
*Fantazia—the Definitive Superhero Magazine*

*Fighting Arts*
*Film Monthly*
*Film Review* (UK)
*Films and Filming*
*Flex*
*Flicks* (UK)
*Frau in Spiegel* (Germany)
*Gala* (Germany)
*Gente Mese* (Italy)
*George*
*Good Housekeeping*
*GQ*
*Hollywood*
*Hollywood Reporter, The*
*Hollywood—Then & Now*
*Imagenes* (Spain)
*Impact* (UK)
*Inside Kung Fu*
*Interview*
*IronMan*
*Karate and Fitness International*
*Ladies Home Journal*
*Life*
*Los Angeles*
*Los Angeles Confidential*
*Los Angeles Family*
*M inc.*
*Maariv La'noar* (Israel)
*Mad*
*Magna*
*Marquee*

*Max Sports & Fitness Magazine*
*Maxim* (Italy)
*Men's Fitness*
*Men's Journal*
*MGF Movies*
*Movie Idol*
*Moviegoer*
*Mr. America*
*Muscle*
*Muscle & Fitness*
*Muscle Builder*
*Muscle Mag 2000*
*Muscle Mag Annual*
*Muscle Mag International*
*Muscle Media 2000*
*Muscle Training Illustrated*
*Muscular Development*
*National Enquirer*
*National Lampoon*
*NewsMax*
*Newsweek*
*Nok Lapja* (Hungary)
*Oui*
*Parade*
*Paris Match* (France)
*PC Premium Channels Guide for HBO*
*People*
*Photoplay*
*Physical Magazine*
*Planet Muscle*
*Popular Mechanics*

*Premiere*
*Rolling Stone*
*Satellite Direct*
*Saturday Evening Post*
*Sciences, The*
*Sci Fi Cinema*
*Set*
*Showbiz Magazine*
*Smart*
*Soldier of Fortune*
*Sports Illustrated*
*Spotlight Casting Magazine*
*Spy*
*Star Fix* (France)
*Star Log*
*Strength & Health*
*Sunday* (UK)
*Sunday Mirror Magazine* (UK)
*Talk*
*Terminator 3: Rise of the Machines Official Magazine*
*Terminator Mag/Comic*
*Time*
*To…* (UK)
*Total Film* (UK)
*TV Guide*
*TV Movie & Video News*
*U Magazine*
*Us*
*U.S. News and World Report*
*Utne Reader*
*V LIFE (Variety Life)*
*Vanity Fair*

*Video* (Germany)
*Video Event*
*Video Play*
*Video Revue* (Czech Republic)
*Vim & Vigor*
*Wired*
*World*
*World Gym*

The spectacle of endless images of Arnold constitutes yet another kind of language—a visual one—whereby we learn by rote about Arnold's prominence in the culture. There are plenty of celebrities whose faces paint the covers of movie and pop-culture magazines. But few stars have had their images directly linked to so diverse a range of disciplines and passions, and almost no one has remained a cover-star for so many years. Since the 1970s, Arnold's face has been used to sell magazines about electronics, martial arts, politics, mass media, sports and fitness, parody and satire, men's and women's fashion, and cigars. Taking advantage of both Arnold's omnipresence in magazines and the public's appetite for things Arnoldian, the Santa Monica–based Center for Media Literacy (CML), whose slogan is "Empowerment Through Education," developed an activity designed for use by students in grades 3–12. The project is called "Deconstructing Magazine Covers: The Reinvention of Arnold Schwarzenegger."[1] According to CML, "Connection to state and national [education] standards can be made to Social Studies, English/Language Arts and Art. Basically, the activity entails studying the covers of two magazines—*Muscle and Fitness* and *Esquire*—that feature large, but very different photographs of Arnold. Students are asked to respond to a set of questions about each cover, such as "What do you think about this person based on the cover of the magazine?" and "How does he look?"

The project is intended to help students understand CML's MediaLit Kit™ Core Concept #2: "Media messages are constructed using a creative language with its own rules." We would agree; the vast array of Arnold magazine covers over more than three decades has helped to produce a kind of media-language fluency in America—a fluency with Arnold Schwarzenegger's image, his persona, face, and body—that lies at the core of its cultural grammar. The CML exercise focused mainly on Arnold's face. But it's time now to examine the phenomenon of what *Time* magazine called Arnold's "cumulonimbus physique."[2]

# CHAPTER 9

# Predator: Arnold's Bodies of Work

## The Biggest Built Body

Arnold has always built his movies around his body. Whether he is a cop fighting the devil, a barbarian fighting enemy hordes, a secret agent fighting mutants, or a Terminator killing machine, somehow he convinces us that an extraordinarily built body is necessary for each story to be plausible. But what good is a pumped-up human body against a force like the Predator? The Predator is an alien whose armored body is capable of invisibility. It haunts the jungles of some unnamed Latin American country, disemboweling or skinning its victims in a gruesome display of alien might. To combat this Predator, Arnold's character "Dutch" must move beyond the expectations of his pumped-up body. A trailer for the movies proclaims, "He must become more than a man, more than an animal. He must become the very spirit of the Predator." Also featuring Jesse "The Body" Ventura, the movie *Predator* (1987) has been called by one reviewer "a male adolescent snapshot of tough-guy heaven."[1]

Dutch accidentally discovers that if his body is covered by mud he can acquire the same characteristic that makes the Predator so dangerous—his invisibility. When a fall in water washes off the mud and the alien finds him, the violent end of this incredible human seems near. But instead of killing Dutch outright, the Predator takes off his high-tech armor and engages Dutch in hand-to-hand combat for reasons not revealed to us in the movie. The Predator made the same mistake about Dutch that political analysts have warned not to make about Arnold: Don't underestimate him or you will suffer the unforeseen consequences. In the hand-to-claw combat, Dutch eventually crushes the ugly Predator beneath a big log.

To lose the visibility of his body may seem an advantage to fighting alien Predators, but for Arnold Schwarzenegger his body's visibility and presence have been his most impressive weapon. At the heart of Arnold's effects on American culture is a remarkable body of work—or more accurately, the work of his body. Arnold's body is the essence of his image to the world. To this day, decades since his body was considered the most perfect in the world, many major news articles written about Arnold will include a photograph of him when he was a bodybuilder. Arnold's body is important for all of the same reasons other bodies are important: They are our interface with the social world. We experience the world through our bodies and these experiences are modified by the body's shape and age and decoration and form.

Bodies provide the canvas on which we paint our selves to share with the world, and they can help or hinder our social functioning on so many levels.

Our bodies always mean something: by what we say and do and by how we appear or move. But Arnold's body acts as more than his personal canvas; he has been, to a great extent, America's mirror, too, a reflection of our culture's fascination with the body and all that it can do. If Arnold's body is so big that it can contain all our bodies and almost every relevant body image this culture has to offer, he can reflect back to us a world of corporeal possibilities. If he can change his size and shape so as to fit into any context he desires, he reminds us that, while he is among us, he also stands apart. That one person can be this dominant in the culture should be more disturbing to Americans, for in this dominance is the license to define what is natural, fit, and human.

Americans have never known Arnold without this anatomically exaggerated, Teutonically proportioned anatomy. He represents a kind of solidity and durability that few humans achieve and sustain in mass culture. The fact that his body has been, for two decades, as large as the grandest movie screens has certainly helped him maintain the sense of bodily grandeur. And the fact that his movies so universally highlight his body, in contexts as diverse as technology, war, romance, espionage, education, criminal justice, bodybuilding, and even male-pregnancy, has only increased our sense that Arnold's physical presence touches so much in our culture.

For over thirty years, Arnold's body has been working its way through the American imagination, shifting the very idea of what a body can and should be, how it should look, and what it can accomplish. Cognitive scientist George Lakoff explains why knowing something about a body is knowing something about the thinking being occupying that body: "Our brains take their input from the rest of our bodies. What our bodies are like and how they function in the world thus structures the very concepts we can use to think. We cannot think just anything—only what our embodied brains permit."[2] Arnold Schwarzenegger's body permits him to think big, to think about defeating alien opponents, to think about being the last male survivor when men confront inexplicable forces. "What the hell are you?" Dutch asks the dying alien. "What the hell are *you*?" the alien retorts before laughing maniacally and blowing up half the jungle and himself. We know the answer: Arnold is his body, and it is that body that triumphs over everything, whether alien or human.

Admire it, be repelled by it, find it beautiful or grotesque. You can gape at it in wonder or gape at it in terror. You can think, like some women did when considering the accusations of groping that were made against him, that he is nevertheless "hot." Or you can be outraged that a man today can still throw his body around in such an arrogant way and not get into very deep trouble over it. No matter what your take is on Arnold's body and what it does, it is something remarkable to behold, and in all its permutations it fascinates in the most unexpected ways.

One source of this fascination is the size of Arnold's body. One thing people always ask us about is: Just how big is Arnold? How big are his arms? How tall is he, really? How bulked up is he? How large are his hands? Sometimes they will reveal their suspicions: He's really only five feet eight inches, right? But few suspect that he is far larger than they could have imagined. For his largeness is now only symbolically represented by his once big body; it is his expansion into so many other fields and into so many minds that really redefines "big" and shows its impressive power. Indeed, as the *Los Angeles Times* reports, Arnold is "larger than larger-than-life"[3] in Japan and this certainly holds true for his image across America. He has been described as "a gargantuan specimen under the public microscope."[4] His photographer friend George Butler once referred to him as "the Mountain" to which the "Muhammad" of the national media would come.[5]

In 1991, Arnold told *Muscle & Fitness* magazine, "I did not want anything about my life to be little. What I wanted was to be part of the big dreamers, the big skyscrapers, the big money, the big action. Everything in the United States was big. That's what I enjoy about this country. And there's no monkey business; I mean, you have to make an effort to be little here."[6] So while some men may be physically larger, some people may be richer, some have more power to influence events, and perhaps a few are more ambitious, scarcely anyone is as recognizable or as familiar, as big in the collective consciousness, looming large in the American imagination. Arnold Schwarzenegger has come to occupy common knowledge and despite being so large, he lives inside each of us every day and all the time.

When you talk about Arnold, you have to adjust your vocabulary to accommodate his largeness. In a National Public Radio interview with NPR's senior Washington editor, Ron Elving, host Alex Chadwick asked about the national impact Arnold's election would have. Elving responded by saying, "It's *extremely* difficult to reproduce both the circumstances of this *extraordinary* victory, and it's probably even more difficult to reproduce Arnold Schwarzenegger... with his *enormous* name recognition, his *enormous* personal resources... his *enormous* worldwide movie fame"[7] (our emphasis). CNN correspondent Bill Hemmer called him "the gargantuan '80s action hero."[8] Actress Jamie Lee Curtis described him as "an enormously talented man with enormous charisma."[9] Tim Shriver, Maria's brother, remarking on first meeting Arnold: "He was huge."[10]

But none of this would be possible if not for the one factor that brought Arnold to national, and ultimately global, attention—his very large and muscularly perfected body—a body whose size quickly became the stuff of myth. From his early days in the American spotlight, Arnold's body extended the known possibilities of the flesh as it bulged in unexpected ways and expanded in every direction through bodybuilding. Bodybuilders are devoted to their muscles for all sorts of reasons that observers have speculated range from obsessive self-control to a desire to hide insecurities about their masculinity or to the proverbial Charles Atlas protection from bullies.[11] Arnold's well-scripted story is that he spent years in sweaty gyms blasting his muscles with stress and pain (and, he has admitted, steroids[12]) because bodybuilding gave him a passport, a chance to cross another boundary: that between postwar Europe and the promising America, between being a nobody in a small town in Austria to being the biggest man in the "biggest" country in the entire world. Mr. Universe wanted that title to be literal; Mr. Olympia intended to be in the pantheon of the gods.

The impact of Arnold's body has indeed been huge. Arnold pushed the limits of what was considered "natural" for a built body to do in what *Muscular Development* magazine describes as "our demented little sport."[13] He also appears to have used every clever trick of the eye and mind to achieve the appearance of being the biggest and most perfect body. His statements in the "documentary" *Pumping Iron* showed that winning at bodybuilding was about creating the impression of bigness by projecting confidence and by posturing more than it was about actual muscle development and physical dimensions. As Peter McGough puts it, "Bodybuilders deal in illusions: trying to accentuate some body parts while de-emphasizing others. It goes with the territory to claim that a 19-inch arm is a 20-inch arm and that a 350-pound bench is a 400-pound bench. Arnold became a bodybuilding champion by mastering the art of making himself appear larger than life." Artie Zeller, who photographed hundreds of bodybuilders for magazines, was convinced that Arnold's body "doubled in size" when he flexed.[14] When *Pumping Iron* producer George Butler showed him some photos taken when Arnold was relaxed, Arnold complained, "These photos are not me… there's no pump. No monster arms. I look tiny."[15]

It was Arnold's body that established the trend in bodybuilding that to this day produces bodies that literally cause one to gasp. Each of these bodies in some way conjures up the image of Arnold who made it acceptable to be big in body as well as everything else. Visit any bodybuilding Web site or buy a bodybuilding magazine and stare in utter disbelief at the images of bodies exploding out of their skins with veins and muscles popping. Arnold's measurements when he was at the top of his form—Height 6'2", Weight 235 pounds, Biceps 22 inches, Chest 57 inches, Waist 34 inches, Thighs 28.5 inches, Calves 20 inches—are minuscule compared to today's champions. All the bodybuilding champions after Arnold have been physically monstrous, outweighing him, outmuscling him, presenting unimaginably gigantic bodies. Just take a look at Marcus Ruhl and be very afraid![16]

On the cover of the February 2004 issue of *Muscle & Fitness,*
Ronnie Coleman, Mr. Olympia for the sixth time, declared,
"I am the World's Biggest Man." At 287 pounds, all hard,
sculpted muscle and no fat, he is huge, as were all the other
Mr. Olympia contestants for 2003. Even some of today's
women bodybuilders, bulked beyond belief, are nearly as big
as Arnold was in his pumping iron days.

Arnold had brought bodybuilding to its peak not in terms
of the size of the contestants but in terms of the significance of the accomplishment; after Arnold, the aura of the
larger-than-life built body began to fade. Lee Haney, who
won the Mr. Olympia title more times than Arnold, achieved
a bigger and more sharply defined body, something Arnold
once said could not be done. But when Haney, a black man,
achieved his remarkable and measurably larger-than-Arnold
body, the significance of the achievement had already been
rendered irrelevant. It was as if America had eyes only for
Arnold and that in the culture's view, Arnold was always
going to be the largest man in the world.[17]

In some ways his body is bigger now than it ever has been,
bigger than when he was Mr. Olympia, with "a physique that
strained the imagination."[18] This may be a curious statement
since anyone who looks at Arnold now could easily see that
in terms of body mass, he has become quite noticeably
shrunken in the last twenty years. It is what Arnold's body
can do now that makes him so big. Arnold's has become a
dominant icon in America because *his* body, more than any
of our puny, flabby bodies (as *Saturday Night Live*'s Hans and
Franz would remind us), can contain or encompass just
about any body he, or we, could imagine. "The Arnold,"
after thirty-five years of permeating the American scene, has

shown that he can hold in his vast interior almost all the things needed to flood the culture, to break down the barriers that would keep him out. Within his muscular frame are images that include the impossibly hard laborer, the immigrant-made-good, the uncannily clever financial planner, the quintessential consumer capitalist who understood how to turn his body into a powerful commodity, and the master planner whose charted course brought him to the capitol of California.

When *Pumping Iron* was filmed in 1975, Arnold had already won his sixth Mr. Olympia title. By the time the film came out in 1977, Arnold had already moved on to other things. And yet, fourteen years later, in 1991, in the well-known magazine *MuscleMag,* Arnold Schwarzenegger dominated the "Second Annual Readers' Poll" on all the various bodybuilding categories. The introduction to the survey told readers, "A few years back, we ran our first, ahem, Annual Readers' Poll (Yeah, we know. Annual. But hey, the magazine was rockin' and before you could say 'Arnold Schwarzenegger' several years had passed. If that ain't good enough sorrcccc...)."[19] The author(s) of the survey then went on to keep Arnold in the foreground even as the survey told readers not to vote for Arnold in categories for which he was no longer eligible. For example, for the category "MuscleMag International Hall of Fame," readers were told, "But, before you grab those pens & pencils and start scribbling that Arnold guy into the 'other' category (as well as notes of death, berating us for leaving him out in the first place) keep in mind that Arnold was inducted into the hall in our last poll. That means he's out of the race this time, so pick someone else. PICK SOMEONE ELSE! We said PICK SOMEONE ELSE!"[20]

For the category "Best Pro Female Bodybuilder," readers were told, "And hey, ain't no way you can pick Arnold for this one." The blurb for "Best Bodybuilding Instructional Video" admonished readers, "*Total Recall* ain't an instructional video. PICK SOMETHING ELSE!"[21] All in all, there were twenty categories, eleven of which were introduced with some kind of remark about the fact that Arnold was either no longer eligible or that he had already won. Of the small photographs sprinkled throughout the survey, a quarter of them were of Arnold. More than ten years after his retirement from bodybuilding, bodybuilders and their fans were still paying homage to Arnold and his unsurpassed body. Not surprisingly, in the January 2004 issue of *Muscular Development,* the "special" treat is a 25-page pictorial tribute to Arnold. No doubt his rise to high political office at age 56 was ample reason to offer the retrospective. Still, not a single photograph was of an Arnold Schwarzenegger older or smaller than his championship years.

Arnold often refers back to bodybuilding not only as his early profession but also as the "great foundation" for everything else he has done.[22] Soon after he was elected governor, Arnold visited the Mr. Olympia contest in Las Vegas and said, "Finally I feel at home again."[23] This message was reiterated by his mentor Joe Weider who said at the same event, "Finally, it's beginning to dawn on the world that bodybuilders are smart. They develop determination. They don't give up. They don't lose. If they ever apply that to any profession… they can be a great success."[24] CBSnews.com posted a story on its Web site a few days later that continued this theme: "Mr. Universe Goes to Washington."[25]

. . .

## Bodily Indiscretions

If bodybuilding was Arnold's foundation, it may also be where he developed his controversial attitudes toward women. In his autobiography, *Arnold: The Education of a Bodybuilder,* he explains:

> I had no difficulty getting girls. I'd been introduced to sex with almost no hang-ups. The older bodybuilders at the gym had started including me in their parties. It was easy for me. These guys always saw to it that I had a girl. "Here, Arnold, this one's for you."
>
> Girls became sex objects. I saw other bodybuilders using them in this way and I thought it was all right.[26]

His claim that "My attitude about all that has changed radically"[27] may be true, but the roots may still be there. In a timeline of his life on his own Web site (copyrighted 2003), Arnold's development in the 1960s is described in these steps: "Discovers he loves pumping up his muscles—Discovers he loves girls—Discovers that girls love his pumped up muscles—Decides his life goal is to be the most pumped up guy in the world."[28]

Accusations of Arnold's groping and humiliating women over a thirty-year period appeared in the *Los Angeles Times* five days before the California recall election, although rumors of the story had been circulating for weeks. But the questions about his relations with women started long before that. First were his comments about a film character, a virtual woman, a robot whom he had to fight in his last movie. Discussing a scene in *Terminator 3* (2003) in which he fights a cyborg that looks like a gorgeous female, Arnold told a reporter well before the election campaign, "I saw this toilet bowl. How many times do you get away with this—to take a woman, grab her upside down, and bury her face in a toilet bowl?"[29] Although the "woman" was a cyborg, and one in a fantasy movie at that, it suggested to some people a more sobering undertone.

This quote was repeated during the election and presented as proof of his disrespect for women, a trait that had been suspected in Hollywood for years. Another story was resurrected from Arnold's bodybuilding days when he described how a black woman appeared in the gym and all the bodybuilders together had sex with her. The story appeared in an interview in a *Playboy* magazine subsidiary publication called *Oui* in 1977 and was, throughout 2003, reported extensively on Web sites and in newspapers. The *Los Angeles Time*s on August 30, 2003, described the contents of the publication this way:

> According to Schwarzenegger, "a black girl" entered the room "naked" and "everybody jumped on her and took her upstairs where we all got together." In another instance, Schwarzenegger recounted an anonymous sexual encounter backstage at a bodybuilding competition that left him feeling "like King Kong."[30]

The Web site thesmokinggun.com reported Arnold's interview in *Oui* this way:

> "Bodybuilders party a lot, and once, in Gold's—the gym in Venice, California, where all the top guys train—there was a black girl who came out naked. Everybody jumped on her

and took her upstairs, where we all got together." Asked by Manso [the *Oui* reporter] if he was talking about a "gang bang," Schwarzenegger answered, "Yes, but not everybody, just the guys who can fuck in front of other guys. Not everybody can do that. Some think that they don't have a big-enough cock, so they can't get a hard-on. Having chicks around is the kind of thing that breaks up the intense training. It gives you relief, and then afterward you go back to the serious stuff."[31]

Before the allegations of inappropriate sexual contact were published in the *Los Angeles Times* on October 2, 2003, the campaign to elect Arnold was already responding to the issue of Arnold's attitudes toward women with signs on campaign headquarters and at rallies, and a section of the official Web site, encouraging "remarkable women" to "Join Arnold." Maria Shriver's campaign speeches and a campaign brochure written in her name all addressed why Arnold would be a good governor for women. "You are welcome here," the cover of the brochure invited.[32] The crusade to win over women voters was in full swing by the time the October 2 article entitled "Women Say Schwarzenegger Groped, Humiliated Them"[33] appeared in the *Los Angeles Times*.

Anonymous and named women in newspaper stories and on television in the next several days described how Arnold had grabbed their breasts, tried to take off their clothing, stuck his tongue down their throats, grabbed their asses, and made lewd suggestions. The *Los Angeles Times* reported:

Six women who came into contact with Arnold Schwarzenegger on movie sets, in studio offices and in other settings over the last three decades say he touched them in a sexual manner without their consent.

In interviews with *The Times*, three of the women described their surprise and discomfort when Schwarzenegger grabbed their breasts. A fourth said he reached under her skirt and gripped her buttocks.

A fifth woman said Schwarzenegger groped her and tried to remove her bathing suit in a hotel elevator. A sixth said Schwarzenegger pulled her onto his lap and asked whether a certain sexual act had ever been performed on her.[34]

A woman who was a waitress when her groping incident took place was not impressed with Arnold's excuse that film sets tend to be rowdy because her incident took place in a public restaurant. She told the *Los Angeles Times:*

One Sunday, she said, she was pouring coffee at the table when Schwarzenegger beckoned her to his side.

"I bent down to listen to him," she recalled. "He said, a little louder than a whisper, 'I want you to do a favor for me.' I thought, OK, maybe he wanted more bread. And he said, 'I want you to go in the bathroom, stick your finger in your [vagina], and bring it out to me.'"

She stood upright. "I was thoroughly disgusted" but said nothing to Schwarzenegger, she recalled. "There was drama in the silence of it," she said. "He looked up, and it looked like I was threatening [him] with the coffee pot."

Everyone at the table then glanced over at the restaurant owner, Andre Driollet. He wagged his finger at the waitress, she said, apparently fearful that she was going to dump the coffee on Schwarzenegger.

"I was so appalled, and when Andre looked at me [as if]

to say you better not, I immediately went to him to tell him what happened," she recounted. What Schwarzenegger had said "was above and beyond what was acceptable. I think he should have had hot coffee poured in his lap."[35]

Arnold went from being the potential "Governator" to being the offensive and definitive "Gropinator." Additional stories painted a picture of Schwarzenegger as a man with an established M.O.: He would make quick gestures that were evaluated by almost all the victims as attempts to intimidate or humiliate the women rather than as violent sexual acts. As several of the women were quoted, it was not like he had raped them but it was definitely something they found degrading and that they didn't forget. For five days before the election, first 6 then 9 then 15 or 16 women said he had made uninvited visits to various erogenous regions of their anatomies.

If all of this were only about bodily indiscretions, it would have expanded into other areas like his steroid use. But Arnold's use of steroids during his bodybuilding years turned out to be another nonissue. Although one article documented the steroid use and attitudes about it,[36] and while it is now generally accepted that virtually all champion bodybuilders have used performance-enhancing drugs, there was no questioning of candidate Arnold during the debate and no news conference called to apologize for steroid use. The only time his body has cast doubt on his fitness for political office was when it was associated with the bodies of women. Yet Arnold's power and influence reside in part in his ability to redirect any doubts so that he and his impressive body of work are in the foreground while any weaknesses he might be accused of having are firmly pushed to the background.

In the days leading up to the election, protesters in Santa Monica near a "Schwarzenegger for Governor" volunteers' headquarters challenged his attitude toward women with signs that read, "No Governor Gangbang" and "Arnold is an Asshole" and a sign with a toilet on it that read, "Flush Arnold, Not Women." The protesters reported that people in cars driving by and honking horns in support of Arnold threw objects at them. But at rallies for Schwarzenegger on the last days of campaigning, thousands of women appeared wearing campaign-produced T-shirts or carrying signs that reiterated that "Remarkable Women Join Arnold." Clearly not all women were in agreement on the importance of these accusations and what they might indicate about the action hero candidate.

The women volunteers at his San Bernardino rally, the very last stop of the campaign, expressed little concern about the Gropinator as they spent hours preparing a festive staging area for Schwarzenegger's last appearance before the election. They all had different reasons for being there, and few of those reasons needed to be reevaluated in light of the harassment charges. As she helped the volunteers hang decorations and hand out signs and brochures, Louise learned that some came just to be involved, some came for the company, some came because they liked Arnold, and some came because they wanted a change. The only reference to the "groping" charges came from a male campaign worker who, looking at the thousands of people waiting to get into the rally, said, "They're groupies." Then, chuckling, he said, "No, they're gropies!"

Yet all predictions that the women's accusations would sink Schwarzenegger's election vanished, and 43 percent of the California women voters chose Arnold, with the rest of their votes spread over the other 134 candidates (Bustamante received 36 percent of the female vote and Tom McClintock 14 percent). In exit polls, those who voted for Schwarzenegger said that where a candidate stands on issues is more important than a candidate's character by a percentage of 44 to 38 percent, and 14 percent said the most important thing was that the candidate share their values.

It is not that Arnold denied that his body participated in this unacceptable behavior, but the remarkable thing is that he was able to contain whatever it was within boundaries that he defined in his public "apology." Announcing with a non sequitur that "Where there's smoke, there's fire," he proceeded to apologize not to the women he touched but more generally to people he may have offended:

> So I want to say to you, yes, I have behaved badly sometimes. Yes, it is true that I was on rowdy movie sets, and I have done things that were not right, which I thought then was playful. But I now recognize that I have offended people. And to those people that I have offended, I want to say to them, I am deeply sorry about that, and I apologize.[37]

Years ago, Arnold told the British men's magazine *Loaded* that "Apologies are for wimps. If you behave like a wimp, you're going to get stiffed, simple as that. If you're a man, then you should behave like a man."[38]

The Schwarzenegger campaign clearly anticipated and prepared for these accusations. There was, after all, the *Premiere* magazine article in March 2001 ("Arnold the Barbarian: Sex, Pecs and the Videotape") that had detailed the same groping accusations when Arnold was previously rumored to be considering a run for governor. The article by

John Connolly, now available on numerous Web sites,[39] begins, "Once, he was a box office terminator. But now that Arnold Schwarzenegger has lost some of his muscle in Hollywood, stories of his boorish behavior can no longer be routinely erased. Then again, he'd make a helluva politician." The article was faxed to news outlets when it first came out, sent by a Gray Davis aide.[40] It claimed to document several incidents of Arnold grabbing the breasts of interviewers, frolicking with a costar, and making lewd comments through the years. One interviewer described Arnold coming into the studio in 2000 as being "like a dog in heat." After this article was published there was a flurry of letters from his female costars and friends supporting him. Arnold's costars Jamie Lee Curtis, Linda Hamilton, Kelly Preston, and Rita Wilson sent letters to *Premiere* and the media, and gave interviews saying that the story was false, outrageous, and politically motivated. All described Arnold as a devoted family man. "What was I supposed to learn from that?" Rita Wilson is quoted as saying about the article.[41]

In a carefully orchestrated interview with Maria's longtime pal Oprah Winfrey, on her season premiere show on September 15, 2003, Arnold and Maria spoke about the election and the difficulty of having their personal life scrutinized. Winfrey, who is acknowledged to have substantial influence over the opinions and tastes of female audiences, carefully led the couple through a series of soft, sympathetic questions. Maria came out alone first and chatted for a while with gal pal Oprah. Then Arnold came out and sat down with Maria in what was billed as their first-ever joint interview. After their performance on Oprah's couch, there was no need to wonder why they had not previously been interviewed together. Too-perfect images of domestic bliss

(Arnold bringing coffee to Maria every morning) were contradicted by the severe expression on Shriver's face when her husband spoke about his past and by the severe angle of her body tilting away from him on the interview couch. Believe in body language or not, this woman was leaning well away from her husband. When he repeated the oft-heard phrase from the movie *Pumping Iron* that pumping weights is like coming sexually, she quickly clapped a hand over his mouth and admonished him that her mother was watching.[42]

When Oprah asked about rumors of Arnold's womanizing, Maria responded, "I know the man I'm married to. I've been with him for twenty-six years. You know, I understand the way the process works. And I understand the man I'm married to."[43] Part of that understanding must be that her husband's movie-screen-sized body is always under America's gaze and embedded in its imagination. There is another clue to how this all played out in the speeches Maria Shriver gave once she joined the election campaign. The video for one speech was carried by the JoinArnold.com official campaign Web site.[44] In the speech, which followed the same format as the campaign brochure directed at women, Maria offered "Ten Things You Should Know About Arnold Before You Go To The Polls." In the brochure she clearly states these as: "Number One: He's smart. Number Two: He's disciplined, determined and decisive. Number Three: He's bold—and follows his gut," and so on. But when she gave her speeches, Shriver inserted another reason. In her speech to the Commonwealth Club on September 23, 2003, she said,

> When I first started going out with him in 1977, people were, I have to say, a little bit confused about the relation-

ship. I think some people probably still are. And they would say to me, "What do you see in this guy?" And I'm like, "Hello, have you checked out the body? You think I'm blind or what?"

After making several faces of wide-eyed, open-mouthed wonder, she continued her talk. But later she brought up his body again, directing our attention to the exact source of the problem her speeches were supposed to deal with. If he lost, she said it would be because people "couldn't see beyond the labels, couldn't see beyond the body, couldn't see beyond the accent." If he wins, she offered, "you win. You get his heart, his brain, his vision, his excitement." She concluded by saying, "You can listen to people who have never sat down to see what is behind the body, behind the accent" or we could listen to her. She wasn't saying he never acted inappropriately with women, she only said that she focused on a bigger picture that was more significant; Arnold is, as she worked hard to make us understand, far larger than any image that meets the eye.

This bigger picture includes a history of both Maria and Arnold always pointing to Arnold's body, to his interest in women's bodies, or women's interest in his body. In a 1990 interview on the *Tonight Show* with Johnny Carson, Shriver tells how Arnold tried to prepare her for the show, which he had appeared on many times. Imitating Arnold's accent, Maria said he told her to "Talk about me, about my movies, about my body, what a big star I am." On the same show a few minutes later, she repeated the often-told story of how, when she was first introduced to Arnold, he said to her in front of her mother, "You have a great ass." So she said to herself, "This man I want to get to know." On a Barbara Walters' special in 1990, Arnold commented, "By the way, a lot of women, of course, when I went out with them says, 'I just want to make sure you understand, that I don't like you just for your body, I love your brain.' Yeah, that's a good one."

If Maria isn't always thinking about Arnold's body, America certainly expects her to be doing so. In an interview in *People* magazine in 1985, when asked what she liked about her husband-to-be, Maria replied that it was his humor and his intelligence. When the reporter asked, "You haven't mentioned the body, what about the body?" Maria answered, "I don't even think about that." The exchange continued:

> "You don't ever think about the greatest body of *all time?*"
> "I just don't think about it."
> Then she starts giggling, as though thinking about Arnold as the most perfect specimen of mankind is too outrageous to consider.[45]

Even in her "denials" Maria manages to make sure Arnold's body is in the foreground. But why did Maria Shriver want to make us pay so much attention to her husband's body during the California gubernatorial campaign? You would think that with all the doubts and issues his actual body had created that she would try to divert attention away from his physical attributes. Yet her message seemed to be, Don't forget the most important thing about Arnold is his body.

## The Virile Body

When he first appeared on the American scene, Arnold Schwarzenegger seemed to be *all* body, a fleshy billboard for the excesses of the '60s and '70s. Unable to speak coherently and possessing a manner that seemed more programmed than spontaneous, he was initially the familiar image of the dumb bodybuilder, all body and no brain. He may have seemed to be a walking advertisement for the brawny, showy hypermasculinity that critics for years had suggested was just a front, a cover for male homoeroticism. But he changed the face of bodybuilding, not just by lifting it out of its seedy history and making a second-rate sport into an art form, but by putting an unambiguous, heterosexual face on it. Bodybuilding had been an activity rumored to attract gays and carried a "suspicion of abnormal sexuality, which had dogged it for a generation or more."[46] In his book *Arnold Schwarzenegger: A Portrait* George Butler tells of one rejection letter from a publisher that said, "no one in America will buy a book of pictures of these half-unclothed men of dubious sexual pursuits."[47] He quotes a book reviewer from the *New York Times* who refused to review the book once it was published as referring to the book of pictures of Arnold as "fag bait."[48]

But Arnold's body—"masculine, dominant, potently virile"[49]—screamed aggressive heterosexuality not just through its appearance but through its actions. The movie *Pumping Iron* provided a powerful example of this effect. Adding to his comments about the erotics of pumping and his brief mention of his girlfriend, the movie images of women hanging onto his body in a photo shoot and at the beach sealed his signature on bodybuilding as an activity that builds real men. Today bodybuilding is promoted in dozens of magazines like *Muscle & Fitness* or *Flex* as much for its potential to build a sexually active and attractive body as it is to build a body that is strong or fit. Many of the magazines feature muscled men admired by attractive women. It is a reminder of the old Charles Atlas ads from the back of comic books and magazines that promised to make "HE-MEN" out of "weaklings."

Part of being a "he-man" is proving that you are more of a man than other men are. Arnold has made this an unwritten agenda item throughout his career. When *Oui* magazine asked Arnold, "This business of feeling like King Kong—is it your act to psych everyone out so they know you're King Kong?" Arnold replied that he simply uses his powerful presence to make others "feel great. I tell a guy that he's never looked better, that he looks brilliant, fantastic.... I'm positive that you'll place.... You can easily beat this guy and that guy. I'm certain you'll go all the way—to second place."[50]

In one of the more bizarre and seemingly out-of-place scenes in *Pumping Iron,* Arnold jokes with federal prisoners while demonstrating bodybuilding poses in their exercise yard. Teasing the men he says, "I know about you guys in here. Come over here and I will give you a kiss." The scene does, of course, have its place: to confirm Arnold's heterosexuality in opposition to these men imprisoned with lesser choices. In the second bodybuilding documentary, *Pumping Iron: The Women* (1985), the controversy shown in the film is about whether Bev Francis, a woman with male features and a hugely developed body, should be allowed in a competition that still wants to promote a more feminine image for its females. Francis loses but not before order is restored and women are clearly distinguished, through their bodies, from men.

By accepting rowdy bodily behavior from Arnold all these years, perhaps America just wanted to make sure our most developed and muscular male icon of the feminist and post-feminist era was truly a man. The question has always been there, in both serious and comic forms. From 1987 to 1991, *Saturday Night Live* featured the recurring characters Hans and Franz as a spoof on the bodybuilding craze but also ultimately as the perfect foil for Arnold's pumped-up hypermale, heterosexual body. Hans (Dana Carvey) and Franz (Kevin Nealon) are Arnold's "cousins" who have come to America to pump us up. According to Hans and Franz, little men who do not exhibit "pumpitude" are girly-men in danger of losing their women:

HANS: ...anyone who calls us "stupid" is really just jealous. Because their girlfriend looks at us, then looks at him, and realizes she's cuddling up with a little girly-man!

FRANZ: Ya. Ya, girly-man. Hear me now and believe me later—but don't think about it ever, because, if you try to think, you might cause a flabulance!

HANS: Ya!

FRANZ: Poor little girly-man, alone in his girly-house!

HANS: Sorry, Mr. Girly-Man, but here's a treat for your girlfriend!

[Hans and Franz flex their muscles][51]

One of the funniest and telling episodes of the Hans and Franz routine (October 27, 1990) featured actor Patrick Swayze. After Swayze leaves the set, Franz begins fantasizing about the man *People* magazine was soon to call "the sexiest man alive." Franz in his sweat clothes and Swayze in a sleeveless muscle shirt are shown at the end of the routine riding away on a white stallion together.

But Hans and Franz's biggest fear was that cousin Arnold would come checking on them and one day he does show up:

VICTOR (Danny DeVito): Okay, I'll see you guys later. Oh, by the way. Your cousin Arnold Schwarzenegger came by today.

HANS: Oh, don't-don't-don't be joking us.

FRANZ: Ya. You'd better not be pulling my rock-hard leg.

Victor: He did! He said he might drop by. All right, he might see your show. Okay, see you later! [exits set]

FRANZ: Arnold?

HANS: Coming here?

FRANZ: Today?

HANS: Today? Oh...

FRANZ: Oh...

HANS: Oh, I don't believe this!

FRANZ: We are not properly pumped up!

[Hans and Franz desperately start flexing and working out their muscles]

HANS: I don't believe this! Oh no, I can't believe it!

[Arnold Schwarzenegger enters the set, his pecs bouncing in rhythm]

ARNOLD: Hello, hello. I am back!

HANS: Oh, Arnold, I can't believe how properly pumped up you really are!

FRANZ: Ya! You are the embodiment of perfect pumpitude!

ARNOLD: No, no, no... relax, fellows, relax.

HANS: Hey, Arnold, look at this! [flexes]

FRANZ: Ya! Look at this! [flexes more vigorously]

ARNOLD: Oh, you guys make me sick. [mimes vomiting] *This* is what you have to do. Like *this*. [demonstrates the proper way to flex his muscles] That's the way to do it! Look at you guys, how pitiful losers you are! You know something? I hate the way you guys talk! What's the matter with you? I mean, I sent you over here from Austria, to become real hard-core terminators, and look what you are—little termites! I wanted you to become real running men; but you are *girly*-men. Oh, come on, you make me sick! And look at those legs, they look like little skinny sticks! And those buttocks. Soft, like marshmallows. You guys are lucky you don't have a campfire here in the background. And believe me— [sees sullen faces] What's the matter?

FRANZ: It's no use, Arnold. Compared to you, we are losers. And not even the grown-up kind, the little baby losers.

HANS: Ya. You know, you could very easily flick us with your littlest finger, and send us flying across the room until we landed in our own baby poop.

ARNOLD: I know. I know, you're right. But don't be downing yourself too much now. Listen to me now, and believe me later: It doesn't matter how much you pump up those muscles, as long as you reach the full pumptential.

FRANZ: Oh, okay.

HANS: Ya, I think I understand, Arnold. 'Sank you.

FRANZ: Ya. Ya, Arnold. You've given us something to hear now, and something to think about later.[52]

Girly-men, even ones with bulging muscles, have always been a problem for bodybuilding. In the same *Oui* magazine article that got him in trouble for comments about women, Arnold makes comments about gays that were just as insensitive but did not stir his campaign to try to assure that "remarkable gays" joined Arnold too. Thesmokinggun.com printed part of the interview that was advertised on the cover as "Arnold Schwarzenegger on the Sex Secrets of Bodybuilders":

Asked whether he was "freaked out" by being in such close contact with guys at the gym, Schwarzenegger said, "Men shouldn't feel like fags just because they want to have nice-looking bodies.... Gay people are fighting the same kind of stereotyping that bodybuilders are: People have certain misconceptions about them just as they do about us. Well, I have absolutely no hang-ups about the fag business...."[53]

Arnold works hard in many of his nondocumentary films to continue the confirmation of his distance from the "fag business." He draws attention to his distinction from the gay world when in *Total Recall* he is asked what his sexual orientation is so that an attendant can inject the correct sexual fantasy into his virtual vacation. She gives a skeptical look when he answers, a little too quickly, "hetero." It should be noted that this is also a film, like several others, that features Arnold in women's clothing and scenes of male birthing. But both eventually support rather than undermine his status as a heterosexual icon.

In the California recall election, he presented this unambiguously heterosexual, virile body to the electorate and they accepted it. It is a very large part of why Maria was able to talk about his body in gushing terms without seeming ridiculous and why the sexual harassment charges didn't mean all that much. He didn't have a problem with being a man and what California needed at that moment was a real man whose body of work was less important than the iconography of his body itself. Consider the alternatives in California: a soft-spoken Cruz Bustamante, a wimpier-than-George-Bush-Senior Gray Davis, a symbolically castrated Larry Flynt, a symbolically castrated Gary Coleman, a neutral Tom McClintock, a raging feminist Arianna Huffington, and a bunch of other unimpressive bodies. Why wouldn't California choose a body that had stood through the years for a restored maleness that promised "to give California back its future" maybe even as it promised to give the rest of America back its men?

As if to provide evidence that Arnold's manliness is powerful enough to restore masculinity to the least likely Americans, a cartoon version of Arnold appeared on FUSE TV's spoof "The Arnold Eye for the Girly Guy."[54] The animated episode takes a satirical swipe at the wildly popular show *Queer Eye for the Straight Guy* on Bravo. Arnold Schwarzenegger leads the transformation team charged with restoring hypermasculinity to Michael Jackson. Along with his animated team of Rosie O'Donnell, Howard Stern, and Snoop Dog among others, Arnold must change Michael from a "girly guy" into a "manly man."

## The Trojan Body

What sort of man are we talking about that can contain, control, and define all kinds of bodies in this way? California state senator and conservative candidate Tom McClintock has called Schwarzenegger a Trojan Horse surrounded by liberals.[55] An article in *Socialist Worker* referred to "Pete Wilson hiding inside the Trojan horse called Schwarzenegger."[56] This is an interesting metaphor for Arnold, and one that has been repeated in on-line Web-logs ("Blogs"), opinions, commentaries, and public debate. If Arnold is a Trojan horse, it is both in the classical Greek sense and in the high-tech computer sense. The Trojan horse was a successful trick used by the Greeks to gain entrance to the city of Troy during a long war. The Greeks built a gigantic horse, filled it with soldiers, and offered it as a gift to their enemies. That night the Greek soldiers emerged inside the city gates and destroyed the Trojans.

In computer jargon, a Trojan horse is any program that is disguised as a benign application that can do damage to your computer's hardware, software, or both. Computer worms and viruses can be Trojan horses if they are disguised as desirable files like movies or pictures or text files.[57] It is a battle between the machine—often the home computer— and the forces trying to subvert it. Arnold is a technological Trojan horse who could be the bearer of a kind of program capable of upsetting the entire American political and cultural machine.

The Trojan Horse cannot be ignored; once it has been let in—either to the machine or to the culture—its very existence constitutes a threat. The *Socialist Worker* remark painted Arnold as the stealth device containing Pete Wilson, the former California governor who was long regarded as a leading cause of California's political and economic troubles. But if the concern is that Wilson's strategies might reenter California, the implication is that Arnold could *contain* and transport those toxic policies, undetected until they are in place. But rather than releasing a flurry of "anti-bodies" to combat this type of incursion, America indulges its appetites for things that look pleasing on the surface even if they are toxic beneath. Our culture's superficial attractions and lax analyses not only prompt us to welcome Trojan horses, but we also willingly execute (that is, run) their programs in virtually every area of life. Arnold has the ability to show up in any cultural setting and establish himself as a seemingly desirable resident.

We have executed cultural Trojan horses during the "culture wars" that have been so prominent in the past few decades. The culture wars are the unending battles over the supposed moral decay in our society, the struggles over defining America's cultural values.[58] The culture wars are about controlling the definitions of who is a good role model, who are the "proper" Americans, who are the "patriotic" citizens, and who are the troublemakers. Arnold Schwarzenegger, on the other hand, is more than ever being promoted by some as the epitome of the American Dream and more and more as a role model despite all we have learned about his function as a Trojan horse.

In the culture wars that have been raging in this country, the body has always been a locus of great dispute. Whoever gets to define what is a proper American body and how it should behave, speak, and look is in a position of great influence. That is why the culture war battles are over issues like abortion rights, nude art, homosexuality, and English-only laws. Arnold hasn't been in the forefront of any of these battles although he is on the advisory board of U.S. English, a conservative organization whose purpose is to keep the country united by enforcing English as a common language (he is joined on the board by such linguistic notables as Arnold Palmer, Alex Trebek, and Charlton Heston). He was also once photographed by the gay photographer Robert Mapplethorpe, whose work has been at the center of battles to ban "obscene" art that was supposedly created with government funding.

Despite the fact that he is a significant model for American behavior, Arnold somehow seems to have transcended the ongoing skirmishes of the culture wars. He provides a model of fitness that may seem less threatening because it is so consistent with the all-American view of the value of the big, strong, clean, nondisruptive, centrist, very white, very male, very heterosexual citizen. The real threat is to all the people this image will leave out. For Arnold the new fitness, and thus the new source of power, is the ability to fit into surprising places—film frames, political parties, after-school programs, the Sacramento statehouse. Arnold is the newly born man, equally imbedded as the larger-than-larger-than-life-sized movie incarnation or the scaled-down, aerodynamic, stealthy statesman, outfitted for the new millennium. A section of his official Web site devoted to his early bodybuilding career is called "Mr. Everything" and this is what his body, the old bulked one as well as the new stealth one, has enabled him to be.

His earlier, "fantastic" films—*Conan the Barbarian* (1982), *Conan the Destroyer* (1984), *Hercules in New York* (1970), and *Red Sonja* (1985)—and his bodybuilding film roles—*Stay Hungry* (1976) and *Pumping Iron* (1977)—demanded a mythically proportioned body and he continued to work out in order to offer this. But for later films, and most recently for his move into the world of politics, Arnold had to get smaller. As he explained in Columbus, Ohio, at the Third Annual Arnold Classic in 1991, he was just too big for the film-frame and needed to reduce his size literally to fit into the picture. Arnold's point made sense; the reason he had to get smaller was because his films had begun, more and more, to bring together cinema and reality—a fusion that demands a smaller, less extraordinary body. His films of the past decade or so required that his characters look more like the Arnold people might encounter on the street. Arnold had to transform himself from mythical status to ordinary human status in films like *Last Action Hero* (1993), *True Lies* (1994), *Jingle All the Way* (1996), *The 6th Day* (2000), and *Collateral Damage* (2002).

## The American Body

Lore about Arnold's body is perpetuated by a culture that for over 100 years has been demanding that men use body sculpting to prove their masculinity. As the nineteenth century turned into the twentieth, a redefinition of American manhood was taking place in an atmosphere of fear about the feminization of American culture. Men could no longer count on their productive economic activities to define themselves. The self-made man became redefined to be one who developed a manly physique. Men flocked to gyms and "a nationwide health and athletics craze was in full swing, as men compulsively attempted to develop manly physiques as a way of demonstrating that they possessed the virtues of manhood."[59]

From the first moment he appeared on American soil, Schwarzenegger has been massaging these categories and pumping them up in his own image. Even today, in his relatively diminished bodily form, Arnold remains the standard by which the real and metaphorical size of others is measured. As Susan Faludi has claimed in her book on American manhood, "The ordinary man is no fool: he knows he can't be Arnold Schwarzenegger."[60] Just as America at the turn of the nineteenth century into the twentieth was anxious about its men's masculinity, the era when Arnold came into cultural prominence also experienced a fear of the feminization of the entire culture.

When the post-Vietnam era issued a renewed call to conquer this feared feminization, Arnold was there to help, but only after Rambo failed to do the job completely. In her analysis of stories about Vietnam and how they reflect our concerns about gender roles in that era, Susan Jeffords[61] showed that the military failures in Vietnam and the home-based protests created a problem for our culture. If war is the best stage to demonstrate the masculine bond,[62] then a failed war is the proof that the bond is threatened. Stories like those in Sylvester Stallone's *Rambo* series (1982, 1985, 1988) act out this crisis and show the need to restore male identity and manhood itself. It was Arnold's films after this that showed in more complex and less hysterical ways how to actually get it done.

But while Arnold was ascending into the highest echelon of male icons, a response to the women's movement was developing across America. In the late 1980s and early '90s, a so-called "men's movement" promoted a vision of a new man that would reclaim his "proper" role in American culture. As Bill Zehme put it, it was

> ...a woeful time to be a man. It is a time when men gather to bemoan all that has become of them. Men, experts believe, went soft somewhere. Now, to correct matters, hordes of them retreat to the woods for strange rituals in which they strut about in loincloths and howl at trees, trying desperately to find the wild man within themselves, previously lost for generations. Men, alas, have forgotten how to be men.[63]

Arnold was not a specific model for this new man and his body was not one that most men could achieve even if they wanted. Instead, Arnold outlasted and usurped this "new man." In Zehme's words, "Arnold shames all men."[64] A chief theme of these new male visions was the concept of the twin, often the twin within. Poet and masculinist Robert Bly talked about a man glimpsing his psychic twin, his "other half, his shadow, or hidden man."[65] Sam Keen suggested that psychological and spiritual integration for twice-born men could be achieved by "re-owning our shadows."[66] Robert Moore and Douglas Gillette encouraged the recognition of the archetypal "Shadow Warrior" who, when properly controlled, instinctively knows when to kick butt and when to hold back.[67] The movement also encouraged men to repair the damage done by their mothers, to reconcile with their fathers, and to give birth to their new selves.

America must be able, somehow, to share the prospects of the ideal American body that Arnold's life seems to offer. He neatly offers us this opportunity in the movie *Twins* (1988), in a story that defines his essence as well as the essential role Americans play in relation to him. In the movie, he is the perfected, godlike man who can see in other men the flaws that have been cleaned from his own system. Arnold plays a young man called Julius Benedict, the product of a genetics experiment conducted by the American government to produce a physically, mentally, and spiritually advanced human being. The purpose of this type of reproduction is not explained, but the scientists, all six of them, are his proud fathers. The mother, we are told, has died (although it is later discovered she is still alive).

Much to Julius's surprise, he learns that he has a twin brother, Vincent, played by Danny DeVito. DeVito's character is a short, balding, loud-mouthed rascal who steals cars and beds married women. Julius, in contrast, is the gentle giant—the flawless human specimen who claims to hate violence, can speak twelve languages (with German the obviously dominant tongue), and is still a virgin. Vincent's girlfriend is a sweet, plain, street-smart woman who puts up with Vincent's slovenliness, his infidelities, and his coarseness. Her sister, who becomes Julius's girlfriend, is the more statuesque, blonde, beautiful half of the sibling pair. She, too, is sweet and generous and finds Julius's purity and power to be the perfect complement to her own characteristics. The physical, moral, and social contrasts between the two brothers provide the humor of the film but also create the message that the high-minded, anatomically marvelous, and eugenically perfect world manifested in Julius is not problematic in any important way.

The genetic scientist in charge of this project to produce the perfect man explains to the two brothers that when their embryo split in two, it did not split equally. All the purity and strength went to Julius and all the "crap that was left over" went into Vincent. The significance of this dawns on Vincent as he responds, "Are you saying I'm a side effect?" The brothers eventually claim to see the other as the missing part of each other's life and their story is one of finding the twin-within who makes a man complete. What twins in general, and Julius and Vincent in particular, provided each other was supplementarity. A supplement is both surplus and substitute.[68] A supplement is (in Vincent's vernacular) the crap left over; it sits next to something that is supposed to be complete except insofar as that completeness is subverted by the very existence of the supplement. The advantage of identifying your supplement/twin is not a renewed or extended camaraderie but a more complete control of those "side effects," the rumors, the fallout of any actions and stories.

DeVito's character is, in effect, all of us, for we are the fallout or side effects of Arnold's incursion into American culture. Vincent is determined not to be overlooked, full of ambition that is often ineffectively or inappropriately applied, and content with relatively small successes. He is inclined to bend plenty of rules, but is ultimately decenthearted and full of unnamed longings. And he is obviously physically inferior to his sibling counterpart. Arnold's character Julius is, in so many ways, *not* us. He is gigantic, a genius, unshakably patient, pure of mind, heart, and—thanks to genetic perfection—breeding. If Vincent represents the "side effects," then Arnold/Julius is the condition itself. The production of the idealized male—large and magnificent—entails the creation of side effects—ordinary people who simply can never quite measure up. Lesser men are "girly," and women even "girlier." Thus, as versions of Arnold's inferior twin, Americans do not have to look like him or be as powerful or charismatic. It is enough to feel we share his cultural DNA.

## The Replicating Body

When we tell stories about our bodies and how they reproduce, and how we create ourselves, we are addressing the very definition of being a human being and defining a meaningful existence. While other men were drumming and chanting to give birth to their "real" selves through some twin entity, Arnold Schwarzenegger was teaching Maria Shriver how to give birth to real babies. In her appearance on the *Tonight Show* eight months after giving birth to her first child, Maria complained about the difficulties of childbirth but then explained how Arnold had participated. Their birthing class teacher, wanting to include Arnold in the experience, said during one class, "Arnold will show you how to push." She explains how the teacher took a doll and, after instructing Arnold to put his legs up in the birthing position (which Maria demonstrates), she put the doll between his legs and yells at him to push. Maria demonstrates Arnold pushing and breathing and delivering the baby doll. Maria comments, "Arnold delivered the little baby and I watched him and knew what to do. That's how I learned how to give birth."

What might be a cute celebrity story in other circumstances here has connections to other birthing representations in Arnold's larger story. This is not the only time Arnold has taken the birthing body under his control. In an example of Arnold as midwife, Kevin Spillane, a Republican strategist working to defeat Democratic senator Barbara Boxer, said, "If Schwarzenegger had lost, Republican donors and activists would have been in fetal position." In winning the election, Arnold, in effect, delivered these fetal Republicans.[69]

In *The 6th Day*, Arnold is Adam Gibson, who comes home to his birthday party only to find that he has been cloned and his duplicate is now living his life. He told *Muscle & Fitness* magazine that "I never worried about cloning; as a matter of fact, at times I've wished I could clone myself [laughs], because there are so many ambitions and so many goals in my life, and there's not enough time to do all those things."[70] In *Total Recall,* Arnold has a scene in which he is trying to escape disguised as a woman. The mechanical mask of the disguise fails and the escaping Arnold is "born" out of her body. Later in the movie, a fetus-like creature emerges from the belly of one of Arnold's allies.

In both of the first two Terminator films, the birthing of both humans and machines is a concern. In *The Terminator* (1984), antimachine freedom fighter John Connor chooses to send Kyle Reese back to the past to become John's father;

by *Terminator 2* (1991), it is the Terminator itself that takes on the fathering role to the now young John Connor, while the "mother of the future," Sarah Connor, has given up all maternal roles and takes on all the killing aspirations of a terminator.

These appropriations of the maternal body are most obviously and dramatically presented in *Junior* (1994). In *Junior,* Arnold plays the scientist Dr. Alex Hesse, who, along with his colleague Dr. Larry Arbogast (Danny Devito again), has developed a promising drug that will help women carry their pregnancies to full term. We are not told how the drug, Expectane, does this or why women would need it. When the team is refused permission to conduct tests on humans, they steal an egg from a female scientist and place the fertilized egg in the abdomen of Dr. Hesse, the last place anyone would look, and administer the drug to him. Although the experiment was supposed to last only through the first trimester, Hesse gets attached to his fetus and refuses to stop taking the drug.

We should point out that Arnold's character, Dr. Hesse, reminds us of another Hesse: Hermann Hesse, the German writer who wrote *Der Steppenwolf,* a novel with a hauntingly relevant plot. In *Steppenwolf* the protagonist, Harry Haller, is a self-absorbed man in midlife crisis who must choose between a life of action and one of contemplation. Haller faces his shadow self, a female named Hermine, who introduces Harry to drinking, dancing, music, sex, and drugs, teaching him to find his liberated self.[71] Like Stevenson's Jekyll and Hyde,[72] Harry and Hermine represent the split nature of human beings. Arnold's *Junior* portrays this split as that between the calm, studied, scientific approach by the male scientists and the liberating-but-chaotic condition of being feminized through pregnancy. It is a condition that the male side of Dr. Hesse must control. Ironically, when the female scientist learns that Hesse is carrying one of her fertilized eggs, she becomes hysterical,[73] yelling "This is so male! Do you think men don't hold enough cards? You have to take this away from us as well?" The tag line in the film's advertisements, "Nothing is inconceivable," is played out not only with a fully pregnant Arnold noticeably glowing and eating for two, but also dressed as a woman, disguised as a former East German athlete who took too many steroids.

In the studio production information packet, director Ivan Reitman is quoted as saying, "If men can carry babies to term, it's going to really confuse our perception of what makes us different as men and women." He continued, "Are we really that different? I think so, but emotionally we have much deeper connections than one would expect. To explore this, I wanted to take Arnold Schwarzenegger, an icon of masculinity, and see what happens when he has to deal with one of the great events of life heretofore reserved for women—giving birth."[74]

The critical reception for the film was surprisingly warm and many critics found it charming. Arnold himself claimed that making the movie gave him a new appreciation for what women go through in childbirth. About his simulated pregnancy he noted, "It's not just stuffing a pillow in your trousers and play-acting."[75] For Arnold, a key moment in the film comes with the line he claims "everyone was waiting for"—when he asks a friend, "Does my body disgust you?" According to Schwarzenegger, what made the line so rich for him was that "I have been working on my body and, by any accounts, from age 15 to 47, people have been telling me it is spectacular. You know, that's been my life. Then I have to have this big belly and feel that, maybe, I'm disgusting. That teaches me something about what a woman goes through. I mean, she must feel the same way."[76] Whatever Arnold may have believed he learned from playing a pregnant man whose "skin glowed,"[77] the description of the movie on Schwarzenegger.com attempts, these ten-plus years later, to distance Arnold from the female roles he took on in the movie. The Web site entry on *Junior* reads:

> "I'm known for being this muscular guy and this heroic movie star, but to run around in dresses and wear earrings—it was fun to be able, in a legitimate way, to play that kind of feminine character, because in real life if I wear or do any of that, they would definately [*sic*] put me away."
>
> But Arnold would be the first to admit he doesn't know if seeing him in make-up really worked for his biggest fans. "One day I was sitting on a life cycle at World Gym... and this guy next to me was just staring at me and shaking his head. 'Nowwwww, you did it,' he said, and I was like, 'Did what?' He looked at me and said, 'You sold out. What happened? You marry a democratic wife and now you have to make nice movies.'" Arnold recalls, "Basically I was verbally attacked, on the life cycle—I'd sold out, I'd become a democrat, I'd become this feminine guy. All of that! So I said 'thank you for you comments' and called Ivan (director Ivan Reitman). I told him, 'Ivan, if the movie doesn't work in my gym, we have a problem.' And sure enough, the guys just wouldn't go for it—they thought it was too far."[78]

Why did we need a pregnant Arnold or a cloned Arnold or a maternal Terminator? Historian David Noble says that the history of science and technology in the Western world is full of male scientists seeking ways to eliminate women from the birthing process, or at least make their contribution irrelevant. While this may seem to be an overbroad brush with which to paint the scientific world, he draws a compelling picture of the history of technologies designed for the "obsessive pursuit" of creating a "motherless child."[79] Arnold's movies coupled with tabloid stories about male birthing[80] certainly are consistent with this pursuit. It was as though Arnold had made sure to have a hand—and sometimes his whole body—in every area of human endeavor. This constant and aggressive reach into new arenas was a sign in itself of Arnold's insistent presence in our culture.

## The Artful Body

After the election, the cartoon strip *Doonesbury* represented Arnold as a disembodied hand and dubbed him "Herr Gröpenfuhrer," a sort of all-groper, all-the-time Arnold. Shown at a news conference, the hand was the living definition of the phrase "talk to the hand." "Talk to the Hand" is an expression that spread on trashy afternoon TV talk shows, with a more complete version of it being, "talk to the hand 'cause the face don't give a damn." The best urbandictionary.com definition is "A saying used to ignore and disregard a comment or an insult when you can't think of a way to counter it."[81] It is also a line from *Terminator 3* (2003), used by a very effeminate male stripper dressed in the leather outfit that Arnold's character needs. When the naked Terminator demands the clothes, which of course are an homage to the previous Terminators, the insulted artist suggests that the Terminator "talk to the hand." Instead of talking to it, however, Arnold crushes it. A bit later in the movie, the Terminator enters a convenience store to gather provisions for his human charges. When the clerk demands payment for the piles of junk food the Terminator has scooped up, Arnold's character restores manliness to both the gesture and the expression when he tells the clerk, "Talk to da hand," before stalking out of the store.

Of course, the Herr Gröpenfuhrer character has National Socialist associations, and this other history of Arnold's body made a brief appearance in the election campaign. Arnold's purported pro-Nazi statements were hard to pin down and the allegations that he looked favorably upon Hitler-style leadership quickly faded. Indeed, Arnold commissioned investigators at the Simon Wiesenthal Center to find out about his father's Nazi history as a way to bring some order to the chaos of rumors circulating about him. But his body and its ability to conjure up the image of the ideal Aryan body are not gone and are a reminder of this connection.

Arnold has always considered his body a sculpture and he remarked in *Pumping Iron* that a "good bodybuilder has the same mind, when it comes to sculpting [the body] as a sculptor has." In February 1976, Arnold participated in a staged posing of sculpted muscle-bodies-turned-art at the Whitney Museum in New York. "You don't really see a muscle as a part of you, in a way. You see it as a thing. You look at it as a thing and you say, well, this thing has to be built a little longer, the bicep has to be longer, or the tricep has to be thicker here in the elbow area. And you look at it and it doesn't even seem to belong to you. Like a sculpture. Then, after looking at it, a sculptor goes in with this thing and works a little bit, and you do, maybe then some extra forced reps to get this lower part out. You form it. Just like sculpture."[82] The Whitney Museum event was a huge success and made built bodies into art.

The images of Arnold posing that were taken by George Butler at the prime of his career could easily be mistaken for the statues that populated Germany during World War II. The sculpted body was the most familiar and imposing form used to present National Socialist ideology in Germany. As one study of the art of that time explains, "it was most of all the virile beauty of the male body that dominated sculptural output. Modeled on antiquity, the sculptures displayed steely masculinity."[83] The sculptures were intended to convey the idea that Germany was creating a new man and the sculpture of the idealized male nude became "the absolute image of the Fascist human being," an ideal not of beauty but of "being."[84]

The early images of Arnold as the self-sculptured man with an inhumanly perfect body have been replaced by an image of the sculpture-come-to-life, the living embodiment of our own American dreams. Americans have always wanted to animate the American Dream, to embody it in a visible way, not with all those messy, confusing multi-skinned poor people, but with the biggest, strongest, cleanest, sleekest, and most statuesque example we could tolerate. And now we have done that. We have animated the perfectly sculpted man and made him a living statue of the American Dream.

The dream of enlivening the statues that we have created, often in our own image, is centuries old. Puppets, marionettes, automatons, robots, cyborgs, Pinocchio, the Golem, Santa's wooden soldiers, Frankenstein's monster, Frosty the Snowman, and Pygmalion all enact it. All have the purpose of granting the sculptor his wish to make the dream real just as Arnold has said many times in his life. We all have collaborated with Arnold on this artistic creation. Neither the citizenry nor Arnold could have done it alone; it is also likely that neither the people nor Arnold knows what to do with it next.

**CHAPTER 10**

# Scavenger Hunt: Toilets and Titles

IN *TERMINATOR 3,* Arnold Schwarzenegger's Terminator converts a toilet into a weapon, plunging the enemy female Terminator's head into it. Arnold was quick to point out that it really wasn't a woman at all but a cyborg, like his own Terminator character. Schwarzenegger's critics locked on to Arnold's expressed pleasure in making that scene, and on to the line's sequel on September 24, 2003, during the one California debate in which Arnold participated. Once again, Arnold brandished a toilet, this time by implication, when he suggested that he might have a fitting part in "Terminator 4" for political opponent Arianna Huffington.

That "toilet" should become a significant term during the gubernatorial campaign is not surprising, given its use in the circumstances mentioned above. Pursuing the issue, the *Los Angeles Times* featured a commentary entitled "Family Values

Down the Toilet: How Can the GOP Women Endorse Schwarzenegger?"[1] The *Modesto (Calif.) Bee*'s local news section sported a brief commentary entitled "California in the Toilet."[2] The *Daily Express* offered a tiny piece called "Arnie's Feeling Flush,"[3] and London's *The Independent* ran a story from Los Angeles entitled "Terminator's Toilet Humor Backfires as Candidates Clash."[4] The "Flush Arnold, Not Women" message written on a toilet seat was yet another indication that, for many, Arnold had become "The Face in the Toilet Bowl."[5] The toilet-as-protest-sign caught on, and across the country, in Suffolk County, Long Island, someone bolted to telephone poles six toilet seats framing pictures of a woman who was running for a position on the town board; beneath each toilet seat were the words, "Flush Away."[6]

If that were the end of it, we might simply chalk up these press clippings and protests to an anomalous "plumbing" phase in Arnold's campaign. However, it turns out that from well before the debate until nearly the end of 2003, there had been a fairly steady stream of toilets, in a much wider variety of circumstances and contexts, connected directly or indirectly to Arnold. Back in August of 2003, Arnold had offered the press a recently honed position statement on the California economy, in which he stated, "From the time they get up in the morning and flush the toilet, they're taxed."[7] The *New York Times* picked up on this comment and ran it again, two months later.[8] Responding to this campaign remark, a reporter from the *Milwaukee Journal Sentinel* wrote that Arnold's point was "Absolutely true. We pay a sewer tax so that we can flush instead of digging a hole in the backyard."[9]

Many sources ran stories about Arnold's childhood in Austria, and a number of them included Arnold's own recollection that "We had no TV at home. We had no flushing toilets."[10] The on-line journal *The Hawk Eye* noted that Arnold "now has lots of flush toilets."[11] Gwyneth Paltrow came forward with a confession that when she was a young girl, she and a friend had played a prank on their neighbor, Arnold Schwarzenegger, covering his shrubs "by throwing rolls of toilet paper over them."[12] And in a bizarre juxtaposition, the *Palm Beach Post* asked readers, "How do you top a product like O. J. Simpson toilet paper? By peddling California Total Recall playing cards."[13]

Of far greater relevance were the toilets that became part of discussions about California's ongoing problem with its water supply. During the gubernatorial campaign, Schwarzenegger said, "California must increase its water supply," but also indicated that he is a proponent of water conservation efforts throughout the state.[14] The Pacific Institute, an Oakland, California, think tank devoted to the issue of water conservation, proposed replacing or upgrading approximately seven million six-gallon toilets with models that use only 1.6 gallons per flush. The Institute claimed that replacement of these antiquated toilets would save California's cities around a third of the water consumed annually.[15] By late 2003, Governor Schwarzenegger had not yet indicated whether he supported investing in these toilets. A U.S. company has created a waterless toilet—a urinal, specifically—and proposed replacing ordinary urinals throughout California, but the initial proposal was rejected by both the city of Los Angeles and the state of California, pending "more research on its long-term maintenance needs."[16]

The toilet connection was in effect in the issue of casinos on Native American land. Part of Arnold's campaign for election included a promise to tax Indian casinos as a way to add to state revenue. In an essay on *Hotel Online: News for the Hospitality Executive,* members of the San Pasqual Indian Reservation were quoted as saying that Arnold and others who have made political attacks on the casinos "think that because there's a casino, people here have all this money.... But that's not the case." One longtime resident suggested that Arnold come to the Reservation to see for himself that the local economy is hardly booming. He recalled a time not long ago when "so many used to live in camper trailers... the kids bathed in the canal... they carried buckets of water to flush their toilets."[17]

And two days after Arnold Schwarzenegger actually took office as California's governor, the Singapore-based World Toilet Organization, which exists to help keep public toilets open and well maintained, declared that November 19 would henceforth be World Toilet Day.[18]

Toilets. A term associated with Arnold that is as arbitrary as, say, ostriches, or microscopes. But we have seen that the term has attached itself to Arnold in a way that has everything to do with how and why he matters so profoundly in America. His presence has so completely saturated the culture, and his influence is so universally felt, that words, ideas, and things we would not normally even consider pertinent to Arnold Schwarzenegger not only become significant but actually work like tiny holograms, each in a way inscribed with an impression of what Arnold has become in the American imagination. In the 1979 movie *Scavenger Hunt,* Arnold plays Lars, one of fifteen people who stand to inherit an eccentric millionaire's estate, if any one of them can succeed in finding, and procuring, a peculiar set of objects indicated in the old man's will. On that list: an ostrich, a cash register, a microscope, and a drive-thru speaker.

As farcical as the film may have seemed, *Scavenger Hunt*'s darker theme comes through as potential heirs of the great fortune begin to murder each other. The message was that people will do anything for money and the power it brings. But a more interesting message of this and every other of Arnold's movies is that the titles themselves are terms that can be used to highlight important aspects of Arnold's life and career. His films somehow demonstrate an eerie foresight into events and activities with which he and/or America will be involved.

When George W. Bush said in early 2003, "The U.N. inspectors were not sent to conduct a *scavenger hunt* of hidden materials across a country the size of California,"[19] he reconnected the idea of the scavenger hunt with an equally dark theme involving murder and death. The phrase gathered some steam; a *Chicago Daily Herald* article, commenting on the U.S. involvement in Iraq, noted, "This scavenger hunt ignores a basic fact… that Iraq must account for weapons of mass destruction or face grave consequences."[20] In December 2003, George W. Bush re-spun the term, arguing now that the United States is on a "scavenger hunt for terror."[21]

It's not difficult to see that Arnold's movie titles seem ingeniously conceived to become part of everyday thinking, sometimes in unexpectedly humorous ways. Even an obscure 1979 movie like *The Villain* offered a glimpse into the future that now seems both ironic and uncanny. In that film, Arnold plays a character known only as Handsome Stranger who ends up protecting Ann-Margret's Charming Jones from would-be double-crossing robbers led by "the villain," Cactus Jack Slater. Why does Handsome Stranger protect Charming? Because he owes his life to her father, Parody. Arnold owes his "life" to Parody and must protect

Charming... some would argue that this describes the basis of his political career.

Arnold Schwarzenegger's presence and influence are so thoroughly available and effective in the culture that the movie titles function as compact translations of the many ways in which Arnold matters. Sometimes the titles are combined in such a way as to create a new and perfectly apt term for Arnold's activities. An article in the *Sunday Tribune* (Dublin) announced, "The Governator: Arnie Enters the 'Recall Carnival.'"[22] In this case, the writer combines *Total Recall* with the name of one of Arnold's little-known videos, *Carnival in Rio*—in which Arnold hosts a "campy, tongue-in-cheek tour of 'Mardi Gras Madness' in Rio de Janeiro... where little is left to the imagination." The resulting term cleverly conveys the campy and frenzied atmosphere of the California recall itself. An article about Arnold's refusal to participate in an early September 2003 candidate forum referred to the "scavenger hunt" all the other candidates would be engaged in as they would have to "poke around at the Walnut Creek debate" for issues other than the man who would have been "the main target."[23]

An August 2003 Op-Ed piece in the *Boston Herald* began:

> Accusing California Gov. Gray Davis of telling True Lies and giving the state a Raw Deal, outraged Republicans demanded a Total Recall. They wanted a Running Man who would be Davis' Eraser, someone who would Stay Hungry through the End of Days of the campaign. Actor Arnold Schwarzenegger, saying he would be the regular Joe's Last Chance, offered himself as Terminator. "Davis has been no better than a Kindergarten Cop," Schwarzenegger said. "Let me be your Commando in chief."[24]

*USA Today*'s Tom Arnold wrote, "Now that the Terminator is the Running Man, Arnold Schwarzenegger is a hot property."[25] The *National Post* of Canada ran the headline "California's New Hercules Has Twin Pillars: Governor-elect Liked by Republicans and Democrats."[26] An attorney from the Philippines wrote in his Web-log: "Conan, the Terminator did it."[27] In a piece entitled "Conan the Candidate," the *New York Post* referred to "Conan-the-Running-Man-Terminator's ride to California's rescue."[28] A piece from the *Washington Post* made the following argument:

> Arnold Schwarzenegger has zero experience in government, but his many film roles may have prepared him well for the task of straightening out California's budget mess. He's been the Terminator, who blows up anything that gets in his way, and Conan the sword-wielding barbarian, who's no doubt a natural at slashing costs. And as the Kindergarten Cop, he met the challenge of winning over people who initially didn't want to listen to him. But perhaps no movie role has better prepared him to deal with California's immense budget problem than his 1994 hall-of-mirrors flick, "True Lies."[29]

What is interesting about these film references is that they work just like "toilets" in that they become inseparable from our sense of how Arnold permeates culture. They are used as a kind of shorthand for aspects of the campaign, or for an aspect of Arnold's worldview that is more easily named than explained. In the *Washington Post* example, it is fairly clear that the references to *The Terminator* and *Conan* are inaccurate as they pertain to the movies, yet effective in communicating an idea about Arnold's dubious qualifications for governing the largest state.

Conan's swordsmanship has nothing at all to do with budgets or politics; the Terminator's elimination of "anything that gets in his way" is not likely to be the literal approach California's governor would take. Arnold's character in *Kindergarten Cop* really does not have to persuade anyone to listen to him; that is not one of his difficulties. But the use of that title in the context of Arnold's political qualifications provides readers with a quick and metaphoric image of a leader who must bring order to his unruly charges. The film title *True Lies* conjures all sorts of paradoxical situations but nothing in the movie is directly applicable to the budgetary problems facing Governor Schwarzenegger. In the movie, the "lies" are the falsehoods that Arnold's Harry Tasker tells his wife to protect her from the dangerous business he's in. His wife's "true lies" are the counter-falsehoods that she tells her husband to keep him from knowing that she has slipped into the same very dangerous business. But the use of "True Lies" in the context of the *Post* article is not intended to be accurate; it is intended to be applicable to an idea of bureaucratic entanglements that are always difficult to sort out with regard to truth and falsity.

In these contexts, and in the many other references to Arnold Schwarzenegger's movie titles that have circulated regularly in political discussions, newscasts, and print articles, the speakers and writers engaged in a kind of "scavenger hunt" to find ways of encapsulating the fascinating trajectory of Arnold's political career. In the earlier *Boston Herald* piece the writer's reference to *Joe's Last Chance*—a movie that never got released—is proof enough that the film titles are being used not as cinematic allusions but as idioms uniquely endowed with authority about one or more aspects of Arnold's life and work. It is perhaps not even ironic, then, that in *Scavenger Hunt* there is one other item that each potential heir must find and "capture": a toilet.

The following list includes the films in which Arnold was either the main character, the director (in one case), or a featured performer—generally as himself. It is not difficult to see the appeal in going through the list to hunt for titles and names that are somehow fitting for Arnold, in any given context, at any given moment. Taken as a whole, the list of films and characters constitutes a fascinating set of elements that can be examined individually, combined, and recombined in what becomes a record of the culture's investment in Arnold and of Arnold's embeddedness in the culture.

| MOVIE | YEAR | CHARACTER(S) PLAYED |
|---|---|---|
| 1. *Hercules in New York* | 1970 | Hercules |
| 2. *The Long Goodbye* | 1973 | One of Augustine's hoods |
| 3. *Stay Hungry* | 1976 | Joe Santo |
| 4. *Pumping Iron* | 1977 | Himself |
| 5. *Scavenger Hunt* | 1979 | Lars |
| 6. *The Villain* | 1979 | Handsome stranger |
| 7. *The Jayne Mansfield Story* (TV) | 1980 | Mickey Hargitay |
| 8. *Conan the Barbarian* | 1982 | Conan |
| 9. *Conan the Destroyer* | 1984 | Conan |
| 10. *Playboy: Carnival in Rio* | 1984 | Himself (host) |
| 11. *The Terminator* | 1984 | Terminator |
| 12. *Red Sonja* | 1985 | Kalidor |
| 13. *Commando* | 1985 | Col. John Matrix |
| 14. *Raw Deal* | 1986 | Mark Kaminsky |

| | | | |
|---|---|---|---|
| 15. | *Predator* | 1987 | Dutch |
| 16. | *The Running Man* | 1987 | Ben Richards |
| 17. | *Red Heat* | 1988 | Ivan Danko |
| 18. | *Twins* | 1988 | Julius Benedict |
| 19. | *Total Recall* | 1990 | Quaid/Hauser |
| 20. | *Kindergarten Cop* | 1990 | John Kimble |
| 21. | *Terminator 2: Judgment Day* | 1991 | Terminator |
| 22. | *Christmas in Connecticut* (TV) | 1992 | [Director] and man in chair |
| 23. | *Lincoln* | 1992 | Voice of John G. Nicolay |
| 24. | *The Last Party* | 1993 | Himself |
| 25. | *Last Action Hero* | 1993 | Himself and Jack Slater |
| 26. | *Dave* | 1993 | Himself |
| 27. | *True Lies* | 1994 | Harry Tasker |
| 28. | *Junior* | 1994 | Dr. Alex Hesse |
| 29. | *Beretta's Island* | 1994 | Himself |
| 30. | *Eraser* | 1996 | John Kruger, the Eraser |
| 31. | *Jingle All the Way* | 1996 | Howard Langston |
| 32. | *Batman and Robin* | 1997 | Mr. Freeze/Dr. Victor Fries |
| 33. | *Arnold Schwarzenegger: Hollywood Hero* | 1999 | Himself |
| 34. | *End of Days* | 1999 | Jericho Cane |
| 35. | *The 6th Day* | 2000 | Adam Gibson |
| 36. | *Dr. Doolittle 2* | 2001 | Voice of White Wolf (uncredited) |
| 37. | *Collateral Damage* | 2002 | Gordy Brewer |

| 38. | *Joe's Last Chance** | 2003 | Hit man |
|-----|---------------------|------|---------|
| 39. | *Terminator 3: Rise of the Machines* | 2003 | Terminator |
| 40. | *True Lies 2*** | 2003 | Harry Tasker |
| 41. | *Around the World in 80 Days** | 2003 | Prince Hapi |

*Not yet released
**Not yet produced and/or completed

# CHAPTER 11

# Christmas in Connecticut: Arnold Dreaming

### LOUISE'S DREAM 7/19/03

There had been a nuclear war and we wanted to see if Arnold had survived. We drove to his fancy neighborhood in Greenwich, Connecticut. Michael went up to the back door of Arnold's house and opened it despite my concern that we would get caught. We heard the sound of a children's birthday party so we knew they were there. Arnold came out and I saw that he had a hole burned all the way through his bare foot. The inside of his foot was hollow. We followed him to a local store and he looked at us but didn't seem to know who we were.

The friendly man behind the airlines counter asked where the family was traveling for the holidays. "Connecticut,"

Louise said. "Connecticut!" he said, surprised (since this was Albuquerque, New Mexico). "I grew up in Connecticut. Where in Connecticut?" "Stamford, Old Greenwich," Louise offered. "Ah," he replied, "Fairfield County, the home of the Schwarzeneggers and the Kennedys; well, maybe not the Kennedys...."

Actually, it was home to some Kennedys, Ethel Kennedy's relatives the Skakels, and Michael Skakel had recently been convicted in a trial in Fairfield County for the 1975 murder of a 15-year-old girl. But people in Albuquerque probably had not heard of that although it was the talk of the town in Connecticut. The Schwarzeneggers have never actually settled anywhere near Connecticut but that fact is irrelevant to the connection made by this airline employee: For him it must have seemed that Arnold Schwarzenegger represented the type of money or prestige or social standing associated with Fairfield County, Connecticut. Despite his Austrian origins and action movie wealth, Arnold easily stands in for this region that houses many of the country's wealthy, powerful, and elite. How Arnold can be this kind of representation says a lot about the influence of the idea of "Arnold" apart from his actual economic or political clout.

Heading for this mythical "Christmas in Connecticut" conjures up scenes of the idealized American family in the perfect domestic setting with a scrumptious home-cooked meal on the finely set table. Connecticut is Martha Stewart country, not just because Martha actually has a home there but because it has epitomized Stewart's lifestyle empire since her first entertaining book in 1982, her magazine debut in 1990, and her television show's premiere in 1993. Love her or hate her, Martha Stewart has done for domesticity what Arnold Schwarzenegger has done for the larger American scene: set an agenda and a style that is impossible to follow but that generates longing and hope along with revenues. Despite her current legal difficulties, Stewart still projects this quest for a piece of the American Dream on her Web site: "When America wants to learn how to make the perfect piecrust, grow an herb garden, create a beautiful flower arrangement, or fix a broken windowpane, America turns to Martha Stewart. Martha's dedication to sharing creative principles and practical ideas has made her the nation's foremost authority on living well."

Stewart, like Schwarzenegger, has made a living out of promoting herself as the hallmark of "living well" in America. But while Martha is the perfect hostess, Arnold is more like the ideal party guest, the one we invite into every aspect of our well-lived lives. Arnold is the guest you want at your party or in your life because his presence jacks up the value and excitement of the life being lived. It is not that he is a well-behaved guest but rather that he is an interesting and enchanting one. He also lets us be in the show with him and that is the most any of us can hope for. This model of living very well and very fit in America is one that few but Arnold can achieve. Even Martha Stewart can only look on in envy.

As Arnold himself describes the situation in a glossy magazine called *Arnold: The American Dream,* "The American Dream is real. I know because it happened to me."[1] The cover of this publication illustrates each of the mileposts toward this "dream": the trophy wife, the iconic hero status, the fame, the handsome body and good looks, the political might. To connect Arnold with this fabricated yet materialized version of the American Dream is to give a physical presence and an indisputable proof to that dream's possibility.

Yet the American Dream is really a practical impossibility and by being out of reach for nearly everyone, the American Dream can be utilized by characters like Arnold Schwarzenegger and Martha Stewart for less than charitable purposes. In Arnold's case it allows him to build on the paternalism of his ruling style and enables him to enlarge his image as a leader in the culture. As in a family with a strong head and docile members, some believe that "good" citizens in a culture are those who have learned self-discipline, who control their own behavior before others have to see it. With Arnold as the director of his own American Dream project, we have someone in control who has constructed himself as the epitome of this ideal and the terminator of all other possibilities.

There is another connection between Arnold and the American Dream in Connecticut at the holidays. The only film Schwarzenegger has ever directed (albeit for television) was a remake of the 1945 Barbara Stanwyck classic *Christmas in Connecticut*. In 1992, Arnold uncannily predicted the meteoric rise of a fabricated ideal television homemaker and cook, foreshadowing the immensity of Martha Stewart and her finely controlled lifestyle empire. Of all the movie stories Arnold could have chosen, with his money and clout and connections (even in 1992), why choose a classic screwball comedy about a domestic diva who lies to the world about what she is really capable of doing and who she actually is? Why not direct an action film or an adventure film or a comedy like *Twins* or *Kindergarten Cop*? Or why not continue directing television episodes like the one for the *Tales from the Crypt* series in 1990 that told the story of an old man bartering to get a new body so that he could woo his dream girl? The answer is that *Christmas in Connecticut* is the perfect story of Arnold's life, not because he has actually shown up for holidays with the Kennedys and Skakels, but because Arnold's is a story of cooking up truths, garnishing reality, and decorating confectionary treats that we swallow like a well-cooked goose at our most important ritual moments.

The essence of both the original and Arnold's exaggerated version of *Christmas in Connecticut* is the power of the fake and the lack of any need for truth-telling in human relations. In both movie versions, lie is built upon lie and the eventual discovery of the deceitful nature of all the relationships and motivations is easily dismissed and forgiven. All the shortcomings shown by the ambitious characters are seen as the inevitable fallout of aggressively pursuing one's goals.

In the 1945 original a starving World War II sailor adrift on a life raft dreams of the perfect meal. The dream is shown in a brief surreal sequence and the pursuit of this dream meal is the initial driving force of the film, because after he is rescued the sailor recounts this dream to everyone. A veteran's hospital nurse tries to get the sailor to marry her just like other nurses have done in this time when men were in short supply. The nurse decides to supply her dream man with that dream meal (focused on the all-American steak-and-potatoes), but that only causes the recuperating sailor to retch. What the nurse doesn't know is that the sailor is faking and that his regurgitation is part of a strategy to lie to her and get rid of her so that the man can stay free. It is a strategy that his buddy calls "the magoo." The magoo is not "baloney" or simple lying but a seductive, well-scripted story that gets you what you want. Just as the magoo can get you into a desired scenario, it can also get you out of a problematic one like an over-romantic nurse. The nurse goes on to arrange the perfect Christmas for the sailor, one in

Connecticut with Elizabeth Lane, the famous homemaker the sailor read about in a magazine, in hopes of convincing the sailor that he too will see the joys of domesticity and want to marry the love-struck nurse.

The difference between the first film and the remake is that a dream is the driving force in the original while mere greed for money, fame, and power is the compelling force in the second. In Arnold's version of *Christmas in Connecticut* we are not offered a hero who has dreams, even dreams of food. Instead he is a recluse park ranger in the mountains of Colorado who has just rescued a boy lost in a snowstorm "on the sixth day." He hates people and has never heard of the famous Elizabeth Blane, the Martha Stewartesque television cook who can't cook. The producer of the television cooking show wants to use the hero to boost ratings. He schemes to have the hero appear in Blane's holiday special. These motivations are much simpler than in the original and money is pushed as the reason or excuse for nearly every character, including the hero, who needs the payoff he will get for appearing on television to rebuild his mountain cabin.

The erasure of the dream from the movie remake is significant. Now, the one creative factor that seemed to motivate a whole range of behaviors, from compassionate to deceitful to silly, was replaced by one unambiguous motivation, greed. The proposition of the dream as a force that can compel many different scenarios is gone. When one disgruntled character in Arnold's version of *Christmas in Connecticut* asks at the dinner table, "Do you dream in black-and-white or in color?" he could be asking whether you buy into the philosophy of the Barbara Stanwyck version or Arnold's remake.

Arnold really magoos us in this remake, weaving a tale that

convinces us of the possibility of a perfected life despite lies, denial of the past, and outright greed. The goal is not to live Arnold's life or even the life depicted in the movie. The goal is not to be Arnold but to live a life well directed by Arnold. The rule of this life-lived-well is "stay hungry," which has been the driving force throughout Arnold's careers. "Stay hungry" states that you need to constantly create new goals and desires and never be satisfied with the accomplishment of previous goals. So the achievement of what appears to be the good life is merely a momentary marker of success, one step in an endless pursuit.

*Christmas in Connecticut* becomes the perfect vehicle for staying hungry: The world is hungry for the life Elizabeth Blane represents yet she is not really married, does not really have the lovely children and grandchildren she talks about, and does not live on a warm, homey farm in Connecticut. The famous cook cannot prepare a proper meal without her assistant and none of the food prepared for her television program is edible anyway. The constructed nature of her reality is emphasized by the hordes of technicians who descend on the set the moment the cameras stop rolling. Everyone is hungry for something even though they seem to have it all, and it is by staying hungry that they seem to be vibrant and alive if needy folks.

By eliminating the dream as the structuring device for the film and replacing it with the stay-hungry motif, Arnold redirects our attention in a way that does not threaten his role as the unachievable model for the good American life. But real dreams, not ones concocted in a faux home, have a way of intruding when they are least anticipated, and this provides them with a unique power to challenge such linear, logical models as "stay hungry."

Despite our growing awareness of Schwarzenegger's amazing reach into virtually all aspects of the culture, we were nevertheless surprised—and to be honest, uncomfortable—when he began reaching into our own lives via actual dreams. It was one thing to have encounters with people who used Schwarzenegger metaphors or created odd Arnold connections like the one to "Christmas in Connecticut" at the airport. It was another thing to dream about Arnold Schwarzenegger more than 200 times in little over a decade, to expect to encounter him while asleep, and to find in these dreams a chance to offer an alternative version of an Arnold-saturated world.

There is no way to erase Arnold from the American scene, from America's common knowledge, from the American language, or from the American Dream. There is no way to keep teachers from using him as an example to punctuate their lessons or children from imitating him when they accomplish something by striking a bodybuilder pose. But it is possible to look at dream narratives about Arnold and see in them a series of choices about how to reinterpret or challenge his dominance of the American imagination. The "stay hungry" motto of *Christmas in Connecticut* can be challenged by the motto "dream on," but only with a thorough understanding of what Arnold dreams are and what they can do.

What crept up on us and took us by surprise were the dreams we began to have about our research subject—dreams that were violent, erotic, funny, absurd, and occasionally disturbing.

### LOUISE'S DREAM 2/1/91

Arnold makes a muscle and I touch it to see how soft his skin was (not to see how hard the muscle was). His skin was amazingly soft. He gave me a lips-barely-touching kiss to prove his lips were soft too. We look out the window and hanging from the tree was the black panther from the movie *Cat People*.

The dreams provided a parallel narrative for our research, an alternative way for us to consider ideas and issues that were hard to bring up in the logical, linear world of everyday life.

### LOUISE'S DREAM 9/24/96

There is a bear trying to break into the house. Then Arnold Schwarzenegger is trying to break in. I regretfully stab him in the stomach with a pie spatula.

This first dream Michael had at the beginning of 1991 suggested a plan for approaching the study of Arnold Schwarzenegger and it provided a place for dreams in that research strategy. Dreams were one piece of an extensive puzzle that had many interrelated pieces. The collected samples from all the areas Arnold dominated—movies, the news, bodybuilding, politics, fitness, and now dreams—all pointed to a cultural phenomenon that in many ways had not been seen before.

### MICHAEL'S DREAM 1/28/91

Arnold Schwarzenegger comes to my door and says, "I hear you are doing a book about me." He then tells me that Maria Shriver thought that she could find out about him by peeling away his layers like an onion. But he says that the only way anyone will really find out about him is by breaking him into little pieces.

Dreaming eventually became our metaphor and model for connecting the disparate aspects of our research on Arnold Schwarzenegger. It is an appropriate and useful approach because it echoes the basic form of our information-laden, postindustrial, postmodern, millennium-straddling culture. With their incongruous connections, indeterminable authors, rapid shifts in time and place, fluidity of ideas and images, emphasis on metamorphosis, nonhuman protagonists, and innumerable border crossings,[2] both the dreams and our weblike culture have complex and intertwined ways of addressing knowledge about Arnold.

### MICHAEL'S DREAM 2/6/93

I was dreaming that Louise had found in a novelty shop a 78 rpm record of Arnold singing Elvis songs—one side was "Love Me Tender" and the other was "Jailhouse Rock," which, she told me, when you played it backward, was also the "preamble" to *Mein Kampf*.

One thing we could see was that the details of these dreams reflected lines of thought we were not achieving while awake. Dreams introduced the element of the irrational and the uncontrollable into academic research that, by tradition, favored order and demanded the rational. Whether this was good or bad, it was still a fact that had something to say about Arnold's reach and how those touched by him found ways to resist and deny him.

### LOUISE'S DREAM 3/20/91

Arnold Schwarzenegger is sitting at my kitchen table. I say to him flirtatiously, "You know we are writing a book about you but we haven't been able to admit it face to face." I tell him I am interested in the President's Council on Physical Fitness. I show him something on a small piece of paper, which he gets up from the table to look at over my shoulder. I know he is looking down my cleavage and I am pleased.

These dreams weren't news items whose veracity could be checked; they weren't fitness regimes whose effectiveness could be tested; they weren't political schemes whose fallout could be measured. What are dreams and what do they tell us about the waking world? If the subject of your study were, say, plant genetics, and you had one or two dreams about killer tomatoes, your dreams might be little more than an odd curiosity or the reflection of hard work, the results of thinking intensively and creatively about your subject.

### MICHAEL'S DREAM 3/3/91
Arnold invites Louise to watch his workout. She brings my video camera. His workout consists of filling out two intricate columns of numbers in a ledger book on a wide table. It looks like a scene from Charles Dickens' A Christmas Carol. When he is finished he says, "Ta da! Debt is now profit!"

Celebrity dreams are a little more complex. Wayne Koestenbaum, when he was studying Jackie Kennedy, had two dozen dreams about her, and he thought this was both telling and delightful. His Jackie dreams, like many celebrity dreams, are based on "imaginary complicity," as if the celebrities reveal that they need us as much as we need them.[3] Dreams about members of Britain's Royal Family have been interpreted as entertainment for the working class;[4] dreams of Madonna have been seen as an indication of the "private language between women."[5] Revealing the seductive nature of celebrity dreams, Koestenbaum both warned and enticed, "If you follow her [Jackie O], in your imagination," he wrote, "she will take you miles away from your original destination."[6] Since 1991, our nighttime tour guide has been Arnold Schwarzenegger, and the 200-plus dreams we have had about him have become a source of endless fascination, confusion, and inspiration. Where was he taking us, how was he misguiding us, and why did he need this "imaginary complicity"?

### LOUISE'S DREAM 7/22/91

I had won a contest to spend the day with Arnold. We were in a shopping mall riding up an escalator and everyone was staring at us, but more at me than at Arnold. Arnold is awkward around people so I am trying to make him comfortable. We stop at a machine that sells postage stamps and Arnold gets enthusiastic like a little kid. He wants to buy one of the stamps that has him on it. I fumble for change and when the stamp comes out I slip and fall on the ground. Arnold is delighted with the stamp. I introduce him to Tony Randall with whom I share a bedroom but not a romantic relation. Tony is hanging down from the upper bunk on our bunkbeds. Tony says, "Hi, I'm Tony Randall. I'm in *M. Butterfly*." Arnold is trying not to make mistakes as we meet and talk to people. I say to him, "That's my job—to make you comfortable."

It turns out that the dreams are evidence of one of the few areas where Arnold Schwarzenegger is out of control in the American imagination. In 1990, British writer Wendy

Leigh produced an unauthorized biography of Arnold that she says Arnold made every effort to stop and keep out of the public eye.[7] This direct control of his image is something even Arnold can't accomplish in dreams.

### LOUISE'S DREAM 5/2/91

I was in a bookstore and the copies of Arnold's biographies that I ordered had come in. But some woman picked them up off the desk and walked out with them. I chased her and chased her and asked her friends where she was. She was in a church playing a guitar, looking at Arnold's book. Then she was at a wild disco that had an electronic message board that displayed the number of foreigners in the United States. I asked her if I could buy one of the books because I had ordered them and was writing a book on Arnold and this was the only thing about him that I hadn't ever read. I knew I was lying but I wanted the book. She agreed to sell one to me.

Many of the approaches to the analysis of dreams that had been so prominent in the last 100 years have proven inadequate for this project. There is no definitive way to analyze or even talk about dreams. Scholars and dream aficionados alike gather each year at the Association for the Study of Dreams conference and seriously debate the value of each of these theories even as they also conduct dream sharing workshops and dress up as their dream characters. Dream analysis has always had a problem with its identity as both a scholarly pursuit and something all of us attempt at some point in our lives.

There are many different approaches to studying dreams. A medical approach to dreams says they are necessary for mental stability but can't explain how and why; an artistic theory says they are a form of inspiration for creative acts; for the occult, the dream can be the remnant or memory of an out-of-body experience; for the religious, the dream is a form of divination and foretells an event or emotional state; for the materialist it is some state of the body (hunger, fear, fatigue) that causes particular types of dreams. But for our purposes, none of these theories explain our dreams in ways that expand our understanding of Arnold's place in American culture or our unique ways of finding him there.

### LOUISE'S DREAM 2/1/91

Arnold and I were talking about women bodybuilders and he wanted to show me what it would look like for me. We were standing in front of a big mirror and Arnold had on his competition trunks. He stood facing the mirror with his hands on his hips and his legs apart. He tilted his head all the way back so that he looked like one of those amusement park displays of bodybuilders that you put your head on and get your picture taken. I put my head where Arnold's used to be and then I put my arms under his and out front like he was a ventriloquist dummy. We laughed.

Our way of looking at dreams is a departure from what may be the most familiar—the psychoanalytic approach, which says dreams are either expressions of wish fulfillment or defense mechanisms for hiding true desires and fears. A psychoanalytical approach interprets dreams and tries to explain their hidden meanings in order to reveal to dreamers their fears and desires. It seemed to us rather unreliable to try to recognize in our Arnold dreams the signs of repressed emotions with hidden symbolic meanings or manifestations of some unconscious desires.

### Michael's dream 3/15/92

Arnold's father sent me a postcard on which was both a swastika and a Star of David. No other marks appeared so I couldn't be sure what it meant. When I called Louise to yell about it she said, "They cancel each other out. Now we have to see if Maria is the Star of David or the swastika." In the dream, this seemed like sheer brilliance.

In a symbolic approach to dreams, for example, it would be fruitful to examine the following dream for hidden content. But there could never be any assurance that the interpretations of those "symbols" would be anything more than another creative narrative and they would have difficulty having these meanings for many other people. But if we take an inventory of the objects and actions and try to imagine how they might be extensions, elaborations, or new categorizations of ideas our research had discovered, the dream becomes more useful to us.

### Michael's dream 6/8/99

I arrive at Louise's house and she is very excited to show me something. We go upstairs to her "inventory room" and Arnold is against the wall, wearing a long T-shirt. I am relieved that I do not see his genitals because I remember that he has gangrene. He is tied to the wall with bungee cords so he can move around a few inches. When he struggles, he bumps into a mobile of glass prisms. The prisms make a kind of clacking noise. I realize this is the sound TV producers use for canned applause. Arnold's mouth is gagged with Louise's gray sweater. One of the sleeves is hanging from his mouth. He looks like an elephant and I start to laugh. Arnold tries to lunge at me but is restrained

by the bungee cords. Louise is hopping around and is saying something but I didn't make sense of it. She grabs my
face in her hands and I notice she has calluses on her finger-
tips and I figure that among her other fields of expertise,
she is probably an accomplished harpist. She makes me
look at her and tells me, "Now we can see his triangles!" I
realize she is referring to the prisms. I look back at Arnold
but I can't see any triangles. I do notice that he has tiny
rainbows on his thighs and figure that's what Louise
meant. Louise is typing up her findings. I try to pour orange
juice into the hanging sleeve so Arnold won't be thirsty.

What connects the objects and actions from the above
dream in any kind of meaningful way is impossible to guess
at first glance. This is a category that is not defined by common properties.[8] It may well be that dreams create categories
following the principle of physical juxtaposition or temporal
similarities, as odd as these may be in the dream world. If we
imagine, then, a category that includes as members bungee
cords, triangular prisms, gray sweaters, orange juice, callused
fingers, and harps, we have a much different kind of interpre-
tive challenge than if we try to see these objects and actions
symbolically. It could be simply that, taken together, they may
be signaling a new category, a unique way of configuring a
particular cluster of information.

Dreaming Arnold is an activity during which our brains
are creatively processing the tremendous amount of information they receive during the day; dreams are where the
mind "digests experience for later use."[9] Dreaming is necessary for patterning and structuring that information, making
it available the next day for use in the real world. So as we
were researching Arnold Schwarzenegger intensively for

days and weeks at a time, it now makes sense that we were so frequently dreaming him. The dreams were the result of our processing Arnold information and fitting it into knowledge schemes we already had. If the dream is a collection of images and ideas that can encourage new ways of thinking and organizing the world, it can offer the observant dreamers some creative alternatives that are not governed by Arnold's "stay hungry" philosophy.

### MICHAEL'S DREAM 11/1/92

I am drinking a cup of coffee and have a number of beer bottles on the table in front of me and I have a terrible hangover. I think I am in a diner until I hear the sound of water running and realize I'm in someone's kitchen. Joan Lunden of *Good Morning America* is making more coffee, cheerfully telling me our interview went very well. I groan and she laughs and says, "Mr. Universe doesn't look much better!" I am suddenly alert and ask her if she means Arnold Schwarzenegger, and she laughs again and says, "Well, since Lee Haney is born again it must be the Terminator." I notice, then, that Joan is topless and when she turns to me, I see that she has enormous pink breasts, which have tattoos on them, but the tattoos turn out to be bite marks. She laughs again and says something like, "He uses his teeth," and I realize or suspect she means Arnold. I notice that her right breast's teeth marks look like a swastika.

Opening up to the possibility that there are many alternative ways to categorize the world is similar to the experience of anthropologists going into a foreign culture and trying to understand how other people make sense of the world by the way they employ their own categories. As George Lakoff explains, "people around the world categorize things in ways that both boggle the Western mind and stump Western linguists and anthropologists."[10] He gives an example from Australia where a category included the following things: women, anything connected with water or fire, bandicoots, dogs, platypus, echidna, some snakes, some fishes, most birds, fireflies, scorpions, crickets, the stars, shields, some spears, some trees. The category is of women, fire, and dangerous or fighting things, but that does not mean that women are dangerous or that the animals listed are considered feminine or that they all fight. Instead Lakoff shows that categories don't have to contain things we find similar in our own culture, only that the grouping somehow makes sense culturally, mythologically, or religiously to the people using the category. There are no "natural" categories but only ones that we as cultural creatures create to invent our worlds.

### MICHAEL'S DREAM 6/6/92

Arnold is demonstrating sign language for the deaf to a crowd of admirers in the parking lot of a grocery store across the street from my house.

The fact that Arnold Schwarzenegger was the single-most recurring element in all of our dreams reinforced for us, again and again, that the constellation of Arnold-related phenomena fits into the culture in innumerably diverse ways. In the aforementioned dream, Louise's "inventory room" becomes a central member of the category created by the dream. As such, it suggests that the various dream-elements are part of a collection that must be studied precisely *as a* collection rather than as separate symbols pointing to something else.

We have found, in considering the many dreams we have had about Arnold, that a "category analysis" yields much more interesting and productive results. We employ categorization when we reason, perform mundane or important actions, speak, listen, write, or do just about anything. Lakoff explains, "Without the ability to categorize, we could not function at all, either in the physical world or in our social and intellectual lives. An understanding of how we categorize is central to any understanding of how we think and how we function, and therefore central to an understanding of what makes us human."[11]

### LOUISE'S DREAM 6/16/91

Arnold and I are at home early in the evening of the awards dinner at the Simon Wiesenthal Center. Arnold is playing with my little brother and sister, who appear to be about 5 years old but in reality are in their 30s. My sister is in a wheelchair but oddly every once in a while she gets up and walks around. My brother was a thalidomide baby but at one point he sprouts new arms. Arnold is looking very thin, then he suddenly changes into different people—the old, consumptive man (Michael Jeeter) in the Broadway show *Grand Hotel*, then the cadet in *Red Dawn* (Patrick Swayze). But the cadet was bald except for a weird tuft of hair on his head. Then Arnold was hiding in the top of a closet and suddenly drops out. He was wearing several layers of nice suits and coats. He is not wearing the tuxedo he needs for dinner. I am hoping he asks me to the dinner. I realize I will have to go rent a gown.

Consider the dream above and the seemingly disparate elements that populate it. Patrick Swayze's apocalyptic movie *Red Dawn* came out the same year, 1984, as Arnold's *The Terminator.* Swayze had already appeared in a Hans and Franz routine on *Saturday Night Live,* connecting him in more than one way directly to Arnold. In the irrational environment of the dream, the other elements taken together serve to concretize a set of misgivings about Arnold, and about our culture's acceptance of such things as universal models of fitness regardless of one's physical condition. In this dream, one of the things that becomes more concrete is the disturbing intersection of Arnold's seemingly wonderful work with the Special Olympics and the implicit suggestion that everyone ought to be willing and able to compete in some sort of competitive athletic pursuit. That Louise dreamed of her brother and sister as disabled and, therefore, potential Special Olympic participants is connected to the fact that these were also the kinds of children who would have been destroyed in Nazi Germany *because* they were deformed and unfit.

The Simon Wiesenthal award shocked us when we heard about it because we were aware of Arnold's rumored admiration of some aspects of the Nazi past. Yet Wendy Leigh had been successfully sued for stating the National Socialist affiliations of Arnold's father even though, right before this awards ceremony, Arnold had commissioned the Wiesenthal Center to see if his father's membership was true. They confirmed it.

The interesting thing for us was to recognize in the act of dreaming the making and remaking of categories. This creative action, performed by the sleeping mind, is in many ways as important as the analyses one makes in waking moments. Any composite that takes place in the dream, any juxtaposition of elements that creates new images or ideas is significant because it is evidence of the making of knowledge—even if we don't always understand it. It's just like reading a book or going to a movie; it's another mechanism for bringing images, concepts, texts, and sounds together to create new ways of fathoming the world. It is also a way to animate a design for a tableau, to bring to life a scenario that had never even existed before. Finding, through dreams, new ways to animate Arnold and to juxtapose him with a host of strange "props" also taught us new ways to track his contagiousness in American culture.

### MICHAEL'S DREAM 9/23/99

I am waiting in line at a book signing. Charles Dickens has been successfully "cloned" and is signing the reissued edition of *A Tale of Two Cities*. The guy in line in front of me is bragging that he has a copy of the original edition by the "original Dickens." His friend is an old man with terrible breath who keeps coughing to the side, which happens to be where I am standing. I say to him, "Cover your mouth when you cough!" and he looks at me with annoyance. His younger friend looks at me and says, "That's how you talk to Walter Benjamin?" I am shocked to find that Walter Benjamin [a famous philosopher/thinker from the early and mid-twentieth century] is still alive and catch myself as I almost say so. The young friend is waiting for me to say something, but Benjamin starts to collapse. His friend can't lift him, and I try to help but Benjamin is incredibly heavy. I wonder if his having lived so long has increased his "governing gravity." The friend and I are sort of holding Benjamin up by his armpits, but he is slipping out of our grasp. His shirt is very sweaty and I am worried that I will not be able to find a place in Manhattan to wash my hands. The Dickens clone stands up to see what is going on at the back of his book signing line, and I see that he has Charles Dickens's body but Arnold Schwarzenegger's face. Walter Benjamin's friend notices me staring at Dickens/Schwarzenegger and says, "They all look like that." I realize he means that all the human clones have turned out looking like Arnold. I suddenly "remember" that there is a black clone of me living in Rwanda. I try to remember if he has Arnold's face as well.

We could say that the dream is the brain's attempt to create a somewhat coherent story out of firing neurons, stored metaphors, persistent visual images, meaningful symbolic associations, emotional baggage, chemical floods, neural reactions, and the events and emotions of our busy lives. If it reflects any need, it is the need to give "narrative order"[12] to the chaos of overwhelming experiences. When we are researching Arnold Schwarzenegger, the dreams have to process the entire complex of Arnold images and experiences that we have accumulated.

Dream theorist Bert States writes, "My hunch is that dreams may be our clearest window into this whole process,"[13] "the process of "seeing ourselves think."[14] The dream does this by creating connections between old and new information, between bits of information whose links may be more intuitive than explicit. The dream creates new metaphors that forge connections we might normally resist as they exercise their "freedom to confuse categories."[15] It is, he states, "the brain doing what it does best without the impediment of actuality."[16] States calls the dream a metaphor machine, and shows how we are "used to thinking in chains of resemblance both in and out of dreams."[17]

These new connections created by the dream process become part of the logic by which we make sense of new experiences, new information. They affect the ways we organize, categorize, and interpret the real, tangible world. It is these metaphors, created silently and while we are asleep, that let us navigate the complexities of culture. Most of us don't remember our dreams, but these dream metaphors, these illogical and creative connections, still have an effect.

### MICHAEL'S DREAM 4/4/93

I am eating an apricot that I have found on Dan Rather's counter. I am not sure why I am in Dan Rather's house, but I walk around as though I am a welcome guest. There are other guests, all of whom either are sipping wine from huge goblets or are eating sloppy-looking sandwiches. I walk to the large glass sliding doors, which look out onto the ocean. I am watching a couple romping on the beach, getting more and more passionate. I suddenly have binoculars, which have a jar of macadamia nuts hanging from them, so I have to use them carefully. I look out to the beach and see, now, that Arnold Schwarzenegger is making out with the woman who plays Roseanne Barr's sister on the *Roseanne* TV show. I want to tell the other guests that Arnold is out there, but I notice that one of the guests is Maria Shriver. She notices me and waves and then looks sad. It dawns on me, for the first time, that I might be someone famous. I look back out to the beach and am startled that Arnold is now at the glass doors. The woman is gone. Arnold is naked and I notice that his neck seems to have rope-burn marks. He waves to me and I hear him saying, "Hi, Dan!" For a second, I am panicking, thinking that I am Dan Rather and why didn't I know this all along? Then I realize that Dan Rather is behind me and Arnold was waving to him as though I weren't even there. Suddenly I realize that Arnold and Dan Rather are lovers and that Arnold had been trying to make Dan jealous by making out with Roseanne's TV sister. I wonder if Maria Shriver knows this, but I see that she is already gone. Dan Rather looks effeminate and I notice that his shoes are purple with rather high heels.

Bert States prods us to remember that "if dreams were primarily instruments of communication, most dreams would be useless."[18] Because they are unconsciously constructing new categories and metaphors, we can't hope to "read" dreams like we can a poem or understand their point like we can with a joke. But we can regard each dream as one more installation in a vast exhibit our minds are always creating. In these installations, real and imaginary parts are set in motion together to form a living tableau. Arnold's role(s) in these tableaus, and our own "costarring" roles, bring to life one-of-a-kind dramatic enactments of information. The job of dreams is to take a sampling from all our life experiences, all our memories, and all our emotions and have them appear together in a series of images. In this sense, the dream is "a combinatory activity."[19] If we wake up and remember those images, we construct them into a nearly linear narrative so that we can make sense of them; they are like homemade movies, private narratives acted on public screens if we remember and choose to exchange them with others. When they are remembered, and recounted as these are recounted here, dreams become a form of cultural exchange. The compulsion of humans to share stories and create meanings is especially compelling with dreams that make no sense and need the help of others to put them into a socially comprehensible context.

### MICHAEL'S DREAM 12/3/94

My poetry class is meeting in the deep end of an Olympic-style swimming pool. We are all treading water with our special plastic-wrapped books and papers floating in the water around us. Our heads gently bob up and down as people take turns reading aloud. Arnold Schwarzenegger is in the class and as the students take turns reading, he makes a more and more derisive face, which I find enormously distracting. At one point, a student is reading and occasionally her mouth dips down below the surface and her words are slightly gurgled. Arnold snorts and lets out a huge belch, mostly below the surface. It results in a large air bubble that floats into the center of our circle and bursts, stinking of old beer. Arnold laughs and says, "Now dat's poetry!"

Through narratives, whether they are dream narratives or have some other motivation, we tell stories in order to make sense of the world, to make some sense of who we are, why we act, and where we are going. Narratives stimulated by iconic characters like Arnold Schwarzenegger are generated not by individuals alone but by individuals in conjunction with their culture and with other storytellers. They help us both transmit and exchange the realities that define our shared world. If, as Hayden White suggests, "To raise the question of the nature of narrative is to invite reflection on the very nature of culture and, possibly, on the nature of humanity itself,"[20] then dream narratives occupied by Arnold Schwarzenegger can tell us much about how we organize our reality. The impetus for these narratives and the dreams that inspired them is the human need to connect, communicate, and make meanings. It is the drama, as Donna Haraway has called it, of "touch across Difference," the desire to have contact with others in order to confirm our own humanity[21] combined with the fantasy of perfect communication and the "immediate sharing of meanings" that is always desired when humans come face-to-face.[22]

Arnold has appeared in our dreams and, in the waking narratives we have exchanged about them, in a striking variety of roles. This is not just a sign of his versatility in our dreams but his versatility in real life as it has always been easy to imagine or observe Arnold taking on any of these roles. For us, the dream mechanism, when it came to defining Arnold, only succeeded in reinstating his idea that he was the largest man in the world, able to encompass all our ideas and notions about him. What these dreams have done is test out Arnold in different roles, different from the ones he has offered us. It has enabled us to direct him so that in this laboratory of our minds we can see what would happen to this omnipresent and omnipotent icon if we, as dreamers as well as members of the culture he has overwhelmed, could control what he did and what he does to us.

Arnold has been a lover:

### LOUISE'S DREAM 4/17/94

I am in the house that I grew up in. I have a newborn baby girl. She is wrapped tight in swaddling clothes. I lay her on a couch between the crack of pillows so she won't fall off.

She is so clever she uses her head to spin herself around and around. Arnold is there. He picks her up in delight and raises the bundle in the air and laughs. When he puts her down I say something like, "You don't remember me." He leans in close to me and whispers, "I remember everything. Every detail. From the very first time I saw you." I realize he means he knows every thought, every dream, every thing I have ever done about him. I look at him and we kiss, lightly at first and then passionately. He stays with me in the house for two weeks and ignores all his work, including a film listed on a bulletin board that he is directing and costarring in with Sylvester Stallone. Finally he has to leave to straighten everything out. We go out the front door and as he gets in his car, he is recognized by the people in the neighborhood. It is the day after Valentine's Day.

A computer technician:

### MICHAEL'S DREAM 10/27/96
Arnold is fixing my computer by installing a "new rubric" into the monitor. I tell him that he may be thinking, mistakenly, that I have a German computer. He laughs and tells me, "All computers are German!"

And a slot machine repairman:

### LOUISE'S DREAM 9/22/02
Michael and I are in Las Vegas playing slot machines. The machines are not close together but about 2 feet apart. Both our machines break and Arnold Schwarzenegger comes over to fix them. He opens Michael's machine and

presses a button so he gets free games that start spinning with the machine cover open. We understand that we will not be able to win money in these free games, but just will be able to watch. On my machine Arnold opens the cover and takes out grapes, which he pops into my mouth. Michael looks over at me and gives me a funny look.

He has been an aggressive consumer:

### LOUISE'S DREAM 2/19/03

Arnold was shopping with his "Finesse" credit card, which apparently is a very elite credit card. He was trying to show up some military general he just met so he spent $15,000. A clerk at the store said, "People with the Finesse card do that!"

He has been a movie star limited by conditions we set:

### LOUISE'S DREAM 7/16/96

Arnold was making his movie comeback. I was able to see the daily rushes by rolling my son's carriage into the screening room. The movie involved Arnold as some type of tough warrior but his entrance in the film has him as a man in a white diaper. The movie was opening the next day in New York where I was for only a day. The ads said it was going to be the biggest premiere since *Eraser* and everyone would try to crash it. There was a promotion—they would let in some men who came dressed as the man in the white diaper. I was going to tell Michael to try it.

He has also been a bowling opponent:

### Michael's dream 4/15/95

I dreamed I was watching a bowling tournament. My brother (who actually was, long ago, a semiprofessional bowler) and his team were waiting impatiently for their competition. My brother was drinking lots of Budweisers and looking toward me, as though I had something to do with the immediate problem. The opposing team arrived—a bunch of loud-mouthed hooligan types. One was Marc Gastineau, the other two were nondescript musclebound Frenchmen (I remembered, in the dream, "Oh yeah, the French are supposed to be great bowlers") and Arnold Schwarzenegger. My brother didn't look at all surprised—in fact, I don't think he knew who he was bowling against—though he and his teammates all recognized Gastineau, who was, as he usually did as an active football player and after, acting like a jerk. Arnold had ridiculously ornate bowling shoes and wore a high-tech half-glove for his bowling hand. His ball had been specially made and was, as the guys were all commenting, an unbelievable 50 pounds (I think the heaviest normal bowling ball is 16 pounds). My brother Jed started and got a strike, as did all the first framers. Arnold predictably crushed the pins with his shot, and immediately ordered a round of beers for both teams. He yelled to the waitress, "Hey, vooman, bring uss some beeeuhs. And no mawr ahf dis pooosy shit," as he tossed a huge handful of empty Bud bottles. The dream shifted to where the tournament was, I guess, over. I don't know how it turned out, but Arnold was furious with one of his own teammates who was evidently arguing that bowling wasn't a fitness sport. Arnold kept saying, "Loook at dese biceps, you asshole!" For some reason, Marc Gastineau spotted me in the "audience" and was furious. He hurled his beer bottle at me.

And a hero:

### LOUISE'S DREAM 10/30/01

News had leaked out that Bill Gates had been killed by terrorists. But the story never appeared in any newspaper. I
was in San Francisco to check it out. There was a crowd of
people and all of a sudden the Arabs in white robes and
turbans filtered out of the crowd and surrounded everyone.
I escaped and came upon a little boy lost in the desert. We
could see a HumVee approaching from far away. It turned
out to be Arnold. He opens the door for us to get in but he
doesn't stop. I shove the little boy in and jump in myself as
the car drives by. Arnold knows who I am.

And a villain:

### MICHAEL'S DREAM 7/1/98

My brother has gotten a job overseas and calls me from the
plane. He tells me, in a stupid-sounding German accent,
"I'll be a Bavarian!" I then hear choking sounds and somehow I know that Arnold Schwarzenegger was on the plane
and overheard my brother and is now choking the life out
of him.

In one dream, Arnold was a virulent homophobe:

### MICHAEL'S DREAM 7/19/95

Arnold and I are interviewing actors for recasting the
*Bonanza* television show. Arnold is aloof and after each
interview mutters to me (about the actor), "Faggot!" He sits
up suddenly when Bruce Lee comes in. Arnold says, "You're
dead!" I am shocked. Lee cannot speak but does a flourish

of karate moves, and Arnold stands up and shoots him. Lee is dead (again). Arnold says to me, "Fucking faggot!" and tosses his pistol onto Lee's corpse.

In another, our private groper!

### LOUISE'S DREAM 6/6/00
Arnold is at a vacation house we own. I decide after several days to show him the scrapbooks I have made about him. I say, "Arnold, it is time." I go upstairs to get them, afraid he will leave. When I get back I sit next to him on a couch/bed. We are watching some runner on TV who happened to be my date at the house earlier in the week. Arnold says, "How did he get to be here?" He was screwing the Warden's daughter and one day decided to enter the race we were watching him in and that he won. All this time, Arnold is holding my breast. He asks if I mind. I say, "No." He asks if I find it unusual. I say, "No."

In another, he was a family member:

### LOUISE'S DREAM 10/7/02
I was at a voting place. There was a list on the wall. Arnold came up to look at it and walked away looking forlorn and kind of hunched over. I said to him, "That's okay because we are cousins."

Dreams frequently bring new experiences together with old, creating new metaphors and reference points in the process, refining and reorganizing our categories.[23] Dreams, then, add variety to the world. They help us create connections between ideas that seem unrelated. They stimulate the imagination, encourage creative thinking, and help us incubate the unthinkable and make it comprehensible. Without dreams we would be stuck in old ways of thinking; without dreams we would be passive recipients of a world created by others; without dreams our minds could not do the work of thinking for themselves. Maybe that is exactly what some people are afraid of.

Dreams, the actual ones that take place during sleep, are not particularly valued in everyday American life. There are certainly people who meet to exchange and analyze dream narratives, and dream books are still commonly used in some ethnic groups, providing easy interpretations of dream images and lucky numbers that can be played in both state and illegal numbers games and lotteries. Some psychics, mystics, and astrologers use dreams to foretell the future or provide personal advice on love, money, and business.

Dreaming and the discussion of dreams may be considered a marginal American act but it is certainly not because dreams are rare or uncommon. Dream researchers estimate that all adults, whether they remember it or not, dream each and every night. Four or five times each sleep period, electrochemical operations and neuron activity get translated into a set of images and impressions known as a dream. Whether a dream researcher believes this process is random or, on the other hand, subject to the unconscious wishes and desires of the dreamer, it nevertheless is a common activity in the body and minds of all human beings. People may not remember their dreams, but they cannot deny that they dream.

We know other people dream about Arnold Schwarzenegger, just not as frequently as we do. Colleagues and students that we have discussed this work with have then had dreams about Arnold after our exchanges. Dream Web sites include Arnold dreams as do fan sites. But taken in isolation, one or two dreams is not the same as 200 and it is our interest in how Arnold has permeated the American imagination that is the common thread in all our dreams about him.

America itself was the result of a dream. America was dreamed into existence over 225 years ago and we have referred to the bundle of values, qualities, and possibilities of this relatively young country as "The American Dream." The original American Dream was a guiding principle for the founding of the nation. As Martin Luther King described it in his famous "The American Dream" speech (commonly called "I have a dream…"), the dream is a simple but elusive one in which all people are created equal and have an equal chance to pursue life, liberty, and happiness.[24] Greill Marcus reminds us that we are still uncertain about what it means to be an American—given our history of crimes, wars, and prejudice but also hope, optimism, and cultural complexity—and that when we are presented with a vision of ourselves, "We feel ennobled and a little scared, or very scared, because we are being shown what we could be, because we realize what we are, and what we are not. We pull back."[25]

The original concept of "The American Dream" has been replaced by a commercial version, very much like the dream of the perfect life depicted in Arnold's remake of *Christmas in Connecticut*. This American dream is now a wish or a desire for some material goods or status that is currently unattainable. It is the wish to be Elizabeth Lane/Blane, to be Martha Stewart before the stock market improprieties. The trajectory through an American life is a series of steps for fulfilling this "dream" and this path places all Americans in competition with each other. This represents a dramatic and damaging change in the concept. As the Web site for the Center for the New American Dream states:

> The American dream. What do those words mean to us?
>
> For our parents and grandparents, the American dream meant hope—an unshakeable belief that happiness and security were truly possible. They knew they had a unique opportunity to make a better life for themselves and their families. That dream still exists. But these days, it has some competition.
>
> The original focus on security and personal well-being is giving way to an obsession with "more." More work. More material goods. Bigger cars, bigger houses... bigger everything.[26]

It is not surprising, given this new definition, that Arnold Schwarzenegger has been called the perfect embodiment of the American Dream more times than anyone can count. It is indeed the perfect role for him: The American Dream is a comprehensive image of the good life, complete with fame, financial success, political power, and endless resources.

### MICHAEL'S DREAM 8/21/91

For a fleeting second, I stood on a riverbank and watched Arnold commandeer a train upon the water! Arnold is now seated, postured nearly like Rodin's *Thinker*. He looks up at me with a weary face—almost sorrowful—and says (not necessarily to me, but to the general air), "You have to love somebody. (pause) I don't know who I love."

It should also come as no surprise that Arnold Schwarzenegger has no interest in the dreams that come during sleep. Arnold said about such dreams, "Some people train themselves to wake up and write them down. Then what? What do you do with that information?"[27] Dreams are too much outside the control of someone who has been called the Master Planner, a control freak, and the ultimate image machine. Schwarzenegger told Studs Terkel in 1980 that "When I was ten years old, I had a dream of being the best in the world in something. When I was fifteen, I had a dream that I wanted to be the best bodybuilder in the world, and the most muscular man. It was not only a dream I dreamed at night. It was also a daydream. It was so much in my mind that I felt it had to become a reality. It took me five years of hard work. Five years later, I turned this dream into reality and became Mr. Universe, the best-built man in the world."[28] This kind of dreaming is much different than the dreams of a restless, creative sleeper. Arnold's reported "dreams" resemble ambitions more than sleeping dreams, and articulating them as actual goals obliterates any creative logic they could have been suggesting.

The only recurring real dream that Arnold remembers having after his youth has to do with the shame and confusion that come from a lack of control. Schwarzenegger reports this dream: "Before I start shooting a film, I sometimes have dreams where you're out there lying totally naked in a forest, and you have no clothes, and you hear somewhere, 'In two minutes we roll.' All of a sudden the lights come on, and you say, 'Wait a minute, what scene are we doing? Why am I lying out here and where's the clothes? What are the lines?' I'm caught totally off guard, like I wasn't prepared."[29] While Arnold may have believed that his "emperor's clothes" dream was about the particulars of moviemaking anxiety, it is probably closer to the truth to see even this dream report as Arnold's way of using the metaphor of dreaming as a means for conveying the sense of chaos that making a movie provokes and that he temporarily does not control.

Dreams are far more obedient to the laws of the cinema than they are to the rationalized orderings of everyday life. Hollywood has often been called the "Dream Machine" because it produces public versions of the private dream. This is not surprising since the cinema elaborates many of the dream's mechanisms, including identification with the image, the articulation of desire, the manipulation of space and time, the condensation of many concepts into one loaded image/vehicle, and the displacement of meaning from its rightful place to a substitute one. The connection between dreams and motion pictures is long-standing. While dreams are presumably private and films have public circulation, they both nevertheless activate similar effects—they present alternative realities that can be used as reference points for everyday decisions, actions, and motivations. The effect of film stories is to provide narratives of what can happen with certain kinds of boundary crossings. What every American Hollywood film must do is provide a resolution to that crossing, but dreams do not have to do that.

### MICHAEL'S DREAM 12/7/94

I am a driver's education instructor and the car has run out of coolant. The student says he will help with the "torque" but instead runs off, inexplicably howling in pain. I am busy under the hood and see Arnold's reflection, somehow, in the oily metallic surface of the engine block. I wheel around and discover that he is actually shorter than I am and has a long handlebar moustache. I realize, then, that in all his films and public appearances, this moustache has been bleached and treated with "poly-ozone" so that it is more or less invisible. I am excited to call Louise to see if I have learned some incredibly secret thing or if she knew all along and assumed I did, too. Arnold seems to be reading my mind, and smiles. He says something like, "You didn't really think I'd shave it off for every film, did you?" I laugh as though he has said something funny but I see that he was not joking. When I start to speak, he pounds his fist into his other hand and back-flips away from me.

Despite his denial of many nocturnal dreams, Arnold is a persistent and prolific user of the term "dream" (as is his wife, Maria Shriver). The glossy *American Dream* magazine utilizes almost all the meanings of the term he has repeated religiously through his life. The dream is a vision, a Master Plan for the future that assures that things get done; the dream is a desire, like his desire for a woman just like Maria, that can get fulfilled; the dream is a goal and the individual is responsible for achieving that goal and making the dream a reality; the dream is an atmosphere of the culture, an optimism that encourages the realization of the other forms of the dream; the dream is a place like California, where anything is possible; the dream is a fantasy, like his dream to come to America and star in a movie. When he was actually asked to be in his first movie it definitely "seemed like a dream." How do these goal-directed "dreams" contrast with real dreams? Real dreams don't have goals. Real dreams are not under our conscious control. Bert States writes, "The dream… is thought as it occurs, not as it has been perfected in another part of the brain";[30] dreams are, according to States, the "essence of imperfection."[31]

## MICHAEL'S DREAM 3/3/91

We are at the Arnold Schwarzenegger Classic bodybuilding competition in Columbus, Ohio. Louise is using a pay phone while I photograph Lou Ferrigno eating fruit salad. As I change the roll of film, Lou says he has to go—his words are strangely minced. Evidently he is trying to tell me something about Arnold. As I realize this and start to question him, Louise returns and says, "You won't believe this!" She has just gotten off the phone with "Eleanor Weider," the wife of the bodybuilding entrepreneur, and she has agreed to be interviewed for our book. As "bait," she told Louise that "Arnold IS married, yes, although the preacher never would have done it had he KNOWN!" Louise thinks this means that the preacher would never have allowed a Kennedy-clan member to marry a staunch Republican. But Ferrigno, having heard this conversation, laughs (his laugh sounds like it is in slow motion) and says, "That preacher broke his vows when he married those two." Louise asks, "What do you mean?" Ferrigno answers, "Maria is no woman! Look at her cheeks!" Later, Louise and I are talking with various bodybuilders and they are giggling over the fact that Maria is a transsexual. Louise and I panic, fearing that WE have leaked this, and that now Arnold's men will come after us.

Dreams are sensational—in two senses of the word. They are like the tabloids and thus embarrassing in their bizarre constructions and illogical, paranoid references. They are also of the senses, without many of the inhibitions of cultural life because there is no one telling you not to do something in your dreams. Dreams cross boundaries (like virtual reality) and this makes some people want to get them under control. *Psychology Today* once featured an article that instructed readers to "repair" their dreams. The authors suggested a "dream therapy" in which the dreamer rewrites "bad dream scripts" to make dreams come out "better."[32]

Beyond the speculations about redirecting dreams is the paranoid possibility that even our dream life can be under an external control. A study of the dreams of 300 citizens of the Third Reich in Germany by Charlotte Beradt in the 1930s provides frightening evidence that even in their dreams people there were afraid to resist the Nazis.[33] Psychologist Bruno Bettelheim, evaluating this evidence, stated that "The regime was successful in forcing even its enemies to dream the kinds of dreams it wanted them to dream: those warning the dreamer that resistance was impossible, that safety lay only in compliance." Beradt found that the "systematic terrorization" of the Nazi regime reflected itself in dreams and that the effective propaganda machine of the Nazi era fulfilled its function even among the sleeping.[34]

Dream training may be the only type of training that Arnold disdains. In his training of the body, Arnold advocates control, rigor, cohesion, growth, development, health, balance, and fitness. Real dreams are the closest thing we have to rejecting this and as a result they are a vibrant source of intellectual and theoretical resistance because they can be wildly imaginative, fragmented, uncontrollable, incoherent, noncumulative, and suspect as commodities for everyday exchange.

### LOUISE'S DREAM 11/17/94

I am at the movies and Arnold and Maria are sitting toward the front of the theatre. There are subtitles to the film (which I believe is one of Arnold's films) but they are going too fast and I can't read them. Some guy, who I think is O. J. Simpson's friend Al Cowlings, is sitting at the side of the theatre playing the guitar. Arnold gets up, walks over to Al, takes his guitar, and walks out with it. Tucked under Arnold's other arm is a violin, which I understand belongs to him. I open the door for Arnold. I also notice that even though this is a movie theatre, no one is eating popcorn in here.

Dreams provide a source of living chaos that always exceeds the previous scope of life and experience. They provide an alternative to our far-too-controlled existence that can be used productively even when put into a comfortable narrative form. The increase in vantage points available through dreams has been reason enough to include them in our work on Arnold. By paying attention to our dreams and their chaos we admit new ideas to our way of making the world. The very narrow appetites and needs we have learned to accept as natural in our waking hours are challenged in dreams. Paying attention to how our minds negotiate and amplify variety in the unnatural world of dreams can be instructive.

Real dreaming seems unnatural and threatening to the goal-oriented—if impossible—American Dream because it puts the body in contact with alternative experiences. The dream, in contrast, engages bodies in decidedly impossible acts including flying, falling without death, metamorphoses, feats of unbelievable strength, and invisibility. The reconstituted American Dream, despite the fact that at least one man, Arnold, seems to have achieved it, currently offers us only disillusionment and failure. What is the consequence of adopting the Arnold Schwarzenegger approach to dreams and abandoning real dream dramas? The consequence is that we forget how to think for ourselves. Instead we take prefabricated "dreams," visions created in a world that always has us looking for the next thing that may not even be there. We are told to stay hungry not for what we ourselves can imagine but for what is fed to us.

Our dreams about Arnold enabled us to rethink the world we were watching, a world that put him at the center and that made him a reference for all types of meanings. Like the Terminator, dreams can't be reasoned with, can't be bargained with, and they absolutely cannot be stopped. As Gaston Bachelard, a French scientist and philosopher of the early twentieth century claimed, "One can study only what one has first dreamed."[35] In his attempts to revalue imagination in scientific thought, Bachelard wanted dreaming—from real nighttime adventure to creative reveries—to be part of the process. His idea was that knowledge is created from the interaction between imaginative thought and experience and that the resulting "poetic image can be the seed of a world"[36] as it has begun to be with these dreams about Arnold Schwarzenegger.

### LOUISE'S DREAM 9/27/03
There were people walking around everywhere carrying clipboards. They were all doing research on Arnold.

# CHAPTER 12

# All We Really Needed to Know Before We Went Out into the World Are the Things We Learned from *Kindergarten Cop*

IN 2000, MARIA SHRIVER wrote a small, intimate book, *Ten Things I Wish I'd Known—Before I Went Out Into the Real World*,[1] that projected her lessons for a worthwhile life. The book offers the refined version of the list that was delivered in a commencement address Shriver gave in 1998 at College of the Holy Cross in Worcester, Massachusetts. Throughout the 2003 California recall campaign, Maria and her husband used many such lists to educate the voters on candidate Arnold's ideas, principles, and accomplishments. The title of Shriver's book recalls the 1986 best-seller that Robert Fulghum published on his list of things he had learned in kindergarten that had guided his life ever since.[2] Four years after Fulghum's life guide, Arnold Schwarzenegger appeared in one of his most popular films, *Kindergarten Cop,* and provided a unique perspective on learning and life as understood from the point of view of participation in kindergarten, the place where we introduce our children to the rites and rules of the educational system.

One of the things that made *Kindergarten Cop* so appealing was that Arnold played a character, Detective John Kimble, who somehow managed to move from hardened L.A. detective to sympathetic teacher in the course of the story. In the process he not only replaced his own original character but filled in the gaps for virtually everything that was missing in the lives around him. The missing parts and their subsequent fulfillment in *Kindergarten Cop* set up Arnold as more than a mere restorer of order and a vanquisher of criminals; he was the Completer, the one without whom entire stories would not make sense.

The gaps and their replacements provide the hole-ridden story with its purpose as well as its structure. Several of the children in the story have missing fathers, including Dominic, who is the child of the criminal that Kimble is seeking; Kimble eventually becomes Dominic's replacement father. Joyce, Dominic's mother, is missing a husband and Kimble becomes Joyce's romantic interest. One little boy in kindergarten has a father who has been beating him. The boy is missing the protection that should have been given him by his parents and by law enforcement; Kimble both provides protection to the little boy and replaces the absent child welfare services and law enforcement procedures by scaring the father away. The elementary school where the Kindergarten Cop goes undercover is missing a kindergarten teacher (who was sent away to make room for the undercover operation); Kimble steps in and becomes one of the school's best teachers, thus also providing the missing model of good teaching for the school. The class of 5-year-olds is missing a mascot, or some kind of warm, fuzzy creature to rally around; Kimble provides the children with his cuddly ferret to pet and adopt.

Detective Kimble's police partner, Phoebe, is missing her lunch because she has been throwing it up from food poisoning. Therefore, she is missing *her* appointment to be the undercover police officer posing as a kindergarten teacher; Kimble rises to the challenge and replaces her. The children in the kindergarten class, who are shown in a chaotic scene when Kimble first arrives, are missing a strong authority figure; Kimble's commanding personality and his use of "tough love" provide just the right admixture of authority and paternal nurturing. Since the same children are also missing discipline, fitness, and purpose, Kimble's militaristic approach to physical fitness, efficiency drills, and chain-of-command inspire the children.

*Kindergarten Cop* sets itself up as a morality tale for the completion of life's inadequacies. Considered in a closely linked triad with Fulghum's and Shriver's books, we see a fascinating set of formulas for living a meaningful life and for filling in the gaps that clearly must be haunting all our existences. Once again connecting a series of "dots," and following Arnold and Maria's campaign lead, what follows are a variety of composite life lessons.

## Lesson 1

FULGHUM: Don't take things that aren't yours.

MARIA: First and foremost: pinpoint your passion.

K-COP: Express your passions even when your girl-friend's child has just disappeared.

When Arnold's character arrives in Astoria, Oregon, he is obligated to go undercover as a kindergarten teacher. His mission is to arrest Crisp, a very bad man who is intent on harming his ex-wife, Joyce, and capturing their son, Dominic. Dominic, a kindergartner, has grown up without a father; his mother has been on the run from Crisp, whose criminal activities had placed her and Dominic in constant danger. Joyce does not consider Dominic to belong at all to Crisp and does her best to give him a safe, healthy life. Kimble gets "involved" with Joyce with the intention of learning where she may be hiding "dirty" money that Crisp had stolen. Joyce starts to fall for Kimble the kindergarten teacher (not knowing that he is really a cop), and Kimble, despite his professional intentions, begins to fall for her, too. When Crisp shows up in Astoria, with his evil mother in tow, he manages to take Dominic from Joyce's house. Kimble shows up a moment too late to catch Crisp, but not too late for Joyce to vent all of her anger and sense of betrayal for Kimble's deception about why he was in Astoria in the first place. As Kimble tries to calm the frantic Joyce, who is terrified that her 5-year-old boy is now in the hands of a truly desperate criminal, the two suddenly kiss passionately, realizing that, in spite of circumstances, they have "pinpointed" true love.

## Lesson 2

FULGHUM: Take a nap every afternoon.
MARIA: No job is beneath you.
K-COP: No job is beyond you if you have a whistle.

Although he collapses in an exhausted heap after the first day of teaching, eventually John Kimble gets his kindergarten brood to become the most efficient, best-behaved, smartest, relationship-savvy group of children at the elementary school. It became clear that the children *liked* having orders barked at them, that they liked responding to the sound of a whistle. One blast tells them to "freeze" or to get a toy and bring it to the carpet. Two blasts is their signal to return the toy submissively to its rightful place without playing with it and then run back to the carpet. The children respond obediently, and Kimble muses, "It works! This is great!" He quickly catches himself, though, and corrects the moment of self-congratulation by announcing: "You are all good deputies." When he has thoroughly worn everyone out with fitness and obedience drills, he commands everyone to lie down on the carpet and to take a nap while he reads to them.

## Lesson 3

FULGHUM: Play fair.
MARIA: Who you work for and with is as important as what you do.
K-COP: Lying is hard work; a ferret helps.

Overcoming his coarse demeanor and pedagogical ineptitude, Kimble manages to persuade everyone that he is a kindergarten teacher. At a restaurant with Joyce, her son Dominic, and Kimble's "sister," Ursula—who is really his police partner Phoebe O'Hara (Pamela Reed)—Kimble tells Joyce that he became a teacher because his mother, father, and brother had all been teachers in Austria. The Austrian custom, he explains, is that the son should follow in the footsteps of his family. At least the custom is true; earlier he had told his partner that his father and brother had been police officers. Soon, he gains everyone's trust, but then he has to tell the lovely, available, and hiding-a-dangerous-secret-of-her-own Joyce the truth, that he and his partner, Phoebe, are cops. Joyce becomes furious, and now has good reason to trust no one, especially in light of the fact that her evil ex-husband now knows where to find her. Eventually, Kimble wins her over. His ferret, about which he lies when he tells the children that "he never bites," ends up biting a criminal, saving Kimble's life.

## Lesson 4

FULGHUM: Say you're sorry when you hurt somebody.
MARIA: Your behavior has consequences.
K-COP: Teach children the importance of being considerate to others by threatening to sever their spinal cords.

While in flight to Oregon to take on the undercover assignment, Kimble and Phoebe are reviewing their case file. Three young children behind them keep kicking the seats, and Kimble is particularly annoyed by this. When he can stand it no longer, he turns to face the three kids and, with pencil in hand, he says, "If you don't stop screwing around back there, this is what I'm going to do to you." At that point he snaps the pencil in half, much to the stunned horror of the children. A corollary lesson: To teach a child the importance of maintaining a healthy diet, lift him up and then drop him. On Kimble's first day of class, he spots a boy sitting with a number of open lunch boxes. Kimble storms over to him, lifts him up, and asks him, "Are these all yours?" The boy shakes his head, no. Exasperated, Kimble lets go, and the boy falls back to the floor. Since this does not recur, we can safely assume that the lesson was successful.

## Lesson 5

FULGHUM: Don't hit people.
MARIA: Be willing to fail.
K-COP: Sometimes you have to hit people.

While waiting to meet the principal on his first day, Mr. Kimble overhears Joyce Palmieri (played by Penelope Ann Miller), another teacher and his future romantic interest, explain to a student that "you shouldn't punch people." It's a lesson Mr. Kimble discovers is insufficient when the crime exceeds having one's hamster poisoned. When one of the young students shows up at school with bruises, Mr. Kimble figures out that the father has been beating his little boy and his wife. After school Mr. Kimble goes out to the father's car and confronts him. When the father does not respond submissively to his warning to stop beating the boy, Mr. Kimble punches the father in the gut. Looking on is the principal, Miss Schlowski (played by Linda Hunt), who, instead of being disturbed at one of her teachers striking a parent—in plain view of students and faculty—is obviously pleased by her newest teacher's masculinity and righteous anger. In her office, later, he apologizes for losing his temper that way in front of the children. She asks with obviously vicarious delight, "What did it feel like to hit that son of a bitch?" Kimble replies, "It felt great." Miss Schlowski is pleased.

## Lesson 6

FULGHUM: Remember... the first word you learned—the biggest word of all—LOOK.

MARIA: Superwoman is dead.... And Superman may be taking Viagra.

K-COP: Boys have a penis. Girls have a vagina.

On Kimble's first day, he tells his new charges, "First I would just like to get to know you." Kimble asks a series of questions, interrupted when a little girl asks to go to the bathroom. As he lets her go, a little boy stands up and announces, "Boys have a penis. Girls have a vagina." Kimble studies the boy very seriously before responding, "Thanks for the tip." It's a bit of anatomical knowledge necessary for men and women, boys and girls, throughout the film and throughout life (both in the film and in reality). Later in the film, Kimble's partner is taught the same information from the same source. The little boy who imparts this wisdom is greeted with the same general laughter, but this time he pumps his fist in triumph. Phoebe looks at Kimble and says, "Well, you taught them the basics." The little boy has successfully sorted male and female for peers and adults alike. It is probably not an accident that we are told that there is a single penis for all boys and a single vagina for all girls since this is the essence of gender sorting.

## Lesson 7

FULGHUM: Live a balanced life—learn some and think some and draw and paint and sing and dance and play and work every day some.

MARIA: Children do change your career (not to mention your entire life).

K-COP: Children will terrify you.

In *Kindergarten Cop,* Kimble must face a classful of children that are so rowdy that the thought of teaching them causes him to start hyperventilating outside the classroom. When he steps into the room at the principal's introduction, he towers over the sitting 5-year-olds who all have to tilt their heads way back to look up at him. He is far taller than their principal who, despite being quite small, is the big boss at the school. Kimble outsizes all the parents, especially the mothers, who look upon him as though he were a god. However, godliness and big muscles are no match against the kindergartners. The moment his back is turned, Mr. Kimble's tiny students erupt into absolute chaos, hurling toys and food and careening around the room at breakneck speed. When Mr. Kimble attempts to regain control by screaming "Shut up!" at the top of his lungs, the children begin, one by one, to sob. Kimble discovers that teaching children is at least as traumatic as chasing and killing bad guys.

## Lesson 8

FULGHUM: Share everything.

MARIA: Marriage is a hell of a lot of hard work.

K-COP: Male kindergarten teachers are either gay or at least willing to share their insights on sex.

After dropping their kindergartners off, a group of mothers stand around gossiping about the new kindergarten teacher. "He's gay!" says one. "What kind of man teaches kindergarten? He's obviously gay!" The second woman says, "A male kindergarten teacher is just not what I'm used to." A third says, "Samantha calls him 'the giant'!" But when the three women spot Kimble and realize that he is their children's teacher, their jaws drop. They are quite obviously struck by his masculine magnificence, and one mother quickly turns away from him so he will not see her. Puzzled, the others ask what she is doing; she tells them that she does not want him to see her without her makeup. When the others remind her that none of them are wearing makeup, her reply provides another important lesson: If you're married, you're allowed to look like a slob.

However, if you are not married, another important lesson applies: Unmarried mothers with good makeup can consult a male kindergarten teacher (whose bodybuilder's physique may have erased any notion that he is gay) about their children's potential gender issues. The one mom who is always (over)made-up approaches Kimble before class begins and asks to talk about her son. Flirtatiously she leans over the desk and tells him that she has a small problem. Her son has been acting a little strange lately: "It seems he is becoming a little obsessed with playing with dolls. It's weird." Kimble responds, "I think I can help you with that." The mother seems somewhat relieved when Kimble explains that "He uses the dolls to look up girls' skirts. I caught him doing it yesterday." Kimble has solved one sexual identity crisis but then refuels another: When the mother tells him that what's difficult for her son is that his father left them for another man, Kimble is silenced for a moment. Another student comes in and shouts, "Are you married, Mr. Kimble?" When he answers "No," the question hangs in the air, "Why not?"

## Lesson 9

FULGHUM: When you go out into the world, watch out for traffic, hold hands, and stick together.

MARIA: Don't expect anyone else to support you financially.

K-COP: If you are going to shoot a bad guy, you should probably also try to eliminate his mother, too.

When Kimble finally corners the bad guy, Crisp, in the school bathroom, Crisp uses his son as a hostage and gets Kimble to throw down his gun. Crisp then points his own gun (given to him by his mother) at Kimble and pulls the trigger. An instant before, however, Kimble's ferret, which had been hiding in Dominic's sweater, emerges to bite Crisp on the neck, causing him to miss Kimble's heart and hit his leg instead. Kimble is able to lunge for his own gun and shoot Crisp dead. Joyce rushes to gather up her son as Kimble rises, painfully, on a wounded leg. At that moment, Crisp's mother enters, stealthily, and shoots Kimble again, wounding him more seriously. Retreating to the shower,

Kimble is powerless against Crisp's mother as she fires shot after shot into the shower wall above his head. Finally, she prepares to kill him, but by this point Phoebe has limped onto the scene (her leg had been broken when Crisp's mother ran her down with a car to keep the policewoman from running to aid her partner). Phoebe has a baseball bat with her and uses it to strike Crisp's mother's gun hand and then swings a second time to knock the mother out, effectively eliminating her. The symbolism is hard to miss. Team-Kimble has not only eliminated the threat from the bad son, Crisp, they have (symbolically) eliminated all possibility of more evil offspring springing from the mother's loins. If this sounds a little like the movie *The Terminator* that's because Arnold is always the Terminator. In *Kindergarten Cop* he rescues the little boy and enables him to live by effectively deleting both the boy's father and the father's mother. In so doing Kimble replaces the father, as though the father never existed—which, in effect, Crisp hasn't since his mother has been erased, as well.

## Lesson 10

FULGHUM: Flush.
MARIA: Laughter.
K-COP: Alter reality.

Arnold's Detective John Kimble becomes the kindergarten teacher in a school that "emphasizes the three C's—caring, courtesy, and courage." When the chaos of working with a large group of 5-year-olds threatens to drive Mr. Kimble to temporary insanity, he gets a grip—and a plan. On his third day with them, he tells the children that they are going to play a "new fun game called Police School." Mr. Kimble will be the sheriff, and all the kids are "deputy trainees." With military precision, he whips the kids into shape by issuing strict orders, instituting militaristic drills punctuated by the sound of his whistle, and speaking to them all as young soldiers. He tells them, "You kids are soft! You lack discipline! Well, I've got news for you. You are mine now, you belong to me." The day before he had been stymied when one little girl told him she had to use the bathroom and could not open her overalls. On this day, however, he tells the class, "No more complaining! No more 'Mr. Kimble, I have to go to the bathroom.' Nothing! There is no bathroom!"

# CHAPTER 13

# Running Man: The Sequel

**IN THE LAST DAYS** of his gubernatorial campaign, Arnold led a four-bus caravan from San Diego to Sacramento. The lead bus, named "Running Man," carried Arnold, "the self-styled saviour of California."[1] A second bus, filled with supporters (including former New York City mayor Rudy Giuliani),[2] was called "Total Recall." The several hundred lucky reporters granted places in the Running Man caravan rode along in trailing buses labeled either "Predator" or "True Lies." Remarkably, Arnold's campaign ride drew such enormous crowds and so much media attention that the only way several dozen other gubernatorial candidates were able to get any exposure to the press was to charter their own buses and tailgate the Running Man's bus tour. Whenever Arnold would stop to meet and greet supporters, the other candidates would get out of their own buses to try to get a sound bite in edgewise. Arnold was on a roll, and it looked like his momentum would carry him right through to the state's top job—and maybe beyond.

But before we can speculate about a sequel to Arnold's remarkable run for the governorship of California, we need to look back to 1987, the year that Arnold Schwarzenegger starred in the movie *The Running Man*. The film is based on an early story by Stephen King and is set in Los Angeles in the year 2017. The world economy has collapsed, and L.A. has become a police state. Mass media are now controlled by the government, and television is dominated by a government-sponsored game show called "The Running Man." The show is actually a hunt for "game"—the latter consisting of convicted criminals who are given a chance to escape by running through a gauntlet of brutal killers known as "Stalkers." Survivors are given their freedom and a condo in Hawaii, but hardly anyone ever survives. When Arnold's character, Ben Richards, is falsely accused of a capital crime, he is forced to become a contestant. The expectation, of course, is that Ben will die a horrible and entertaining death. But when Arnold is the running man, it's time to revise our expectations.

Ben Richards not only survives the gauntlet of "stalkers," he manages to defeat the entire slate of bizarre hunters—a man hard-wired with electrical charge, another who uses freezing as his death-weapon, and an ice skater capable of dealing death by skate-blade. If this sounds like the cast of candidates from the California recall election, we shouldn't be surprised. Arnold's movies almost always anticipate cultural events of one kind or another, and *The Running Man* is no exception. Both the irony of Ben Richards's line "I'm not into politics. I'm into survival!" and the movie's title itself foreshadow by sixteen years Arnold's determination to "run" for powerful office, to maintain his good public image, and to defeat a cast of characters worthy of an Arnold film.

In the movie, Ben Richards's appearance on "The Running Man" television show made him so popular a figure in 2017 L.A. that he could have parlayed his celebrity into political office, replacing one exercise of autocratic power with another. What can be the sequel to Arnold Schwarzenegger as California's running man?

Before he'd even taken up residence in the governor's office, speculation—and excitement—over a grand-scale Arnoldian political sequel had already begun. What about Arnold Schwarzenegger for president? The 1993 Sylvester Stallone movie *Demolition Man* featured a scene—set in the year 2026—in which Sandra Bullock's character explains to Stallone that thirty years earlier Arnold Schwarzenegger had been elected president of the United States. She tells him, "Even though he was not born in this country, his popularity at the time caused the 61st Amendment." Nine years before that, in 1984, Sydney Schanberg of the *New York Times* joked that if the presidential elections were run more like beauty contests, "Arnold Schwarzenegger could become President."[3]

While many political analysts quickly pointed out that such speculations were frivolous—Arnold cannot become president as a foreign-born citizen—the mere suggestion of the possibility was sufficient to generate heated and lengthy debates on Web-logs, in chat rooms, on television magazine programs and newscasts, and of course in the press. Time for one more headline list!

**Arnold for President?** (Daily Kos.net)[4]
**Pres. Schwarzengroper** (*Washington Post*)[5]

**Arnie for Prez: A Novel Idea** (*New York Post*)[6]

**President Schwarzenegger** (Press action.com)[7]

**President Schwarzenegger?** (*San Francisco Chronicle*)[8]

**Law-makers Take Aim at Ban on Foreign-Born Presidents**
(*Seattle Post-Intelligencer*)[9]

**Immigrants for President?** (*The Daily Standard*)[10]

**Let Immigrants Run** (*Washington Post*)[11]

**Drop Bar to Presidency, Some Say: Effort Afoot to Let
Immigrants Have a Shot at Oval Office** (*Atlanta Journal-
Constitution*)[12]

**Recall Spotlights Drive to Let Foreign-Born Citizens Run for
President** (*San Jose Mercury News*)[13]

**Proposed Law Change Would Make President
Schwarzenegger a Possibility** (Agence France-Presse)[14]

**Arnie Could Break Presidential Mould** (*Irish News*, Belfast)[15]

**Senator Hatch Wants Arnold for President** (The Mail
Archive)[16]

**Claim Arnold—Arnold Schwarzenegger Pres. USA**
(ideosphere.com)[17]

**Arnold for President! We Want a Presidator! Jawoll Ja!**
(Sandorian Grove newslog)[18]

The election of the Terminator to govern the largest and
wealthiest state in the United States may be a sign that
America, now more than at any other time, is attracted to the
idea of a leader whose power is so compelling that he can
simply ignore the usual protocols—and sometimes the
expressed intentions—of both major political parties. On
December 18, 2003, just a month after taking office,
California's new governor unilaterally replaced billions of
dollars in the budgets of cities and towns throughout the
state that had lost revenue when he cut car taxes.[19] The

Democratic-controlled legislature had opposed this revenue-replacement, arguing that it would mean dramatic cuts in state services and funding to pay for Arnold's plan.[20] Arnold simply bypassed the will of the state assembly by declaring California to be in a fiscal crisis, allowing him to invoke emergency powers. In this way, he could impose huge spending cuts without legislative approval.[21]

The money put back into local governments may have met with legislative disapproval, but Arnold's unilateral fiscal gambit was met with enthusiastic approval from local leaders. The Los Angles County Chief Administrative Officer, David Janssen, said of Arnold, "His action was great for local government."[22] Los Angeles mayor James K. Hahn added, "We haven't seen this kind of bold leadership in Sacramento for a long, long time, and we are really grateful for it."[23]

Contemplating a sequel to his term(s) as governor, America may be anticipating—or longing for—leadership by someone who can unite us in a wave of emotion. As the *Los Angeles Times* put it, in just the one powerful act of stepping right over the state government, Schwarzenegger "obliterated any lingering doubts... that he is the supreme political force in the Capitol."[24]

As stirring as it may seem to imagine the classic fulfillment of the American dream in which the underdog rises to become the president himself, it is worth bearing in mind that Hollywood, Disney, and Madison Avenue figured out, long ago, how to manipulate our emotions and mass-produce our appetites. A product of all of those American institutions, Arnold relied on his substantial gift for arousing goodwill at the same time that he obliterated the rest of the electoral field.

America was completely taken in by Arnold's sensational celebrity appeal. California, and by extension all of America, *felt like* electing Arnold Schwarzenegger despite an abundance of rational reasons not to. People across the state and across the country seemed to be agreeing with *New York Newsday*'s Paul Vitello: "Arnold Schwarzenegger *is* California."[25] In his postelection stumping at shopping malls throughout the state, Arnold was able to keep crowds of energized consumers cheering and wanting him to succeed.

His spokesman warned not to make too much of it,[26] but who could resist the rich significance of Arnold continuing to spread via the malled cathedrals of American consumer identity. His threat to clean house in Sacramento, in practical terms, meant going directly to the people of the state and urging them to do his dirty work for him. As the *Los Angeles Times* reported, "No matter the town, Schwarzenegger headed straight to the mall"[27] to deliver his message in front of large but tightly controlled crowds, urging them to contact their state representatives to do his bidding.

Why shopping malls? Malls are a comforting expression of American culture no matter where you go across the nation. Familiar stores, familiar foods, and familiar layouts say, "You are still in America, the America you share with so many others." The mall compresses several different experiences (eating, moviegoing, shopping, playing) into a carefully designed space with limited access and egress and multiple ways to be consumers.

In his insightful analysis of Arnold's campaign, Frank Rich of the *Los Angeles Times* explained, "up until Arnold Schwarzenegger, no one has succeeded (though many have tried) in creating a powerful political movement according to the Disney Park aesthetic."[28] The Disney aesthetic, exemplified in the original Main Street in Disneyland (California), involves simplifying, scaling, cleansing, hiding disorder, creating harmony, guiding behavior at every corner, and controlling it after every turn. But it is not simply the case, as Rich claimed, that Arnold does not have "passionate ideological convictions"[29] to go with his showmanship; rather the showmanship contains those convictions for all to see.

The theme-park aesthetic ensures that malls do not have a genuine sense of place but are generic experiences, that they are obsessed with security and surveillance, and that they simulate community life without its messy attachments. Michael Sorkin explains that both the theme park and the mall present a "happy regulated vision of pleasure... as a substitute for the democratic public realm"; speech of any political sort is restricted in both malls and theme parks and there is no evidence of the real nitty-gritty aspects of democracy.[30] Schwarzenegger's staff confirmed the appeal of the mall's controlled space when they said that malls were "convenient, safe, easily located."[31] The aesthetic of Disney's America is Arnold's not-so-hidden passion, and the sculpting of the rest of America into this model seems to be his goal.

Just as malls have borrowed this aesthetic to make happy places to meet, eat, and spend, an America in this mode will create a certain set of expectations and behaviors. Strict order and regimentation, while a proven strategy for theme parks and shopping malls, can be devastating to American democracy. If we are redefining democracy in what are essentially militaristic terms and if Kevin Baker is correct that "many—perhaps most—Americans now see the military as the last refuge of many *democratic* values in a society that seems ever more shallow and materialistic,"[32] then the theme park/mall aesthetic of Schwarzenegger's election and postelection is not to be dismissed lightly.

As Michael told the *Los Angeles Times,* "Everything in a mall is designed to attract and excite people, and that's the same thing Arnold is trying to do."[33] But shopping mall democracy, as comforting and euphoric as it may seem, comes dangerously close to connecting with a powerful political movement that forgets where American democratic values really need to reside.

Writing on fascism in London's *The Times,* William Reese-Mogg put it this way: "The core of all fascist movements is the direct relationship between the leader and the masses, not mediated through the institutions of democracy."[34] In this model, what a leader does most is lead, and he does so not through his policies or philosophies, but by the strength of his will. Evidence of the leader's will is "the exciting feeling he creates of ultimate ruthlessness." Schwarzenegger, according to Reese-Mogg, shows this ruthlessness in his most well-known and compelling role as the Terminator—a soul-less cyborg that kills indiscriminately.[35] Reese-Mogg offered this conclusion: "The politics of mass emotion are the politics of fascism."[36]

We are not arguing that Arnold Schwarzenegger is a fascist. That somewhat hysterical argument has been made by people on both the political left and right, but it is, we suggest, the wrong one to make. Instead, we have tried to present a compelling picture of America's response to Arnold—a response that has all the earmarks of a society ready and willing to embrace leadership that is far less interested in preserving individual rights and liberties than it is in promoting itself and exercising its will to greater and greater power.

George Lakoff, professor of linguistics and cognitive science at U.C. Berkeley, distinguishes two different worldviews: The progressive worldview "is modeled on a nurturant parent family... it assumes the world is basically good and can be made better and that one must work toward that." On a more political level, this worldview holds that government best protects the people by providing for "universal education,... civil liberties,... accountability,... public service,... open government,... and the promotion of an economy that benefits all."

The conservative worldview, according to Lakoff, takes the strict paternalistic model and "assumes that the world is dangerous and difficult and that children are born bad and must be made good." In this view, it is the father who is "the ultimate moral authority" who controls both his wife and his children through "painful discipline—physical punishment that by adulthood will become internal discipline." As Lakoff puts it, "The good people are the disciplined people."[37]

So, project this onto the nation and you see that to the right wing, good citizens are the disciplined ones—those who have already become wealthy or at least self-reliant—and those who are on the way. Social programs, meanwhile, "spoil" people by giving them things they haven't earned and keeping them dependent. The government is there only to protect the nation, maintain order, administer justice (punishment), and to provide for the promotion and orderly conduct of business.[38]

From this, it is not difficult to see why Arnold Schwarzenegger's candidacy appealed to a wide slice of Californians, as well as other Americans. Schwarzenegger's image—from his role as fitness czar to nearly every one of his movie characters—provides a clear example of the paternal position designed to maintain order and fitness in the culture. Lakoff noted, "He didn't have to say a word! He just had to stand up there, and he represents Mr. Discipline. He knows what's right and wrong, and he's going to take it to the people. He's not going to ask permission, or have a discussion, he's going to do what needs to be done, using force and authority."[39]

We have said, throughout this book, that Arnold matters, not simply because he is a constant presence in the culture and not just because he exerts a profoundly powerful influence on so many facets of the culture. Arnold matters so much because his entire career, from sensational bodybuilding champion to real estate tycoon to blockbuster movie star to storybook governor, has been simultaneously both the creation of American culture and a constant cause for the culture to reshape itself in his images and submit to his professed ideals. One such ideal is that what matters is the present and, of course, the future; history cannot teach us. Arnold's close friend and collaborator, George Butler, explains that "The past meant nothing to Arnold because it was over."[40] For Americans, the idea of such a famous leader who could keep making things new was clearly an exciting one.

Arnold's ability to generate excitement and a desire to trust him with leadership is matched by American culture's decades-long willingness to grant him wide access to our imaginations. In 1991, a letter to the *Los Angeles Times* suggested that Arnold run for president in the year 2000, that by then we could get rid of the prohibition against foreign-born citizens running for the office. "As President, he could intimidate heads of state as well as enemies in Congress.... And it would be refreshing to have a legitimate he-man at the helm instead of all these puffed-up Yalies."[41] One of those "Yalies," George W. Bush, responding to a *People* magazine question about whether there is any longer a good reason that foreign-born citizens should not become president, said, "You're not referring to Governor Schwarzenegger, are you? [*laughter*] That's an interesting question. We ought to look at it and examine it as a country."[42]

It is not at all surprising, then, that Americans would consider extending the potency of their own creation by holding him up to the idea of the presidency, to see if it might be a good fit. As we said to various interviewers throughout the recall campaign, it didn't really matter whether Arnold was elected. America's willingness to elevate him to candidacy had transformed him into a statesman—a power broker who can no longer be ignored by any political party.

Less than a year before the California recall election, in a remark betraying just a hint of things to come, Arnold himself said, "That's the great thing about this country, that as a foreigner... I can come here and say, 'Maybe some day I'm going to run this state.' It's a big state. Then we can buy Austria."[43] The Running Man made his jog into Sacramento look almost too easy. His election was, as the *New York Times* pointed out before the recall vote, immediately after the election, and again when Arnold took office, the completion of Arnold's "master plan."[44] This plan, formulated in the 1970s, was simple: Arnold would become a movie star, make millions of dollars, marry a glamorous wife, and hold political power.[45]

But we would argue that Arnold's plans are never "complete." As George Butler has said of Arnold, "This is a man of bottomless ambition."[46] There is no reason to believe that his role as governor will not have a remarkable sequel. That Arnold Schwarzenegger cannot, at this time, be elected president of the United States should not be seen as a permanent condition.

·   ·   ·   ·   ·

Article II, Section 1 of the United States Constitution:
No person except a natural born citizen, or a citizen of the United States at the time of the adoption of this Constitution, shall be eligible to the Office of President; neither shall any person be eligible to that office who shall not have attained the age of thirty-five years, and been fourteen years a resident with the United States.

IN THE HOUSE OF REPRESENTATIVES
FEBRUARY 29, 2000
Mr. [Barney] **FRANK** of Massachusetts introduced the following joint resolution, which was referred to the Committee on the Judiciary

JOINT RESOLUTION
Proposing an amendment to the Constitution of the United States to make eligible for the Office of President a person who has been a United States citizen for twenty years.

*Resolved by the Senate and House of Representatives of the United States of America in Congress assembled (two-thirds of each House concurring therein),* That the following article is proposed as an amendment to the Constitution of the United States, which shall be valid to all intents and purposes as part of the Constitution when ratified by the legislatures of three-fourths of the several States within seven years after the date of its submission for ratification:

Article—
"A person who is a citizen of the United States, who has been for twenty years a citizen of the United States, and who is otherwise eligible to the Office of President, is not ineligible to that Office by reason of not being a native born citizen of the United States."

Mr. **FRANK.** Thank you, Mr. Chairman. Thank you for giving us this hearing. The gentleman who suggested the amendment to me, Mr. Raimundo Delgado, is here and will be testifying. I bring it forward for a very simple reason: It does not seem to me that there ought to be as a general principle any barriers to treating people who choose to come here and become Americans differently than people who were born here. I am also a great believer in democracy virtually untrammeled.

Now, on the first point, we have had in recent years some legislation, which seems to me unfortunately to reflect some animus toward immigrants. I think the reaction to that nationally has been a good one, and we are in the process of unwinding some of that. But the essential premise of this constitutional provision is that there is some reason to distrust the complete patriotism of people who were born elsewhere, and I have not found that to be the case as a general rule.

Secondly, I support this for the same reason that I oppose term limits and other restrictions on people's ability to choose. Obviously we do not directly elect the President of the United States, and I notice Professor

McDonald in his defense of the existing system cites our system for selecting a President as, to use a technical historic term, cockamamie. I think it is wise to remember that it was, in fact, the result of one of those political compromises that we always find useful. And one of the interesting things about political compromises is that contemporaneously they are always condemned as sellouts. Historically they often take on the patent [sic] of wisdom. I think that is the more accurate view; that is, political compromise is a very honorable part of a system of democracy.

But whatever the rules are by which we elect people, I do not favor putting obstacles on the ability of the people to choose who they wish under those rules. I think the American public is perfectly capable of making those decisions, and for both those reasons I think the amendment is a good idea. And I particularly think it is a good idea for us to begin to discuss this, which obviously is what we are doing, since I have advised people that the likelihood that we are going to pass the constitutional amendment along to the States in the remaining few weeks of the legislative session is highly unlikely since we aren't going to do very much either. People who are in favor of the amendment should not feel discriminated against on that ground.

Thank you, Mr. Chairman.


STATEMENT OF FORREST McDONALD, HISTORIAN AND PROFESSOR OF HISTORY, UNIVERSITY OF ALABAMA

Mr. **MCDONALD.** All right. I could give what I consider the definitive argument against the proposed amendment in two words: Arnold Schwarzenegger, but I have been allotted 5 minutes, so I will take the 5. I will explain the reference, if it does not follow.[47]

．　．　．　．

IN THE SENATE OF THE UNITED STATES
July 10, 2003
Mr. [Orrin] HATCH introduced the following joint resolution, which was read twice and referred to the Committee on the Judiciary.

JOINT RESOLUTION
Proposing an amendment to the Constitution of the United States to make eligible for the Office of President a person who has been a United States citizen for 20 years.

*Resolved by the Senate and House of Representatives of the United States of America in Congress assembled (two-thirds of each House concurring therein),* That the following article is proposed as an amendment to the Constitution of the United States:

Article—
SECTION 1. A person who is a citizen of the United States, who has been for 20 years a citizen of the United States, and who is otherwise eligible to the Office of President, is not ineligible to that Office by reason of not being a native born citizen of the United States.
SECTION 2. This article shall not take effect unless it has been ratified as an amendment to the Constitution by the legislatures of three-fourths of the several States not later than 7 years from the date of its submission to the States by the Congress.

STATEMENTS ON INTRODUCED BILLS AND JOINT RESOLUTIONS (Senate—July 10, 2003)

Mr. **HATCH.** Mr President, I rise today to introduce the "Equal Opportunity to Govern" Amendment, which would amend the Constitution to permit any person who has been a United States citizen for at least 20 years to be eligible for the Office of President. The Constitution, in its current form, prohibits a person who is not a native born citizen of the United States from becoming the President.

The purpose of the native born citizen requirement has long passed, and it is time for us—the elected representatives of this Nation or [sic] immigrants—to remove this impediment. While there was scant debate on this provision during the Constitutional Convention, it is apparent that the decision to include the natural born citizen requirement in our Constitution was driven largely by the concern that a European monarch, such as King George III's second son, the Duke of York, might be imported to rule the United States.

This restriction has become an anachronism that is decidedly un-American. Consistent with our democratic form of government, our citizens should have every opportunity to choose their leaders free of unreasonable limitations. Indeed, no similar restriction bars other critical members of government, including the Senate, the House of Representatives, the Supreme Court, or the President's most trusted cabinet officials.

Ours is a Nation of immigrants. The history of the United States is replete with scores of great and patriotic Americans whose dedication to this country is beyond reproach, but who happen to have been born outside of Her borders. These include former secretaries of state Henry Kissinger and Madeleine Albright; current Cabinet members Secretary of Labor Elaine L. Chao and Secretary of

Housing and Urban Development Mel Martinez; as well as Jennifer Granholm, the Governor of Michigan and bring [sic] young star of the Democratic party. As our Constitution reads today, none of these well-qualified, patriotic United States citizens could be a lawful candidate for President.

Perhaps most disturbing is that the scores of foreign-born men and women who have risked their lives defending the freedoms and liberties of this great nation who remain ineligible for the Office of President. More than 700 recipients of the Congressional Medal of Honor—our Nation's highest decoration for valor—have been immigrants. But no matter how great their sacrifice, leadership, or love for this country, they remain ineligible to be a candidate for President. This amendment would remove this unfounded inequity.

Today I ask the members of this body if we desire to continue to invite these brave men and women to defend this Nation's liberty, to protect Her flag, to be willing to pay the ultimate sacrifice, and yet deny them the opportunity to strive for the ultimate American dream—to become our President? I respectfully submit that we should not.

My proposal to amend the Constitution is not one I take lightly. As our founding fathers envisioned, our Constitution has stood the test of time. It has remained largely intact for more than 200 years due to the careful, deliberative, and principled approach of the framers. This is truly an extraordinary achievement. On a few appropriate occasions, however, we have generated the will to surmount the cumbersome, but no doubt necessary, hurdles to amend the Constitution. I believe the time has now come to address the antiquated provision of the Constitution that requires our President to be a natural born citizen. It has long outlived its original purpose.

I ask my colleagues to join me in supporting the Equal Opportunity to Govern Amendment.[48]

• • • • •

**Arnold Schwarzenegger:** Born 1947, resident of the United States since 1968, became a naturalized citizen on September 16, 1983.

# Notes

## Introduction

1. http://www.hollywoodthing.com/actors/index.shtml
http://film.guardian.co.uk/quiz/questions/0,5952,113133,00.html
http://www.ccvideo.com/actorprofile.cfm?actorid=55
http://www.steffensiebert.de/amdb/schw.txt
http://www.theindependent.com/stories/081503/opt_cico15.shtml
http://www.scms.ca/hbarnd.html
http://www.gay.com/entertainment/celebrities/package.html?sernum=226
http://www.bodybuilders.com/arnold.htm
[There are dozens of Web sites like these that refer to the Guinness quote.]
2. Richard R. Lingeman, "Books: Story of a Bodybuilder," *New York Times*, February 10, 1978, p. C21.
3. We have tried to indicate the most current, active links; however, inevitably links are removed or changed, and this may affect whether some of the Web sites listed in these notes are still accessible.
4. http://www.robert-fisk.com/robert_elias_25sept2001.htm
5. Ryan Murphy, "Arnold Schwarzenegger: No Sweat," *Saturday Evening Post*, March 1989, p. 48.
6. Film critic Sean French makes a connection between Schwarzenegger and Hobbes in his booklet *The Terminator* (London: British Film Institute Modern Classics, 1996).

With regard to the film *The Terminator* he speculated that "Fritz Lang might have grimly approved of a film that seems to preach peace while depicting a future of Hobbesian struggle for survival between Psychopathic machines and a tribe of Nietzschean human warriors." George Butler also makes a connection between Schwarzenegger and the Leviathan, including the Biblical passage Job 41, as a kind of preface to his book *Arnold Schwarzenegger: A Portrait* (New York: Simon and Schuster, 1990). Butler does not, however, explore this connection or discuss the political implications of the analogy.

7. Aaron Lathan, "Schwarzenegger for Governor?" *M inc.*, October 1991, p. 114.

8. "Profile: Arnold Schwarzenegger," *U.S. News and World* Report, November 1990.

9. Suzanne Fields, "Climbing 'Golem' Heights in California," on-line at http://www.townhall.com/columnists/suzannefields/sf20030818.shtml.

## ONE. Crusade for Kahl-eee-fohr-nya

1. http://www.thearnoldfans.com/movies/crusade/crusade.htm

2. http://www.bubblegun.com/features/arnie.html

3. http://thezreview.co.uk/comingsoon/c/crusade.htm

4. http://oakland.8k.com/voting.html

5. http://www.thearnoldfans.com/movies/crusade/crusade.htm

6. Martin Wroe, "Christians Attack Arnie's Crusade," *The Observer* (London), August 6, 1995, p. 3.

7. http://www.avoncompany.com/women/avoncrusade/

8. http://www.worldliteracy.org/

9. http://www.childrenscrusade.org/

10. http://www.patrickcrusade.org/mission_statement.htm

11. Fran Spielman, "Arnie Recruits Fitness Army Among Kids," *Chicago Sun-Times*, March 26, 1993, p. 4.

12. http://www.washingtonpost.com/ac2/wp-dyn/A1012–2003Apr9 ?language=printer

13. Tim Goodman, "Candidates' Debate—All Sizzle, No Steak," *San Francisco Chronicle*, September 25, 2003, p. A15.

14. Jim Rutenberg, "The California Recall: The News Media," *New York Times*, October 2, 2003, p. A28.

15. Susan Crabtree, "D.C. Spin," *Variety*, August 18, 2003, p. 17.

16. Beth Barret, "Major Crusade for Charter Schools Is On," *Los Angeles Daily News*, October 22, 2003, p. N3.

17. Mira Katz, "Woman Wins License Fee Money," *Ontario (Calif.) Inland Valley Daily Bulletin*, August 15, 2003.

18. Matt Carter, "Pleasanton Manager's Pay Raises Put on Hold; Ayala Continues Crusade Against Rising Salaries for Employees," *Pleasanton (Calif.) Tri-Valley Herald*, October 9, 2003.

19. Frank Rich, "The Audio-Animatronic Candidate," *New York Times*, October 12, 2003, Sect. 2, p. 1.

20. "New Ad Unveils California's Unholy Trinity: Pro-Abortion 'Catholics' Schwarzenegger, Davis and Bustamante," U.S. Newswire, September 11, 2003.

21. Brad Stone and Elisa Williams, "Venture Capitalists Are Betting on Fuel-Cell and Solar-Cell Technologies," *Newsweek*, November 17, 2003, p. 40.

22. Vicki Haddock, "President Schwarzenegger?" *San Francisco Chronicle*, November 2, 2003, p. D1.

23. "Nobel Crusades," *Sunday Tribune* (Dublin), October 12, 2003, p. 21.

24. http://edstrong.blog-city.com/read/224646.htm

25. http://www.hevanet.com/peace/paz/bush_supported_israel.htm

26. http://www.marxist.com/MiddleEast/bush_crusades.html

27. http://www.firstthings.com/ftissues/ft0003/opinion/riley-smith.html

28. http://www.firstthings.com/ftissues/ft0003/opinion/riley-smith.html

29. http://www.strategypage.com/onpoint/articles/20020814.asp

## TWO. Total Recall: Conan vs. the Terminator, California 2003

1. *Los Angeles Daily News*, October 8, 2003, p. 1.

2. *New York Post*, Late City Final, October 8, 2003, p. 1.

3. *People*, October 20, 2003, p. 108.

4. *New York Sun*, October 8, 2003, p. 1.

5. *USA Today*, October 8, 2003, p. 1.

6. Clark Rhodri, "The Predator," *Western Mail* (Cardiff, Wales), October 9, 2003, p. 13.

7. *New York Times*, October 8, 2003, p. 1.

8. CNN.com/Inside Politics, October 8, 2003, at http://www.cnn.com/TRANSCRIPTS/0310/08/ip.00.html

9. Brian Flynn, "Arnie the Termwinator," *The Sun* (London), October 9, 2003.

10. Dan Whitcomb and Arthur Spiegelman, "California Has a New Strongman. Schwarzenegger," originally a Reuters story, October 8, 2003, at http://www.networkirc.com/hood/modules.php?name=News&file=article&sid=180

11. *Newsday*, October 9, 2003, p. A34.

12. *Los Angeles Times*, October 8, 2003, p. 1.

13. *Orange County Register*, October 8, 2003, p. 1.

14. *Long Beach (Calif.) Press Telegram*, October 8, 2003, p. 1.

15. David Schwartz, "Inland Empire Basks in Schwarzenegger Victory," *Pasadena (Calif.) Star News*, October 14, 2003.

16. Joe Matthews, "From Novice to Governor in Two Months," *New York Newsday*, October 12, 2003, p. A4.

17. Roger Simon, "Victory for Arnold." *U.S. News and World Report*, October 20, 2003, p. 16.

18. Peter Kiefer and Jesse Hiestand, "Production Starts on Arnold's Next Big Role,"

HollywoodReporter.com, October 8, 2003 (requires subscription to service) at http://www.hollywoodreporter.com/thr/search/search_results.jsp?vnu_old_search =true&vnu_results_page=4

19. Howard Fineman and Karen Breslau et al., "Arnold's Earthquake," *Newsweek*, October 20, 2003, p. 26.

20. Matt Labash, "Arnold Uber Alles," *The Weekly Standard*, October 20, 2003.

21. Todd S. Purdum, "Fame=Power=Fame; Government by Celebrity Is Already Asserting Itself," *New York Times*, October 12, 2003, Sect. 4, p. 1, Week in Review.

22. Mick LaSalle, "Schwarzenegger Steals Recall Scene," SFGate.com, August 7, 2003, at http://www.sfgate.com/cgi-bin/article.cgi?file=/chronicle/archive/2003 /08/-07/MN109521.DTL

23. Michael E. Ross, "A Governor Terminated by Style," MSNBC.com, October 7, 2003, at http://msnbc.msn.com/id/3340937/

24. David K. Li, "Nixon Stoked Arnie's Fire," *New York Post* on-line edition, September 3, 2003, at http://www.nypost.com

25. Sharon Waxman, "From Pumping Iron to Pushing Political Ideas," *Washington Post*, September 28, 2003, p. A7.

26. Sharon Waxman, "From Pumping Iron to Pushing Political Ideas," *Washington Post*, September 28, 2003, p. A7.

27. At the Arnold Classic 1997, he received the IFBB Gold Order Award, proclaiming him the greatest bodybuilder of the twentieth century.

28. Sharon Waxman, "From Pumping Iron to Pushing Political Ideas," *Washington Post*, September 28, 2003, p. A7.

29. Joe Matthews, "So Familiar Yet So Unknown," *Los Angeles Times*, October 8, 2003, p. A1.

30. Annie Brown, "Arnold Schmalzenegger: Film Star Steps Straight into Cheesy Politician Role as He Begins His Term-inator in Office," *Daily Record* (Glasgow), October 9, 2003, p. 1.

31. Mark Lawson, "Some Mistake?" *The Guardian* (London), October 9, 2003, p. 2.

32. Mark Lawson, "Some Mistake?" *The Guardian* (London), October 9, 2003, p. 2.

33. American Media, Inc., *Arnold: The American Dream*. Boca Raton, Fla.: American Media, Inc., 2003, p. 93.

34. http://www.marycareyforgovernor.com

35. http://vote2003.ss.ca.gov/Returns/gov/00.htm

36. http://www.cbsnews.com/stories/2003/09/03/politics/main571480.shtml

37. http://politicalhumor.about.com/library/blschwarzeneggerjokes.htm

38. Paul Krugman, "Conan the Deceiver," *New York Times*, August 22, 2003, p. A23.

39. Andrew Donaldson, "Pass the Popcorn Please—It's Conan the Governor," *Sunday Times* (South Africa), October 12, 2003, Opinion & Editorial, p. 18.

40. Andrew Donaldson, "Pass the Popcorn Please—It's Conan the Governor," *Sunday Times* (South Africa), October 12, 2003, Opinion & Editorial, p. 18.

41. Aaron Latham, "Schwarzenegger as California Governor?" *M inc.*, October 1991, p. 114.

42. Bill Zehme, "Mr. Big Shot," *Rolling Stone*, August 22, 1991, p. 41.

43. Aaron Latham, "Schwarzenegger as California Governor?" *M inc.*, October 1991, p. 115.

44. Aaron Latham, "Schwarzenegger as California Governor?" *M inc.*, October 1991, p. 115.

45. Peter McGough, "Anatomy of an American Icon," *Flex*, July 1997, p. 64.

46. Jill Stewart, "L.A. Times Editor Responds to Charges," *American Reporter*, October 30, 2003 (see also http://www.american-reporter.com)

47. Jill Stewart, "L.A. Times Editor Responds to Charges," *American Reporter*, October 30, 2003 (see also http://www.american-reporter.com)

48. Arnold's roles in *Kindergarten Cop* (1990), *Jingle All the Way* (1996), *The 6th Day* (2000), and *Twins* (1988), respectively.

49. "Schwarzenegger No Barbarian at Finances," *Daily Mail* (Pakistan), August 11, 2003, at http://dailymailnews.com/200308/11/news/show05.html

50. Bradley R. Gitz, "Conan's Dirty Laundry," *Arkansas Democrat-Gazette*, September 7, 2003, p. 87.

51. Kenneth Turan, "Taking 'Conan' Seriously: At the Edges of Arnold Schwarzenegger's Onscreen Persona Are Telling Hints of the Real Man," *Los Angeles Times*, August 24, 2003, p. E6.

52. Kenneth Turan, "Taking 'Conan' Seriously: At the Edges of Arnold Schwarzenegger's Onscreen Persona Are Telling Hints of the Real Man," *Los Angeles Times*, August 24, 2003, p. E6.

53. Tom Kentworthy, "Mr. Governor," *Toronto Sun*, October 9, 2003, p. 3.

### THREE. Around the World in (Almost) 80 Days

1. http://english.pravda.ru/world/20/91/368/11038_arnie.html, October 8, 2003.

2. Terry Jones, "La La Land Loony over Schwarzenegger," *Winnipeg Sun*, October 9, 2003, p. 17.

3. Greg Walters, "Schwarzenegger Win: 'It's OK for America,'" *Moscow Times*, October 9, 2003.

4. "Schwarzenegger Overpowers Davis," *Taipei Times*, October 9, 2003, p. 1.

5. Don Melvin, *Austin American-Statesman*, October 9, 2003, p. A9.

6. BBC News, October 8, 2003, at http://newsvote.bbc.co.uk/mpapps/pagetools /print/news.bbc.co.uk/1/hi/world/europe/3173898.stm

7. http://dailynews.muzi.com/ll/english/1282786.shtml

8. Peter Hartcher Washington, "Arnie—It Could Only Happen in America," *Australian Financial Review*, October 9, 2003, p. 10.

9. Terry Jones, "Those Crazy Californians," *Edmonton Sun*, October 9, 2003, p. 9.

10. BBC News, October 9, 2003, at http://newsvote.bbc.co.uk/mpapps/page tools/print/news.bbc.co.uk/1/hi/world/africa/3178476.stm

11. Maarten Rabaey, "Arnold, de Powerman," *De Morgen* (Brussels), October 11, 2003, p. B1.

12. Vanessa Gera, "From Moscow to His Hometown, World Marvels at Schwarzenegger's Victory," Associated Press, October 8, 2003.

13. "Arnold Schwarzenegger est élu gouverneur de la Californie," *Le Monde* (Paris), October 8, 2003.

14. *Business Day* (Johannesburg), October 9, 2003, Opinion and Editorial, p. 8.

15. Mark Ellis, "Hasta la Victor: Arnie Joy at New Role as Governor of California," *Daily Mirror*, October 9, 2003, p. 18.

16. Global News Wire—Asia Africa Intelligence Wire, Copyright 2003, BBC Monitoring/BBC, BBC Monitoring International Reports, October 9, 2003.

17. Jan Tromp, "Dromen van Arnold," *de Volkskrant* (Amsterdam), October 7, 2003, p. 13.

18. Tom Tugend, "California's Jewish Republicans Hail Schwarzenegger Win," *Jerusalem Post*, October 9, 2003, p. 1.

19. Alex Massie, "The Tidal Wave That Swept Schwarzenegger to Victory Was Powered by a Policy of Letting Arnold Be Arnold," *Scotland on Sunday*, October 12, 2003.

20. Jean-Louis Santini, "Schwarzenegger's Victory Bodes Well for Republicans in 2004," Agence France-Presse, October 8, 2003.

21. "Terminator 4: Arnie's Victory Is a Triumph of Populism over an Incumbent," *Financial Times* (London), October 9, 2003, p. 22.

22. Tom Chorneau, "Schwarzenegger Sworn In," *St. John's (Newfoundland) Telegram*, November 18, 2003, p. D6.

23. *The World*, Latest Editions, October 8, 2003, at http://www.theworld.org/latest editions/20031008.shtml

24. http://www.newsobserver.com/24hour/politics/story/1024698p–7189835 c.html

25. "Schwarzenegger Wins Election," *Irish News* (Belfast), October 9, 2003, p. 22.

26. News Digest, *Saigon Times Daily*, October 9, 2003.

27. "World of the High and Mighty," *National Business Review* (New Zealand), October 17, 2003, p. 28.

28. "Schwarzenegger Is Significant Investor in Israel's CellGuide," *Globes (Online) Israel's Business Arena*, August 13, 2003, and also http://israpundit.com/archives/ 002363.html

29. Cintia Cardoso, *Folha de S. Paulo* (Brazil), October 2003.

30. Jan Tromp, "Dromen van Arnold," *de Volkskrant* (Amsterdam), October 7, 2003, p. 13.

31. Maarten Rabaey, "Arnold, de Powerman," *De Morgen* (Brussels), October 11, 2003.

32. NetWerk—Channel 1 Dutch Television, October 5, 2003, Freke Vuijst, producer.

33. Maarten Rabaey, "Arnold, de Powerman," *De Morgen* (Brussels), October 11, 2003.

34. Mark Lawson, "Some Mistake?" *The Guardian* (London), October 9, 2003, p. 2.

35. "Terminator 4: Arnie's Victory Is a Triumph of Populism over an Incumbent," *Financial Times* (London), October 9, 2003, p. 22.

36. "Terminator 4: Arnie's Victory Is a Triumph of Populism over an Incumbent," *Financial Times* (London), October 9, 2003, p. 22.

37. "Baja Gov. Congratulates Schwarzenegger," Associated Press Online, October 9, 2003, International News.

38. "Mexico's Foreign Relations Secretary Meets California Governor-elect," Associated Press Online, October 22, 2003, International News.

39. http://www.albawaba.com/main/index.ie.php3?lang=e

40. "Road to Governor: Arnold's Affiliation with Jews, Israel," *Al-Bawaba* (Amman/London), August 19, 2003.

41. N. Vidyasagar, "Terminator 3: The Rise of the Moolah," *The Times of India*, July 30, 2003.

42. "A New Career?" *The Hindu* (India), August 14, 2003.

43. Ramola Talwar Badam, "Actors-Turned-Pollies Warn: More to Lose Now Than Applause," *Canberra Times* (Australia), October 11, 2003, p. B06.

44. Fredricka Whitfield and Jeanne Moos, "Boom in So-Called Arnold-Speak," CNN Daybreak, September 9, 2003, Transcript #090910CN.V73.

45. http://everything2.com/?node=chan

46. Kiyoharu Hatano, "Governor," October 9, 2003, at http://www.hatanoes.com /kiyo/journal/archives/000398.html

47. Richard Roeper, "You Know You're Hot When You're in a Japanese TV Ad," *Chicago Sun-Times*, August 24, 2003, p. 11.

48. http://www.glocom.org/media_reviews/s_review/20031201_special_review17/

49. http://www.glocom.org/media_reviews/s_review/20031201_special_review17/

50. Hilary E. MacGregor, "In Japan, He's Larger Than Larger-Than-Life," *Los Angeles Times*, November 19, 2003, p. E2.

51. "Schwarzenegger, Matsui Featured on This Year's Battledores," Japan Economic Newswire, December 2, 2003.

52. Sam Cheong, "Most Singaporeans Happy with Decision," *New Straits Times Press* (Malaysia) Berhad, *Malay Mail*, October 10, 2003.

53. Sam Cheong, "Most Singaporeans Happy with Decision," *New Straits Times Press* (Malaysia) Berhad, *Malay Mail*, October 10, 2003.

54. Sam Cheong, "Most Singaporeans Happy with Decision," *New Straits Times Press* (Malaysia) Berhad, *Malay Mail*, October 10, 2003.

55. "Governor-Elect Arnold Schwarzenegger (R-CA) Holds News Conference," FDCH Political Transcripts (Federal Document Clearing House, Inc.), October 8, 2003 (see also "Bush and Mandela Among First to Congratulate Arnie," *Birmingham (Ala.) Post-Herald*, October 10, 2003, p. 10).

56. Tonye David-West, Jr., "Schwarzenegger's Election: A Cogent Lesson for the Nigerian Polity," October 9, 2003, at http://www.nigeria.com/cgibin/dcforum /dcboard.cgi?az (Web site no longer available)

57. Tonye David-West, Jr., "Schwarzenegger's Election: A Cogent Lesson for the Nigerian Polity," October 9, 2003, at http://www.nigeria.com/cgibin/dcforum/ dcboard.cgi?az (Web site no longer available)

58. M. Kagwe, "Kenya: How the Media May Be Failing Kenyans," *Africa News*, November 13, 2003.

59. M. Kagwe, "Kenya: How the Media May Be Failing Kenyans," *Africa News*, November 13, 2003.

60. "Kenyan Paper Urges Legislators to Learn from California Recall Vote," *East African Standard* (Nairobi) (Web site), Nairobi, October 10, 2003, reprinted/supplied by BBC Worldwide Monitoring.

61. "Kenyan Paper Urges Legislators to Learn from California Recall Vote," *East African Standard* (Nairobi) (Web site), Nairobi, October 10, 2003, reprinted/supplied by BBC Worldwide Monitoring.

62. "Ugandan Politicians Should Take Note of the California Result," BBC Monitoring International Reports, October 9, 2003.

63. "Ugandan Politicians Should Take Note of the California Result," BBC Monitoring International Reports, October 9, 2003.

## FOUR. Collateral Damage: Connecting the Dots

1. ttp://www.villagevoice.com/issues/0149/fhoberman.php

2. Margaret Talev and Dale Kasler, "Rivals Open Fire on Actor," *Sacramento Bee*, August 11, 2003, at http://www.sacbee.com/content/politics/vprint/story/7205259p–8150974c.html

3. http://rogersimon.com/archive/2003_10.html

4. News from CNN, August 18, 2003, Transcript #081805CN.V95.

5. Lisa Leff, "Schwarzenegger's Stand on Gay Rights Puts Him in the Middle of the Road," Associated Press, September 29, 2003.

6. http://www.allhatnocattle.net/8–12–03-ken-lay-bush-schwarzenegger.htm

7. Bill Bradley, "Connecting the Dots," *LA Weekly*, October 3–9, 2003, at http://www.laweekly.com

8. Rob Reynolds, "Connecting the California Dots: Rove to Arnold," BuzzFlash Reader Commentary, August 8, 2003, at http://www.buzzflash.com/contributors/03/08/08_dots.html

9. http://209.157.64.200/focus/f-news/995772/posts

10. Rachel Konrad, "Clinton Blasts California Recall, Predicting 'Long-Term Damage,'" Associated Press, September 16, 2003.

11. http://www.chronwatch.com/content/contentDisplay.asp?aid=4390

12. Beth Fouhy, "California's Davis Mulls His Impact as Job Soon Ends," *Seattle Times*, November 9, 2003, at http://www.seattletimes.com

13. Howard Fineman, "The Democrats' Mr. Right," *Newsweek*, July 22, 1991, p. 23.

14. Bill O'Neill, "72-Year-Old Granny Is a Champion Bodybuilder," *National Enquirer*, August 10, 1993, p. 33.

15. http://www.cigaraficionado.com/Cigar/CA_Profiles/People_Profile/0,2540,39,00.html

16. Roxana Kopetman, "Long Beach Shaken by 3 Slayings," *Los Angeles Times*, April 16, 1993, p. B1.

17. KCRW Press Release, November 7, 2000, at http://www.kcrw.org/about/press releases/001107Studio360.html

18. Bill Whalen, "Scavenger Hunt," *The Daily Standard*, September 2, 2003.

19. http://www.cs.virginia.edu/oracle/arnie.html

20. Emily Yoffe, "Valley of the Silicon Dolls," *Newsweek*, November 26, 1990, p. 72.

21. L. T. Reissner, "In High Gear in Heidi Country," May 14, 1998, at http://www.math.science.unitn.it/Bike/Countries/Switzerland/Tour_Reports/Gruy eres.html

22. Associated Press, May 29, 1993.

23. Steve Weinstein, "TV Anchor Finds a Voice on Radio," *Los Angeles Times*, June 17, 1992, p. F1.

24. "Blitzkriegs," *Village Voice*, August 10, 1993.

25. "Broncos Hope Raging Bull Will Grab Opponents by the Horns," *Sydney Morning Herald* (Australia), August 30, 2003.

26. Carol Biliczky, "Librarics Book Spot on Ballot for Levies," *Akron Beacon Journal*, October 22, 2003, p. B1.

27. Sharon Waxman, "From Pumping Iron to Pushing Political Ideas," *Washington Post*, September 28, 2003, p. A7.

28. As it appeared in *Hemispheres,* June 1996, p. 60.

29. Terril Yue Jones, "Sport-Brutes: Like Schwarzenegger with Bumpers," *Los Angeles Times*, May 2, 2001, p. G1.

30. Terril Yue Jones, "Sport-Brutes: Like Schwarzenegger with Bumpers," *Los Angeles Times*, May 2, 2001, p. G1.

31. "2003 Lingenfelter Hummer H2," *Motor Trend*, August 2003, p. 118.

32. "2003 Lingenfelter Hummer H2," *Motor Trend*, August 2003, p. 118. (In the televised debate among the top gubernatorial recall-election candidates, Arnold told Arianna Huffington, "You have the biggest tax loophole. I can drive my Hummer through it.")

33. Pamela Ann Campbell, "Amazing Darwin's Finches" at http://www.travel-travel-travel.com/out/archives/16/DARWINS_FINCHES.htm

34. http://www.abc.net.au/rural/news/stories/s680496.htm

35. Catherine Moy, "Fairfield Ready for Politics to Get Pumped Up," TheReporter.com, August 9, 2003, at http://www.thereporter.com/

36. Campaign brochure (2003), "You Are Welcome Here." Santa Monica, Calif., Californians for Schwarzenegger.

37. *Entertainment Weekly*, June 11, 1993.

38. Charles Olson, "The Kingfishers," in *The Collected Poems of Charles Olson*, George Butterick, ed. Berkeley: University of California Press, 1987, p. 86. See also J. Hoberman, "Nietzsche's Boy," *Sight & Sound*, 8 (1991), 22–25. Hoberman makes the case that Arnold has dramatically enacted Nietzsche's idea of the "will to power."

39. Larry Tye. *The Father of Spin: Edward L. Bernays & the Birth of Public Relations.* New

York: Crown Publishers, 1998, p. 52.

40. http://www.msnbc.com/news/976299.asp
41. http://slate.msn.com/id/31868/
42. Charles Siebert, "The Way We Live Now: 10–19–03; Wild Thing," *New York Times*, October 19, 2003.
43. http://www.stevefriess.com/archive/theadvocate/SIG&ROYGAY.htm
44. Mireya Navarro and Laura M. Holson, "Onstage Attack Casts Pall over Las Vegas Strip," *New York Times*, October 6, 2003.
45. http://www.stevefriess.com/archive/theadvocate/SIG&ROYGAY.htm
46. Roland Barthes. *Mythologies*. New York: The Noonday Press, 1957, p. 20.
47. Roland Barthes. *Mythologies*. New York: The Noonday Press, 1957, p. 20.
48. Roland Barthes. *Mythologies*. New York: The Noonday Press, 1957, p. 18.

## FIVE. Dave

1. Lisa Denton, "Punchline," *Chattanooga Times Free Press*, August 22, 2003, p. H31.
2. Appears many places in national media.
3. References to Schwarzenegger as "Arnie" are rare in the United States but common in Europe and other parts of the world.
4. *The Australian*, Nov. 1, 2003, at http://www.theaustralian.news.com.au/print page/0,5942,7682854,00.html
5. Tom Green, "Arnie, the Class Clown," *USA Today*, December 20, 1990.
6. E-mail, March 1991.
7. Hugh Downs on *20/20*, December 2, 1988.
8. http://bakiwop.f2o.org/115.asp (Web site no longer on-line)
9. American Media, Inc. *Arnold: The American Dream*. Boca Raton, Fla.: American Media, Inc., 2003, p. 1.
10. Annie Brown, "Arnold Schmalzenegger; Film Star Steps Straight into Cheesy Politician Role as He Begins His Term-Inator in Office," *Daily Record* (Glasgow), October 9, 2003, pp. 1, 11.
11. E-mail, March, 1991.
12. http://www.dctalksolo.com/boards/ubb-get_topic-f–17-t–002517.html
13. http://www.emu-farm.net/
14. http://www.stevenmaginnis.blogspot.com/2003_10_01_stevenmaginnis_archive.html
15. Rob Harvilla, "Get to the Chopper! Cleaning Up the Mythology and Mayhem Surrounding ArnoCorps. Fantastic Exactly," *Emeryville (Calif.) East Bay Express*, December 17, 2003.
16. *People*, January 21, 1991, p. 118.
17. http://www.allhatnocattle.net/zelda_morgan_hollywood_dreams.htm
18. Frank Rich, "The Audio-Animatronic Candidate," *New York Times*, October 12, 2003, Sect. 2, p. 1.

19. American Media, Inc. *Arnold: The American Dream*. Boca Raton, Fla.: American Media, Inc., 2003, p. 8.

20. Bob Keeler, "Asides," *New York Newsday,* October 12, 2003, p. A33.

21. *Boston Phoenix*, June 7, 1991, Sect. 3, p. 1.

22. Amanda Onion, "Big Green Governor? Environmentalists, Republicans Eager to See How Green Schwarzenegger Can Be," November 17, 2003, at http://abcnews.go.com/sections/SciTech/US/Schwarzenegger_environment_0311117.html

23. http://www.encapsulator.com/archives/000003.html

24. Helen Kennedy, "Ah-nold to Pump W for Aid," *New York Daily News*, October 15, 2003, p. 6.

25. Bill Bradley, "Conan the Governor," *LA Weekly* at http://www.laweekly.com/ink/03/47/election-bradley.php

26. Steve Lopez, "Another Actress Makes the Case for Conan the Gentleman," *Los Angeles Times*, October 7, 2003, p. B1.

27. Bill Bradley, "Conan the Governor," *LA Weekly* at http://www.laweekly.com/ink/03/47/election-bradley.php

28. Tom Farrey, "Conan the Politician," October 17, 2003, at http://espn.go.com/columns/farrey_tom/1655597.html.

29. Susan Faludi, "Conan the Vulgarian," *Los Angeles Times*, October 5, 2003, p. M1.

30. http://www.blackenergy.com/index.php

31. Julietta Jameson, "Determinator—How an Austrian Bodybuilder Muscled His Way into the American Dream—Relentless Rise of the Last Action Hero," *Daily Telegraph* (Sydney, Australia), October 11, 2003, p. 25.

32. Michael Wilmington, "Kitschy, Kitschy Goo," *Los Angeles Times*, December 21, 1990, p. F1.

33. Manohla Dargis, "The Incredible Shrinking Hulk," *LA Weekly*, 1996.

34. http://www.urbandictionary.com/define.php?term=Schwarzenegger

35. http://www.latimes.com/news/local/politics/cal/la-me-arnold3dec03,1,1577704.story?coll=la-news-politics-california

36. Editorial, "Gov. Hollywood," *New York Newsday*, October 10, 2003, p. A40.

37. Appears in hundreds of places, for example, http://www.guardian.co.uk/g2/story/0,3604,1014398,00.html

38. http://sandiego.indymedia.org/en/2003/09/100677.shtml

39. *USA Today*, August 7, 2003.

40. This is one of the most common of Arnold's nicknames. See, for example, Paul D. Colford, "All Over L.A. Times for Gropinator Expose," *New York Daily News*, October 9, 2003, p. 6.

41. Popularized in the *Doonesbury* comic strips by Gary Trudeau.

42. http://www.hsbr.net/servlet/readGenome?stock=CRUSD

43. Jonathan Rowe, "Gubernatorial Goldrush: Why the Terminator Is No Gipper," *Washington Monthly*, December 2003, p. 51.

44. http://bakiwop.f2o.org/115.asp (Web site no longer on-line)

45. http://bakiwop.f2o.org/115.asp (Web site no longer on-line)
46. Arnold Schwarzenegger, "Kindergarten Cop Lays Down Law on Exercise," *New York Times*, Education Life End Paper, January 6, 1991, p. 58.
47. http://bakiwop.f2o.org/115.asp (Web site no longer on-line)
48. http://www.imao.us/cgi-bin/mt-comments.cgi?entry_id=1034
49. *M inc.*, October 1991.
50. E-mail, February 1991.
51. http://www.berkeley.edu/news/media/releases/2003/10/27_lakoff.shtml
52. Randy Jennings, "Chill, Mr. Freeze on Vacation!" at http://www.thearnoldfans.com/news/archives/2002/29.htm
53. http://la.indymedia.org/print.php?id=86714
54. Susan Wloszczyna, "'Terminator 2': Rampage Deluxe," *USA Today*, April 13, 1991.
55. Greg Palast, "Arnold Unplugged," October 4, 2003, at http://www.mike hersh.com/ARNOLD_UNPLUGGED.shtml
56. "Arnold Talks!" *Playboy*, September 1976, p. 208.
57. *Star* (Canada), "Hasta La Vista, Baby," March 17, 1992.
58. This was a name Arnold gave himself in jest, as quoted in Erica Werner, "Schwarzenegger: Big Name, No Experience," *New York Newsday*, August 7, 2003.
59. "Governor of California Election Brought to a Halt," Radio transcript at http://www.abc.net.au/am/content/2003/s946716.htm
60. http://www.iompao.com/schwarzenegger.html
61. http://sandorian.us/newslog2.php/_d245/_v245/_show_article/_a000245–0 00061.htm
62. http://www.indybay.org/news/2003/10/1652671_comment.php
63. David Lindorff, "Lights Out, Baby: Where's Arnold When We Need Him?" at http://www.counterpunch.org/lindorff08162003.html
64. Michael Wilmington, "Kitschy, Kitschy Goo," *Los Angeles Times*, December 21, 1990, p. F1.
65. E-mail, March 1991.
66. Christina Valhouli, "Arnold Schwarzenegger," at http://archive.salon.com/people /conv/2001/01/29/schwarzenegger
67. http://www.allocine.fr/article/fichearticle_gen_carticle=18358304.html
68. J. Hoberman, "The Self-Made Man: Arnold Schwarzenegger Über Alles," *Village Voice*, February 12, 1991, p. 53.
69. http://www.bild.t-online.de/BTO/news/2003/10/04/sexinator/sexinator.html
70. http://www.bubblegun.com/features/arnie.html
71. http://www.latimes.com/news/local/politics/cal/la-et-macgregor19nov19,1,42 64760.story?coll=la-news-politics-california
72. Michael Wilmington, "Kitschy, Kitschy Goo," *Los Angeles Times*, December 21, 1990, p. F1.
73. Maynard Good Stoddard, "'Kindergarten Cop': A Classroom Caper," *The Saturday Evening Post*, Jan./Feb. 1991, p. 60.
74. Tim Grieve, "The Teflon Groper," at http://archive.salon.com/news/feature/

2003/10/06/recall/index_np.html

75. http://www.dvdmoviecentral.com/ReviewsText/terminator_3.htm

76. Brian Flynn, "Arnie the Termwinator," *The Sun* (London), October 9, 2003.

77. "The Tool-E-Nator: Guilt by Association?" MotherJones.com, September 8, 2003, at http://www.motherjones.com/news/dailymojo/2003/09/we_543_01c.html

78. Michael Wilmington, "Kitschy, Kitschy Goo," *Los Angeles Times*, December 21, 1990, p. F1.

79. J. Hoberman, "The Self-Made Man," *Village Voice*, February 12, 1991, p. 53.

80. *Daily Californian*, September 8, 2003, at http://www.dailycal.org/article.asp?id=12611

81. *California Journal*, April 1, 2001.

## SIX. Eraser: The Schwarzenegger of All Metaphors

1. http://www.schwarzenegger.com/en/actor/filmography/erase.asp

2. George Lakoff and Mark Johnson. *Metaphors We Live By*. Chicago: University of Chicago Press, 1980, p. 3.

3. George Lakoff and Mark Johnson. *Metaphors We Live By*. Chicago: University of Chicago Press, 1980, p. 4.

4. http://www.amazon.com/exec/obidos/ASIN/0689845324/ref=ase_bridge bookss/102-1677621-2666515

5. http://www.marychen.com/archives/000025.html

6. http://www.dianaslegacy.net/ The link to the sesame Street page no longer exists.

7. John Anderson, "Ustinov Recalls Clash of the Togas," *New York Newsday*, April 25, 1991, p. 79.

8. http://www.westnet.com/~crywalt/pregnancy/pediatrician.html

9. http://www.trainingforclimbing.com/html2/htc512-second-ed.shtml

10. http://www.avninsider.com/stories/lead072902.shtml (also see http://www.enquirer.com/editions/1999/05/02/loc_technology.html)

11. Kathryn Koegel, "Biceps and Ballroom Bulge for Schwarzenegger Speech," *UCLA Daily Bruin*, April 15, 1983, p. 1.

12. http://www.slobrews.com/slostyles.html

13. http://www.northwest-wine.com/kiona-cabernet-sauvignon-reserve.html

14. http://twmwine.com

15. http://www.winepros.com.au/jsp/cda/wine/wineprofile.jsp?ID=4569

16. http://www.bronsonpianostudio.com/reviews/101803r1.htm

17. http://www.nick-cave.net/board/posting.php?mode=quote&p=4785

18. http://oyt.oulu.fi/tbl/archive/VOL1/1100-1171/hl1154.hunl

19. http://naturalolympia.com/html/profile.htm

20. http://ipm.ncsu.edu/current_ipm/03PestNews/03News17/resident.html

21. http://www.writersmonthly.us/pages/wm_library/poets_workshop/speculative_poctry.html

22. http://www.mcgill.ca/news/archives/spring2002/bisson/two/

23. http://www.betterbeef.com/news_montana_range.html

24. http://www.iptv.org/mtom/archivedbazaar.cfm?Bid=2

25. http://www.gene.ch/gentech/1997/Sep-Oct/msg00011.html

26. http://www.meandmephoto.com/Africa/Pages/Lions/LionF7.html

27. http://www.shanmonster.com/archives/20011109.html

28. http://hometown.aol.com/wienerdox/dachshund.html

29. http://www.hollywoodteenmovies.com/ScoobyDoo.html

30. http://www.leeislandcoast.com/everything_to_do/softshellturtle.php3

31. http://www.diveatlas.com/travel/florida5.asp

32. http://county.ces.uga.edu/habersham/spm/spring.html

33. http://www.packllama2000.com/conformation.html

34. http://llamabreeders.com/Sires/Domino.htm

35. http://www.komotv.com/features/aroundthehouse/gardening-story.asp?ID=70

36. http://list.k12.ar.us/pipermail/science/2001-April/001348.html

37. Daniel Butler, "Pretty in Pink, but a Poisonous Enemy," *The Independent* (London), July 4, 1998, p. 13.

38. http://www.adn.com/adn/email/fullemail.html

39. http://www.pecos.net/news/arch98/062998p.htm

40. http://www.agintheclassroom.org

41. David Feldman. *A World of Imponderables: The Answers to Life's Most Mystifying Questions.* New York: Galahad Books, 2000, p. 239.

42. http://www.post-gazette.com/movies/20020315showtime8.asp

43. http://www.mainichi.co.jp/english/travel/stories/991022–1.html

44. http://www.reviewjournal.com/lvrj_home/2000/May–31-Wed–2000/news/13681740.html

45. http://verizonsupersite.com/prospectcyclescom/cruisers

46. http://suntimes.co.za/1999/10/03/motoring/motor18.htm

47. http://technologymeetings.com/magazinearticle.asp?magazinearticleid=95261&magazineid=280&siteID=28&releaseid=6059&mode=print

48. http://www.onlineathens.com/ns-search/stories/042001/mer_01-mb-s600.shtml?NS-search-set=/3ff78/aaaa13173f78bfb&NS-doc-offset=0&

49. http://tampabayillustrated.com/index.cfm?fuseaction=display_article&whicharticle=324

50. Jacques T. Godbout with Alain Caillé. *The World of the Gift,* translated by Donald Winkler. Toronto: McGill-Queen's University Press, 1998, p. 12.

51. Mark Johnson. *Moral Imagination: Implications of Cognitive Science for Ethics.* Chicago: University of Chicago Press, 1993, p. 192.

52. http://fablog.ehrensteinland.com/archives/2002_11.shtml

53. http://www.tellicochurch.org/Archives/980510.html

54. http://www.homileticsonline.com/nonsubscriber/back_page/janfeb04.asp

55. Leslie Brothers. *Friday's Footprint: How Society Shapes the Human Mind.* New York: Oxford University Press, 1997, p. 82.

56. http://www.roxie.com/archive/Sep00.html

57. http://cargo.ship-of-fools.com/Features00/Features/Dominus.html

58. http://whyfiles.org/coolimages/index.html?id=1016768446

59. http://bio-e.epfl.ch/page31414.html

60. http://www.migraine—headache.com/migraine_questions.html

61. Dick McCullough, "Vernon," at http://www.macroinc.com/html/art/s_ver.html

62. http://www.scripps.edu/newsandviews/e_20021125/schmid.html

63. Gaston Bachelard. *The Psychoanalysis of Fire*, translated by Alan C. M. Ross. Boston: Beacon Press, 1964, p. 109.

64. http://www.os2ezine.com/20020416/page_5.html

65. http://exothermic.com.au/articles/oz/packardbell.html

66. http://www.dazmeister.co.uk/review/serioussampc.htm

67. http://lists.evolt.org/archive/Week-of-Mon–20010226/026504.html

68. http://lists.evolt.org/archive/Week-of-Mon–20010226/026525.html

69. http://www.resumemaker.com/ResumeMaker/company/nytarticle.jsp

70. David Pogue and Joseph Schorr. *Macworld Mac & Power Mac Secrets*, 2nd ed. New York: IDG Books, 1994, p. 987.

71. http://www.guardian.co.uk/print/0,3858,4763849–103550,00.html

72. http://www.nzfirst.org.nz/content/display_item.php?t=1&i=1006

73. http://www.2theadvocate.com/stories/080803/new_race001.shtml (link is no longer available)

74. http://www.geocities.com/socialist_action/tories.html

75. http://www.matthewyglesias.com/archives/001353.html

76. http://demsjapan.typepad.com/blog/2003/09/armchair_progno.html

77. http://www.robert-fisk.com/robert_elias_25sept2001.htm

78. http://www.parliament.the-stationery-office.co.uk/pa/cm199798/cmhansrd/vo970611/debtext/70611–01.htm

79. http://www.mips1.net/mgn03.nsf/0/80256DCE0038757A85256DD1007219CD?OpenDocument

80. http://www.bestsyntheticoil.com/amsoil/automatic_transmission_fluid.shtml

81. http://www.powerbookcentral.com/columns/kravitz/ipodcasesb.shtml

82. http://www.cathedralstainedglass.com/saws28.html

83. http://www.buyers-advantage.com/#6

84. http://www.budgetrobotics.com/shop/index.php?shop=1&cat=81

85. http://www.audioholics.com/FAQs/RBHSoundT–2FAQ.html

86. http://www.midi-classics.com/c/c27215.htm

87. Philip Fisher. *Wonder, the Rainbow, and the Aesthetics of Rare Experiences*. Cambridge: Harvard University Press, 1998.

**SEVEN. The Terminator: 3D Icon**

1. Joe Matthews, "So Familiar Yet So Unknown," *Los Angeles Times*, October 8, 2003, p. A1.

2. Marsha Kinder, "Back to the Future in the 80s with Fathers & Sons, Supermen & PeeWees, Gorillas & Toons," *Film Quarterly*, 42:4 (Summer 1989), 2.

3. http://www.cnn.com/TRANSCRIPTS/0310/11/cg.00.html

4. Clinton speech on October 25, 1992.

5. Mark Leibovich, "Political Muscle: When It Comes to a Possible Run for Governor, Arnold Is Acting Coy," *Washington Post*, July 8, 2003, p. C01.

6. *Empire*, June 2003, p. 112.

7. http://www.enquirer.com/editions/2003/07/02/tem_wedlede02terminator.html

8. Mark Leibovich, "Political Muscle: When It Comes to a Possible Run for Governor, Arnold Is Acting Coy," *Washington Post*, July 8, 2003, p. C01.

9. Chris Chase, "Stardom, a Glitzy Stepping Stone to Mediocrity," *New York Times*, October 20, 1991, p. 26.

10. http://www.imdb.com/title/tt0088247/board/nest/2161064 or at http://www.eterminator.com

11. Greill Marcus. *Dead Elvis: A Chronicle of a Cultural Obsession*. Cambridge: Harvard University Press, 1991, p. 3.

12. Victor Turner. *The Forest of Symbols: Aspects of Ndembu Ritual*. Ithaca: Cornell University Press, 1967, pp. 30–33.

13. A fascinating example is from the April 1992 issue of *Premiere*. Schwarzenegger was about to make his directorial debut—*Christmas in Connecticut* (1992)—and *Premiere* magazine wondered, "What does Hollywood think about the Terminator trying to make it as a director?" Caroline Kirk Cordero, "Cable Ready," *Premiere*, April 1992, p. 124.

14. Dan Geringer, "As They Say in Hollywood, Pex Sell Tix," *Sports Illustrated*, December 1987, p. 90.

15. http://www.theage.com/au/cgi-bin/common/popupPrintArticle.pl?path=/articles/2003/08/08/1060145859748.html (Web site had been deactivated)

16. http://www.vh1.com/news/articles/1479631/20031008/schwarzenegger

17. Peter Nicholas, Carla Hall, and Michael Finnegan, "Schwarzenegger Tells Backers He 'Behaved Badly,'" *Los Angeles Times*, October 3, 2003, p. A1.

18. http://www.cbsnews.com/stories/2003/10/05/politics/main576596.shtml

19. http://www.mtv.com/news/articles/1475982/08072003/id_0.jhtml

20. http://www.cbsnews.com/stories/2003/10/05/politics/main576596.shtml

21. http://www.mtv.com/news/articles/1479631/20031008/schwarzenegger_arnold.jhtml?headlines=true

22. http://www.townhall.com/columnists/robertnovak/rn20030814.shtml

23. http://www.cbsnews.com/stories/2003/10/05/politics/main576596.shtml

24. Karen Breslau, "Cut! No Sequels, Please," *Newsweek*, October 6, 2003.

25. Sophronia Scott Gregory, "Hasta La Vista, Bobby," *Time*, June 14, 1993, p. 31.

26. Oren Rawls, "In Other Words...," *Forward*, August 15, 2003, at http://www.forward.com/issues/2003/03.08.15/otherwords.html

27. Tim Harper, "Terminator Wants to Be Governor," *Toronto Star*, August 7, 2003, at http:///www.thestar.com

28. Kevin Mitchell, "Hypocrisy at the Heart of the Affair," *The Observer* (London), October 19, 2003, at http://observer.guardian.co.uk/print/0,3858,4777758–102283,00.html

29. "FPJ and Loren: 'Blockbuster Team? Roco Isn't Worried," *Halalan 2004: News Issues & Commentaries,* October 23, 2003, at http://houseonahill.net/halalan2004/old news/2003/10/000694.html

30. "Enter the Terminator," *News International–Internet Edition,* October 10, 2003, at http://www.jang.com.pk/thenews/oct2003-daily/11–10–2003/oped/o2.htm

31. Robert Lusetich, "Terminator Wins Toughest Battle," *The Australian*, October 9, 2003, at http://www.theaustralian.news.com.au/printpage/0,5942,7504338,00.html

32. "World Press Digests Arnie's Latest Role," BBC News, at http://news.bbc.co.uk/go/pr/fr/-/1/hi/world/americas/3177916.stm

33. http://www.bayarea.com/mld/mercurynews/news/6243700.htm

34. http://www.theindependent.com/stories/093003/opi_ayoub30.shtml

35. http://www.buzzle.com/editorials/10–9–2003-46281.asp

36. http://www.latimes.com/news/politics/recall/cl-et-rivenburg10oct10,1,2041116.story

37. http://www.urbandictionary.com

38. Harold R. Isaacs. *Idols of the Tribe: Group Identity and Political Change.* Cambridge: Harvard University Press, 1989, p. 71.

39. Dominique Audibert, "Californiator," *Le Point* (Paris), October 10, 2003, p. 1.

40. Tom Shields, "The Tartanator: If America Can Have Arnie, Scotland Should Have Shir Sean for Firsht Minishter," *Sunday Herald* (Glasgow), October 12, 2003, at http://www.sundayherald.com/37279

41. Karen Breslau, "The First Lady: The Inoculator," *Newsweek*, October 20, 2003, p. 32.

42. Karen Breslau, "California: From Terminator to Communicator?" *Newsweek*, November 24, 2003, p. 10.

43. Caroline Kirk Cordero, "Cable Ready," *Premiere*, April 1992, p. 124.

44. http://www.scoop.co.nz/mason/stories/HL0310/S00087.htm

45. James Cameron, "Terminator" fourth draft, April 20, 1983, at http://heim.ifi.uio.no/~haakonj/Terminator/Scripts/t1script.txt

46. http://www.gregpalast.com/detail.cfm?artid=283&row=1

47. http://www.trommetter.com/log/archives/2003/10/08/Hasta_La_Vista_Davy _2416.php

48. http://www.hollywood.com/news/detail/article/1730107

49. Thomas H. Maugh II, "HIV Researchers Struggle to Hit Their Moving Target," *Los Angeles Times*, August 8, 1994, p. A13.

50. Sheryl Stolberg and Patt Morrison, "In Landers, Temblors Are the Talk of the Town," *Los Angeles Times*, June 29, 1992, p. A7.

51. Steven Clarke, "The Methylator Meets the Terminator," *Proceedings of the National Academy of Sciences of the United States of America*, February 5, 2002, at http://pubmed central.nih.gov/articlerender.fcgi?artid=122150

52. Robert L. Forward, Robert Hoyt, and Chauncey Uphoff, "The Terminator Tether™: A Low-Mass System for End-of-Life Deorbit of LEO Spacecraft," Tether Technical Interchange Meeting, Huntsville, Ala., September 10, 1997. Publication 98–3491. Birmingham: Alabama Aerospace Industry Association.

53. Anup Shah, "What Is the Purpose of Switching Off Seed Germination?" July 14, 2001, at http://www.globalissues.org/EnvIssues/GEFood/Terminator.asp

54. Michelle Malkin, "Terminate This, Arnold," Townhall.com at http://www.town hall.com/columnists/michellemalkin/printmm20020425.shtml

55. http://www.vop.com/previous_broadcasts/2003/may/03194.htm

56. http://eutopia.cua.edu/article.cfm?ID=61

57. http://www.touchandchange.com/artman/publish/article_456.shtml

58. http://www.all.org/crusade/caltrio.htm

59. http://techupdate.zdnet.com/techupdate/stories/main/0,14179,2914623,00_print.html

60. Terry Costlow, "SCSI–2 Horror Show: The Terminators," *Electronic Engineering Times*, June 28, 1993. Reprint.

61. http://www.mcmenamins.com/Brewing/Ales.html

62. Robert Moritz, "Terminators," *Parade Magazine*, August 3, 2003, p. 16.

63. "Ask Therminator; He Knows Comfort," *Los Angeles Times*, March 23, 1993, p. 1.

64. Anthony Ramirez, "Blab-o-matic" Sales Pitches," *New York Times*, November 5, 1992, p. A1.

65. http://www.suite101.com/article.cfm/Southwest%20Outdoors/92584

66. http://www.businessweek.com/2000/00_17/b3678187.htm?scriptFramed

67. *LA Weekly*, 13:3 (July 19–25, 1991).

68. Eric Mankin, "Terminating the Terminator," *L.A. Reader*, July 12, 1991.

69. George J. Church, "Inflation Terminator," *Time*, March 7, 1994.

70. Jonathan Gold, "Chu-minator II," *Los Angeles Times*, June 25, 1992, p. H29.

71. Sherry Suib Cohen, "Cher Magic," *New Woman*, December 1991, p. 64.

72. David Mermelstein, "Menace to Society," *LA Village View*, no date.

73. *City Sports Magazine*, July 1993, p. 20.

74. Ross Newhan, "Hasta la Vista, Baby," *Los Angeles Times*, October 17, 1992, p. C1.

75. Randy Harvey, "For Lipinski, This Gold Medal Is Child's Play," *Los Angeles Times*, February 21, 1998, p. N4.

76. http://www.dailybruin.ucla.edu/news/articles.asp?ID=18343

77. Jay Boyer, "Junior," *Orlando Sentinel*, November 25, 1994.

78. "A Doctor's Misconception," *People*, January 4, 1993.

79. http://www.discogs.com/artist/Sperminator

80. http://www.tvtome.com/tvtome/servlet/GuidePageServlet/showid–183/epid–22712/

81. http://www.hollywood.com/celebs/detail/celeb/190190

82. http://www.mtbreview.com/dream/bikes/1026.html

83. http://www.toyboxxx.com/products/230145.htm

84. http://www.utne.com/webwatch/2003_101/news/10814–1.html

85. Bill Zehme, "Mr. Big Shot," *Rolling Stone*, August 22, 1991, p. 79.

86. http://www.thehamsters.co.uk/videos/verminator.html

87. http://www.boltontech.org.uk/verminator.htm

88. http://www.verminatorpredatorcalls.com

89. Daryn Guarino, "To Gel and Back: Men's Shower Gels," at http://www.suds report.com/12–01/mens_shower_gels.htm

90. http://www.worminatorlures.com

91. Christina Manz, "6 Frauen beschuldigen als Grabscher Arnold Schwarzenegger— der Sexinator," at http://www.bild.t-online.de/BTO/news/2003/10/04/sexinator /sexinator,templateId=renderKomplett.html#

92. Ronni Sayewitz, "'Sturminator' Replacing Miller on 'The Ticket,'" *Dallas Business Journal,* at http://dallas.bizjournals.com/dallas/

93. http://www.afn.org/~afn41941/strmtor.htm

94. Bill Zehme, "Mr. Big Shot," *Rolling Stone*, August 22, 1991, p. 42.

95. K. W. Woods. *Schwarzenegger: Muscleman to Terminator (An Unauthorized Biography).* Lincolnwood, Ill.: Publications International, Ltd., 1991, p. 6.

96. Knute Berger, "Why Arnold Matters: The Terminator Is Such a Tool (Against Democracy)," *Seattle Weekly* online, August 13–19, 2003, at http://www.seattleweekly. com/features/0333/news-mossback.php

97. Dani Cavallaro. *The Body for Beginners.* New York: Writers and Readers Publishing, Inc., 1998, p. 120.

98. Donna Haraway, "A Manifesto for Cyborgs: Science, Technology and Socialist Feminism in the 1980s," in *Coming to Terms: Feminism, Theory, Politics,* Elizabeth Weed, ed. London: Routledge, 1989, p. 173.

99. Donna Haraway, "A Manifesto for Cyborgs: Science, Technology and Socialist Feminism in the 1980s," in *Coming to Terms: Feminism, Theory, Politics,* Elizabeth Weed, ed. London: Routledge, 1989, p. 174.

100. Bill Zehme, "Mr. Big Shot," *Rolling Stone*, August 22, 1991, p. 41.

101. "Enter the Terminator," *News International–Internet Edition,* October 11, 2003, at http://www.jang.com.pk/thenews/oct2003-daily/11–10–2003/oped/o2.htm

102. http://www.Terminator3-themovie.co.uk/history.html

103. Bill Zehme, "Mr. Big Shot," *Rolling Stone*, August 22, 1991, p. 41.

104. Bill Zehme, "Mr. Big Shot," *Rolling Stone*, August 22, 1991, pp. 41, 79.

105. Sean French. *The Terminator.* London: British Film Institute, 1996, p. 39.

106. Tony Allen-Mills Washington, "Dean Takes Tip from the Terminator with Power Lunge," *Sunday Times* (London), October 19, 2003, p. 28.

107. "T4: Rise of a Governor," at http://www.theage.com.au/articles/2003/08/08 /1060145859748.html

108. Gary Clement, *Toronto National Post,* at http://cagle.slate.msn.com/news/ Schwarzenegger/Schwarzeneggergifs/arnoldgifs/clement.gif

109. Jim Borgman, *New York Newsday,* October 25, 2003, p. A18.

110. Jim Borgman, *New York Newsday,* October 25, 2003, p. A18.

111. "T4 Medical Killing Program," at http://www.remember.org/witness/wit.vic.med.html


EIGHT. Stay Hungry: Appetites for Arnold

1. "Deconstructing Magazine Covers," The Center for Media Literacy (CML) at http://www.medialit.org/pdf/CML_DeconstructionMags.pdf
2. Richard Lacayo, "The Mind Behind the Muscles," *Time*, August 18, 2003, p. 28.


NINE. Predator: Arnold's Bodies of Work

1. http://us.imdb.com/title/tt0093773/
2. http://www.edge.org/3rd_culture/lakoff/lakoff_p1.html
3. Hillary MacGregor, "In Japan, He's Larger Than Larger-Than-Life," *Los Angeles Times*, November 19, 2003, p. E2.
4. Jerry Schwartz, "Schwarzenegger: From Mr. Universe to Governor," *Sacramento Bee*, October 8, 2003.
5. George Butler. *Arnold Schwarzenegger: A Portrait*. New York: Simon and Schuster, 1990, p. 13.
6. Julian Schmidt, "Arnold," *Muscle & Fitness*, August 1991, p. 91.
7. "How the California Recall Election May Change the Nature of National Politics," National Public Radio, *Day to Day*, October 8, 2003.
8. Bill Hemmer, CNN People in the News profile of Venus Williams, Serena Williams, and Arnold Schwarzenegger, July 12, 2003.
9. Bill Hemmer, CNN People in the News profile of Venus Williams, Serena Williams, and Arnold Schwarzenegger, July 12, 2003.
10. Bill Hemmer, CNN People in the News profile of Venus Williams, Serena Willliams, and Arnold Schwarzenegger, July 12, 2003.
11. Alan M. Klein, "Of Muscles and Men: An Anthropologist Examines Bodybuilding and Masculinity in America," *The Sciences*, 33:6 (November/December 1993).
12. George Butler. *Arnold Schwarzenegger: A Portrait*. New York: Simon and Schuster, 1990, p. 13.
13. Ron Harris, "Don't Ruhl Me Out: How the German Beast Hits It in Das Gym," *Muscular Development*, December 2003, p. 214.
14. Bill Dobbins, "Road to Greatness," *FLEX*, July 1997, p. 84.
15. George Butler. *Arnold Schwarzenegger: A Portrait*. New York: Simon and Schuster, 1990, p. 16.
16. Ron Harris, "Don't Ruhl Me Out: How the German Beast Hits It in Das Gym," *Muscular Development*, December 2003.
17. In an e-mail dated March 7, 1991, Michael reported a pair of dreams to Louise:

"Both dreams were rapid-fire images of speeches, poses, and long waitings-around for Arnold to show up, and in one dream he did not. In the other he did, but just to announce his upcoming film for which he planned to 'once again, be the largest man on earth.'" In the on-line magazine *The Rockall Times,* Nick Thomson calls Bill Gates the "largest man in the world with a voice like Kermit the Frog"(March 25, 2002, at http://www.therockalltimes.co.uk/2002/03/25/ms-cock-up.pub.html). However, in most un-Arnold–like fashion, according to Thomson, Gates "broke down in tears" when he lost an early round in court over an injunction against other software companies using names similar to "Windows." The story may be apocryphal, but whereas Gates may be fair game to fictionalize as a crying "girly-man," few if any would tell such a tale about Arnold.

18. Bill Hemmer, CNN People in the News profile of Venus Williams, Serena Williams, and Arnold Schwarzenegger, July 12, 2003.

19. "Second Annual Readers' Poll," *MuscleMag,* September 1991, p. 18.

20. "Second Annual Readers' Poll," *MuscleMag,* September 1991, p. 18.

21. "Second Annual Readers' Poll," *MuscleMag,* September 1991, p. 20.

22. http://uttm.com/stories/2003/10/22/politics/main579444.shtml

23. http://uttm.com/stories/2003/10/22/politics/main579444.shtml

24. http://uttm.com/stories/2003/10/22/politics/main579444.shtml

25. http://www.cbsnews.com/stories/2003/11/07/politics/main582392.shtml

26. Arnold Schwarzenegger and Douglas Kent Hall. *Arnold: The Education of a Bodybuilder.* New York: Fireside Books, 1977, p. 27.

27. Arnold Schwarzenegger and Douglas Kent Hall. *Arnold: The Education of a Bodybuilder.* New York: Fireside Books, 1977, p. 27.

28. http://www.schwarzenegger.com/en/life/hislife/index.asp?sec=life&subsec=hislife

29. http://www.mercurynews.com/mld/mercurynews/news/local/states/california/peninsula/6919164.htm

30. Tim Rutten, "Arnold's Past Now His Present?" *Los Angeles Times,* August 30, 2003, p. E1.

31. http://www.thesmokinggun.com/archive/arnoldou1l.html

32. Campaign brochure, "You Are Welcome Here," Californians for Schwarzenegger, 2003.

33. Gary Cohn, Carla Hall, and Robert W. Welkos, "Women Say Schwarzenegger Groped, Humiliated Them," *Los Angeles Times,* October 2, 2003, p. 1.

34. http://www.latimes.com/news/local/la-me-women2oct02,1,4154043.story?coll=la-home-headlines

35. http://www.latimes.com/news/local/la-me-women2oct02,1,4154043.story?coll=la-home-headlines

36. Mark Arax, "Recall Campaign: An Ethos Developed in the Gym," *Los Angeles Times,* September 29, 2003, p. A1.

37. Peter Nicholas, Carla Hall, and Michael Finnegan, "Schwarzenegger Tells Backers He 'Behaved Badly,'" *Los Angeles Times,* October 3, 2003, p. A1.

38. As quoted in Sharon Waxman, "From Pumping Iron to Pushing Political Ideas," *Washington Post*, September 28, 2003, p. A7.

39. http://www.livejournal.com/users/scripty/66604.html

40. Ann O'Neill, "Schwarzenegger's Friends Swoop In to Defend His Honor," *Los Angeles Times*, March 21, 2001, p. E1.

41. Ann O'Neill, "Schwarzenegger's Friends Swoop in to Defend His Honor," *Los Angeles Times*, March 21, 2001, p. E1.

42. The Oprah Winfrey Show, September 15, 2003.

43. The Oprah Winfrey Show, September 15, 2003.

44. http://www.womenjoiningarnold.com/video.html

45. Alan Richman, "Commando in Love," *People,* October 14, 1985, p. 128.

46. Kenneth Dutton. *The Perfectible Body: The Western Ideal of Male Physical Development.* New York: Continuum, 1995, p. 145.

47. George Butler. *Arnold Schwarzenegger: A Portrait.* New York: Simon and Schuster, 1990.

48. George Butler. *Arnold Schwarzenegger: A Portrait.* New York: Simon and Schuster, 1990.

49. George Butler. *Arnold Schwarzenegger: A Portrait.* New York: Simon and Schuster, 1990.

50. Colette Bancroft, "Arnold the Contender: King Kong or Fay Wray?" *St. Petersburg (Fla.) Times Online*, September 5, 2003, at http://www.sptimes.com/2003/09/05/news_pf/Floridian/Arnold_the_contender_.shtml

51. *Saturday Night Live*, December 3, 1988.

52. *Saturday Night Live*, December 3, 1988.

53. http://www.thesmokinggun.com/archive/arnoldoui1.html

54. "'The Arnold Eye for the Girly Guy' Kicks Off 'Behind the Music That Sucks' Marathon" on Fuse, November 8, 2003.

55. Christopher Ruddy and James Hirsen, "McClintock: Schwarzenegger Not Qualified," NewsMax.com, September 4, 2003, at http://www.newsmax.com/archives/articles/2003/8/31/141018.shtml

56. Mike Davis, "Californian Election—Is It Just About Schwarzenegger?" *Socialist Worker*, September 20, 2003, p. 10.

57. http://www.irchelp.org/irchelp/security/trojanterms.html and http://www.webopedia.com/TERM/T/Trojan_horse.html

58. http://www.publiceye.org/theocrat/Schapiro.html

59. Michael S. Kimmel, "Consuming Manhood: The Feminization of American Culture and the Re-creation of the Male Body, 1823–1920," in *The Male Body: Features, Destinies, Exposures*, Laurence Goldstein, ed. Ann Arbor: University of Michigan Press, 1994, p. 22.

60. Susan Faludi. *Stiffed: The Betrayal of the American Man.* New York: William Morrow and Company, 1999, p. 35.

61. Susan Jeffords. *The Remasculinization of America: Gender and the Vietnam War.* Bloomington: Indiana University Press, 1989.

62. Susan Jeffords. *The Remasculinization of America: Gender and the Vietnam War.* Bloomington: Indiana University Press, 1989, p. 73.

63. Bill Zehme, "Mr. Big Shot," *Rolling Stone*, August 22, 1991, p. 41.

64. Bill Zehme, "Mr. Big Shot," *Rolling Stone*, August 22, 1991, p. 41.

65. Bill Zehme, "Mr. Big Shot," *Rolling Stone*, August 22, 1991, p. 51.

66. Sam Keen. *Fire in the Belly: On Being a Man.* New York: Bantam Books, 1991, p. 237.

67. Robert Moore and Douglas Gillette. *King Warrior Magician Lover: Rediscovering the Archetype of the Mature Masculine.* San Francisco: HarperSanFrancisco, 1991.

68. Josué V.Harari, "Critical Factions/Critical Fictions," in *Textual Strategies: Perspectives in Post-Structuralist Criticism*, Josué V. Harari, ed. Ithaca: Cornell University Press, 1979, pp. 34–36.

69. http://www.gmax.co.za/feel/10/20-schwarzenegger.html

70. Jeff O'Connell, "The 6th Day," *Muscle & Fitness*, January 2001, p. 88.

71. Hermann Hesse. *Steppenwolf.* New York: Picador, 2002.

72. Robert Louis Stevenson. *The Strange Case of Dr. Jekyll and Mr. Hyde.* New York: W.W. Norton and Co., 2002.

73. It is worth noting that the word "hysteria" derives from the Greek word *hystera*, meaning "womb."

74. Universal Studios *Junior* Production Information, Universal Studios, Universal City, Calif., p. 3.

75. "What If Men Had Babies?" see http://www.geocities.com/CapitolHill /1396/babies.html

76. "What If Men Had Babies?" see http://www.geocities.com/CapitolHill/1396/babies.html

77. "What If Men Had Babies?" see http://www.geocities.com/CapitolHill/1396/babies.html

78. http://www.schwarzenegger.com/en/actor/filmography/index.asp?sec=actor&subsec=filmography

79. David F. Noble. *A World Without Women: The Christian Clerical Culture of Western Science.* New York: Alfred A. Knopf, 1992.

80. June Sawyer, "Man Gives Birth to a Healthy Baby Boy," *Weekly World News*, July 7, 1992, p. 19.

81. http://www.urbandictionary.com/define.php?term=talk+to+the+hand

82. "Bodybuilding: Is It Sport? Art?" *New York Times*, April 13, 1975, p. 216.

83. Peter Adam. *Art of the Third Reich.* New York: Harry N. Abrams, 1992, p. 177.

84. Peter Adam. *Art of the Third Reich.* New York: Harry N. Abrams, 1992, p. 178.

## TEN. Scavenger Hunt: Toilets and Titles

1. Robert Scheer, "Family Values Down the Toilet," *Los Angeles Times*, September 23, 2003.

2. Michael Sundquist, "California in the Toilet," *Modesto Bee,* October 4, 2003, p. B7.

3. "Arnie's Feeling Flush," *Daily Express* (London), September 26, 2003, p. 24.

4. Andrew Gumbel, "Terminator's Toilet Humor Backfires as Candidates Clash," *The Independent* (London), September 26, 2003, p. 16.

5. Judith Lewis, "The Face in the Toilet Bowl: Why Arnold Could Flush the Feminists," *LA Weekly,* October 10–16, 2003.

6. Bart Jones, "Issue Jumps to Exec Race," *New York Newsday,* October 23, 2003, p. A22.

7. CNN Money & Markets Transcript #082207cb.107, August 22, 2003.

8. Charles LeDuff, "The California Recall: The Governor Elect, Seizing the Moment, and Defying Expectations," *New York Times,* October 9, 2003, p. A33.

9. Patti Morrison, "For Schwarzenegger, Life Itself Is Way Too Taxing," *Milwaukee Journal Sentinel,* August 30, 2003, p. 17A.

10. John Marelius, "Hollywood Big Gun Casts Himself as Political Outsider," *San Diego Union-Tribune,* October 2, 2003, p. A1.

11. Mike Sweet, "Saving California," *Burlington (Ia.) Hawk Eye,* August 10, 2003, at http://www.thehawkeye.com/columns/Sweet/Sweet_0810.html

12. "The Stirrer," *Daily Star* (London), July 10, 2003, p. 12.

13. "Nothing Sells Like a Goofy Election!" *Palm Beach (Fla.) Post,* September 12, 2003, p. E1.

14. Stuart Leavenworth, "Study Shows Toilets a Drain on Water," Scripps Howard News Service, November 19, 2003.

15. Stuart Leavenworth, "Study Shows Toilets a Drain on Water," Scripps Howard News Service, November 19, 2003.

16. "New Toilets 'Don't Need Water,'" *news.com.au,* November 19, 2003, at http://www.news.com.au/common/story_page/0,4057,7913003%255E13762,00.html

17. Peter Larsen, "California Tribes Say Schwarzenegger Should Visit, Then Talk About Casinos," Hotel Online, November 16, 2003, at http://www.hotel online.com/News/2003_Nov_16/k.OCT.1069084159.html

18. Brealeys, "We All Use Them," *Eastern Daily Press* (England), November 29, 2003.

19. "Courting History's Verdict," *New York Post,* January 29, 2003, p. 24.

20. R. P. Whalen, "Why Wage War on Third World Country?" *Chicago Daily Herald,* February 20, 2003, p. 14.

21. Beth Gorham, "Bush Sees More Bloodshed in Iraq," *Daily Herald Tribune* (Grande Prairie, Alberta), December 16, 2003, p. 9.

22. Marion McKeone, "The Governator: Arnie Enters the 'Recall Carnival,'" *Sunday Tribune* (Dublin), August 10, 2003, p. 18.

23. Bill Whalen, "Scavenger Hunt," *The Daily Standard,* September 2, 2003.

24. Thomas M. Keane, Jr., "On Arnold Coattails Mitt's Hopes Rest," *Boston Herald,* August 13, 2003, p. 31.

25. Thomas K. Arnold, "At the DVD Polls, Arnold Is the Candidate to Watch," *USA*

*Today*, August 19, 2003, p. D3.

26. Sheldon Alberts, "California's New Hercules Has Twin Pillars: Governor-elect Liked by Republicans and Democrats," *National Post* (Canada), October 11, 2003, p. A14.

27. October 8, 2003, at http://houseonahill.net/archives/2003/10/0000601 print.html (no longer online)

28. "Conan the Candidate," *New York Post*, August 9, 2003, p. 16.

29. Allen Sloan, "Varied Scripts for Schwarzenegger," *Washington Post*, October 14, 2003, p. E3.

### ELEVEN. Christmas in Connecticut: Arnold Dreaming

1. American Media, Inc. *Arnold: The American Dream*. Boca Raton, Fla.: American Media, Inc., 2003, inside cover.

2. Richard Catlett Wilkerson, "Postmodern Dreaming: An Introduction," *Electric Dreams*, 4:5 (May 28, 1997), 2.

3. Wayne Koestenbaum. *Jackie Under My Skin: Interpreting an Icon*. New York: Farrar, Straus and Giroux, 1995, pp. 21–22.

4. Brian Master. *Dreams about H.M. The Queen and Other Members of the Royal Family*. London: Blond & Briggs Ltd., 1972, p. 1.

5. Kay Turner, ed. *I Dream of Madonna: Women's Dreams of the Goddess of Pop*. San Francisco: Collins Publishers, 1993, p. 20.

6. Wayne Koestenbaum. *Jackie Under My Skin: Interpreting an Icon*. New York: Farrar, Straus and Giroux, 1995, p. 198.

7. http://www.democracynow.org/article.pl?sid=03/08/26/1430228&tid=25

8. George Lakoff. *Women, Fire and Dangerous Things: What Categories Reveal About the Mind*. Chicago: University of Chicago Press, 1987, p. 96.

9. Bert O. States. *The Rhetoric of Dreams*. Ithaca: Cornell University Press, 1988, p. 121.

10. George Lakoff. *Women, Fire and Dangerous Things: What Categories Reveal About the Mind*. Chicago: University of Chicago Press, 1987, p. 92.

11. George Lakoff. *Women, Fire and Dangerous Things: What Categories Reveal About the Mind*. Chicago: University of Chicago Press, 1987, p. 6.

12. Bert O. States. *Dreaming and Storytelling*. Ithaca: Cornell University Press, 1993, p. 4.

13. Bert O. States. *Seeing in the Dark: Reflections on Dreams and Dreaming*. New Haven: Yale University Press, 1997, p. 3.

14. Bert O. States, "The Dream as Metaphor Machine," *Dream Time*, 17:2 (Spring 2000), 8.

15. Bert O. States. *The Rhetoric of Dreams*. Ithaca: Cornell University Press, 1988, p. 91.

16. Bert O. States. *The Rhetoric of Dreams*. Ithaca: Cornell University Press, 1988, p. 128.

17. Bert O. States, "The Dream as Metaphor Machine," *Dream Time*, 17:2 (Spring 2000), 9.

18. Bert O States. *The Rhetoric of Dreams*. Ithaca: Cornell University Press, 1988, p. 19.

19. Bert O States. *The Rhetoric of Dreams*. Ithaca: Cornell University Press, 1988, p. 143.

20. Hayden White. *The Content of the Form: Narrative Discourse and Historical Representation*. Baltimore: Johns Hopkins University Press, 1987, p. 1.

21. Donna Haraway. *Primate Visions: Gender, Race, and Nature in the World of Modern Science*. London: Routledge, 1989, p. 149.

22. Donna Haraway. *Primate Visions: Gender, Race, and Nature in the World of Modern Science*. London: Routledge, 1989, p. 135.

23. George Lakoff. *Women, Fire and Dangerous Things: What Categories Reveal About the Mind*. Chicago: University of Chicago Press, 1987, p. 5.

24. http://www.stanford.edu/group/King/publications/sermons/650704_The _American_Dream.html

25. Greill Marcus. *Dead Elvis: A Chronicle of a Cultural Obsession*. New York: Doubleday, 1991, pp. 30–31.

26. http://www.newdream.org/thedream/

27. Bill Zehme, "Mr. Big Shot," *Rolling Stone*, August 22, 1991, p. 42.

28. Studs Terkel. *American Dreams: Lost and Found*. New York: Ballantine Books, 1980, p. 140.

29. Bill Zehme, "Mr. Big Shot," *Rolling Stone*, August 22, 1991, p. 42.

30. Bert O. States. *The Rhetoric of Dreams*. Ithaca: Cornell University Press, 1988, p. 50.

31. Bert O. States. *Seeing in the Dark: Reflections on Dreams and Dreaming*. New Haven: Yale University Press, 1997, p. 10.

32. Rosalind Cartwright and Lynne Lamberg, "Directing Your Dreams," *Psychology Today*, 25:6 (1992), 32–37.

33. Charlotte Beradt. *The Third Reich of Dreams*. New York: Quadrangle Books, 1966.

34. Charlotte Beradt. *The Third Reich of Dreams*. New York: Quadrangle Books, 1966, pp. 38–40.

35. Gaston Bachelard. *The Psychoanalysis of Fire*, translated by Alan C.M. Ross. Boston: Beacon Press, 1964.

36. Gaston Bachelard. *The Poetics of Reverie: Childhood, Language, and the Cosmos*, translated by Daniel Russell. Boston: Beacon Press, 1960, p. 1.

**TWELVE. All We Really Needed to Know Before We Went Out into the World Are the Things We Learned from *Kindergarten Cop***

1. Maria Shriver. *Ten Things I Wish I'd Known—Before I Went Out into the Real World*. New York: Warner Books, Inc., 2000.

2. Robert Fulghum. *All I Really Need to Know I Learned in Kindergarten*. New York: Ivy Books, 1986.


## THIRTEEN. Running Man: The Sequel

1. Oliver Poole, "Running Man Arnie Dodges the Pickets," *Daily Telegraph* (Sydney), October 4, 2003, p. 19.

2. Karen Breslau, "Cut! No Sequels, Please," *Newsweek*, October 6, 2003, p. 40.

3. Sydney H. Schanberg, "Mondale Has Great Legs," *New York Times*, May 19, 1984, p. 23.

4. Daily Kos: Political analysis and other daily rants on the state of the nation, October 9, 2003, at http://www.dailykos.net/archives/004502.html

5. *Washington Post*, October 11, 2003, reprinted at http://sf.indymedia.org /news/2003/10/1652671.php

6. *New York Post*, October 18, 2003, p. 10.

7. Press Action.com, October 8, 2003, at http://www.pressaction.com/ pablog/archives/001053.html

8. *San Francisco Chronicle*, November 2, 2003, p. D1 (also at *counterpunch—Out of Bounds Magazine*, October 9, 2003, at http://www.counterpunch.org/hand10092003.html

9. *Seattle Post-Intelligencer*, October 10, 2003, at http://seattlepi.nwsource.com/national/ 143275_prez10.html?searchpagefrom=1&searchdiff=88

10. *The Daily Standard*, October 24, 2003.

11. *Washington Post*, October 10, 2003, p. A26.

12. *Atlanta Journal-Constitution*, October 10, 2003, p. A8.

13. *San Jose Mercury News*, October 9, 2003.

14. Agence France-Presse, October 9, 2003.

15. *Irish News* (Belfast), October 14, 2003.

16. The Mail Archive, October 7, 2003, at http://www.mail-archive.com/ctrl@list serv.aol.com/msg108429.html

17. http://www.ideosphere.com

18. The Sandorian Grove newslog, October 8, 2003, at http://sandorian.us/ newslog2.php/_d245/_v245/_show_article/_a000245-000061.htm

19. Steve Geissinger, "Governor Helps Cities, but Angers Dems," *Pleasanton (Calif.) Tri-Valley Herald*, December 19, 2003.

20. David M. Drucker, "Dems Punish Arnold," *Daily News of Los Angeles*, December 14, 2003, p. N1.

21. Peter Nicholas and Joe Matthews, "Schwarzenegger Seizes Reins of Power in Capitol," *Los Angeles Times*, December 19, 2003, p. A44.

22. Michelle Rester, "Governor's Mandate Saves County Jobs," *Daily News of Los Angeles*, January 1, 2004, p. N4.

23. Peter Nicholas and Joe Matthews, "Schwarzenegger Seizes Reins of Power in Capitol," *Los Angeles Times*, December 19, 2003, p. A44.

24. Peter Nicholas and Joe Matthews, "Schwarzenegger Seizes Reins of Power in Capitol," *Los Angeles Times*, December 19, 2003, p. A44.

25. Paul Vitello, "Arnold in Wünderland," *New York Newsday*, October 7, 2003, p. A6.

26. Joe Matthews, "Schwarzenegger Sells His Agenda in Malls: The Shopping Centers Offer Practical and Symbolic Advantages to a Governor Enlisting Public Support," *Los Angeles Times*, December 8, 2003, pp. B1, B6.

27. Joe Matthews, "Schwarzenegger Sells His Agenda in Malls," *Los Angeles Times*, December 8, 2003, p. B1.

28. Frank Rich, "The Audio-Animatronic Candidate," *New York Times*, October 12, 2003, Sect. 2, p. 20.

29. Frank Rich, "The Audio-Animatronic Candidate," *New York Times*, October 12, 2003, Sect. 2, p. 20.

30. Michael Sorkin, "Introduction," in *Variations on a Theme Park: The New American City and the End of Public Space*, Michael Sorkin, ed. New York: The Noonday Press, 1992, pp. xiii–xv.

31. Joe Matthews, "Schwarzenegger Sells His Agenda in Malls," *Los Angeles Times*, December 8, 2003, p. B1.

32. Kevin Baker, "We're in the Army Now: The G.O.P.'s Plan to Militarize Our Culture," *Harper's Magazine*, October 2003, p. 37.

33. Joe Matthews, "Schwarzenegger Sells His Agenda in Malls," *Los Angeles Times*, December 8, 2003, p. B6.

34. William Reese-Mogg, "The Fascist Spectre That Stands Behind Arnie," *The Times* (London), October 6, 2003, p. 18.

35. William Reese-Mogg, "The Fascist Spectre That Stands Behind Arnie," *The Times* (London), October 6, 2003, p. 18.

36. William Reese-Mogg, "The Fascist Spectre That Stands Behind Arnie," *The Times* (London), October 6, 2003, p. 18.

37. http://www.berkeley.edu/news/media/releases/2003/10/27_lakoff.shtml

38. http://www.berkeley.edu/news/media/releases/2003/10/27_lakoff.shtml

39. http://www.berkeley.edu/news/media/releases/2003/10/27_lakoff.shtml

40. Bernard Weinraub and Charlie LeDuff, "Schwarzenegger's Next Goal on Dogged, Ambitious Path," *New York Times*, August 17, 2003, p. A1.

41. *Los Angeles Times*, September 15, 1991, p. 4.

42. *People*, December 29, 2003, p. 58.

43. Erica Werner, "Schwarzenegger: Big Name, No Experience," *New York Newsday*, August 7, 2003.

44. Bernard Weinraub, "Hollywood Is All Eyes as One of Its Own Takes a New Stage," *New York Times*, August 8, 2003, p. A14; Bernard Weinraub and Charlie LeDuff, "Schwarzenegger's Next Goal on Dogged, Ambitious Path," *New York Times*, August 17, 2003, p. A1; Charlie LeDuff, "The California Recall: The Governor-elect," *New York Times*, October 8, 2003, p. A26; and Charlie LeDuff, "For a Day, at Least, Stars Shine on Sacramento," *New York Times*, November 18, 2003, p. A16.

45. George Butler. *Arnold Schwarzenegger: A Portrait.* New York: Simon and Schuster,

1990, pp. 21–22.

46. Bernard Weinraub and Charlie LeDuff, "Schwarzenegger's Next Goal on Dogged, Ambitious Path," *New York Times*, August 17, 2003, p. A1.

47. http://thomas.loc.gov/cgi-bin/query/z?c106:H.J.+Res.+88:

48. http://www.congress.gov/cgi-bin/query/z?c108:S.J.RES.15:

# Acknowledgments

OUR BOOK IS A COLLABORATION involving not only the two of us, but people behind the scenes who have contributed to the project in a variety of ways. Jody Hendrickson, Vrindavan Gabbard, and Laura Webber provided excellent research assistance through the years. To Jim DeFelice—the Schwarzenegger of novelists—we owe our deep gratitude for his friendship and advice throughout the writing process.

A long list of people offered ongoing support, enthusiasm, and care: colleagues in the Thematic Studies Program at John Jay College of Criminal Justice, especially Darryl Westcott-Marshall, Abby Stein, Dennis Sherman, Shirley Sarna, Jerry Markowitz, Carol Groneman, Betsy Gitter, Geoff Fairweather, Meghan Duffy, Fritz Umbach, Priscila Acuna, and Provost Basil Wilson. Many, many thanks to our friends and family members who have stuck by us as we immersed ourselves in everything-Arnold and contributed their Arnold-insights: Diana Orozco-Garrett, Kerri Cottle, the Stetsons, Mary Torok, the Krasniewiczs, Bonnie MacDougall, Mom & Pop Director, Marcy, Jody, and Jed, the Dayans—especially Alan, Mitch, and Bonnie (always a source of inspiration)—Claude Mark Hurlbert, Derek Owens, Mark "Blaze" Dalton, Alan "Sensei" Predolin, Jim Gelb, Linda Goodman, Joe Cubells, Alice Beresin, and Douglas Rothschild. Thanks also to Nancy Owen-Lewis at the School of American Research, to the staff at Krav Maga Long Island (KMLI), especially Bill Primavera for filling in at critical times, to Drs. Martin Weinberg and Linda Peltz for working a few miracles, to our attorney Jim Snead, and to our agent Caroline Herter. Thanks also to reporter Alan Zarembo of the *Los Angeles Times* for his interest in, and insightful story about, our work.

We want to especially thank the people at Basic Books, particularly our editor, Megan Hustad, for her hard work and for pushing us to write the kind of book about which we could be proud, and Liz Maguire for providing the right combination of guidance and encouragement.

Most of all, we want to thank our wonderful spouses, Mozelle Dayan and Richard M. Leventhal, and our terrific crew of kids: Daina and Cory Blitz, Drew Leventhal, and Celine and Rene Dayan-Bonilla. We love you.

# Index